COMMON
CENT$

COMMON C€NT$

How the Economy Really Works—
from the Global Market to the Supermarket

NANCY J. KIMELMAN, PhD

STERLING

New York / London
www.sterlingpublishing.com

STERLING and the distinctive Sterling logo are registered
trademarks of Sterling Publishing Co., Inc.

Library of Congress Cataloging-in-Publication Data

Kimelman, Nancy J.
  Common cents : how the economy really works—from the global market to the supermarket
/ Nancy J. Kimelman.
    p. cm.
  Includes index.
  ISBN 978-1-4027-5256-8
  1. Economics. I. Title.
  HB171.K477 2008
  330--dc22
                                        2008003301

10 9 8 7 6 5 4 3 2 1

Published by Sterling Publishing Co., Inc.
387 Park Avenue South, New York, NY 10016
© 2008 by Nancy J. Kimelman
Distributed in Canada by Sterling Publishing
c/o Canadian Manda Group, 165 Dufferin Street
Toronto, Ontario, Canada M6K 3H6
Distributed in the United Kingdom by GMC Distribution Services
Castle Place, 166 High Street, Lewes, East Sussex, England BN7 1XU
Distributed in Australia by Capricorn Link (Australia) Pty. Ltd.
P.O. Box 704, Windsor, NSW 2756, Australia

Book design and layout: Jill Anderson

Manufactured in the United States

Sterling ISBN 978-1-4027-5256-8

For information about custom editions, special sales, premium and
corporate purchases, please contact Sterling Special Sales
Department at 800-805-5489 or specialsales@sterlingpublishing.com.

For Jessie, Cassie and Jeff

CONTENTS

Part II: Explaining the Past, Predicting the Future, and Tackling the Hard Problems   171

Why Play Dumb?

Here's what I don't get:

You get up each day and go to work, which means you're active in the job market.

You have a credit card, a car loan, or a mortgage, which means you're active in the credit markets.

You own your home or rent, or perhaps live in a college dorm, which means you're active in the real estate market.

You save for retirement, college expenses, or maybe nowadays a tank of gas, which means you're active in the financial markets.

You shop for things: groceries, home goods, cars, summer vacations. This means you play the role of consumer in many, many markets each and every day.

How can you do all this, lead life in the twenty-first century, without a good understanding of how markets work, and how a market economy works? Aren't you scared by the gyrations in stock prices and the ups and downs of interest rates? How do you judge whether you're fairly paid or have a future in your current line of work? And how can you tell which political candidate has the better economic platform?

Or let's take the high road here. Middle East politics. It's about religion, race, and economic opportunity. The battle over immigration, which has shifted to the front burner recently, is about changes in our nation's demographics, but it's also about the very real fear that immigrants will take jobs away from people who were born here. Our growing reliance on all things made in China. What is that if not economics?

My point is that to live in this world of ours, you need to know more than just a smattering of economics. Now, knowing more economics may not make you richer or happier. Those are not things that I, or any other author, can legitimately promise you. But reading this book will make you better informed and considerably more comfortable wading through the decisions that fill your days, and hopefully let you sleep better at night. Which would you rather have: a better night's sleep or a million bucks? Well, me too. I'd rather have the million bucks. Since that's not an option, though, my advice is that you give this book a try. After all, why play dumb if you don't have to?

What to Expect from This Book

I know that, for most people, economics is something you take in college. Or not. Preferably not. The word conjures up images of complicated graphs, high-powered math, and word problems that would make your high school algebra teacher blush. Unfortunately, all this is true. The formal study of economics does use a lot of algebra, geometry, and calculus, which is why few people actually understand economics.

Luckily, there is another way. You may not know that the early economists considered themselves philosophers. They wrote extensively about the way people lived out their lives, the way markets worked, and the reasons why some people and some societies were better off than others. These are all economic topics, but in the old days they were explained with words and logic rather than equations and graphs.

One of the secrets that we economists keep to ourselves (I may be excommunicated from the American Economics Association just for saying this) is that good economics is very close to common sense. Were you to read some of the writings of those early economists, you would shake your head in agreement with practically everything they said because it would all sound like common sense to you.

This is the key to my approach. You'll find no math in this book (except for the price on the jacket, which I hope you paid in full). You will find economic common sense to answer important questions of our day, like these: How is it that OPEC (the Organization of Petroleum Exporting Countries) exerts such influence over oil prices? Why are jobs moving overseas and what can—and should—we do about it? Is foreign trade good or bad? How do I make the big decisions affecting my retirement or saving for my kids' education? And many, many more.

Before we can tackle those questions, we'll have to run through some basic economic concepts, things like supply and demand, consumption and production, and government finance. We'll also need to understand the basics of personal finance and learn how the financial system works. Even if you think you have a pretty good understanding of some of these concepts, I encourage you to read these chapters anyway. Not only will you learn some new stuff, but you may *unlearn* some things you take for granted that aren't quite right (and besides, I worked hard to write these chapters!).

Once the basic skills have been covered, we're free to explore the issues that make the front page of the newspaper every day and affect your life very directly. So, sit back, get comfortable, and open your mind to the possibilities of seeing life from a different perspective—that of a somewhat irreverent, maybe occasionally witty, but experienced economist who's been on the front lines, lived through the wars, and is ready to spill the beans on all she's learned.

PART I

Basic Skills

1

Supply and Demand: The Foundation of All Things Economic

Imagine a white sand beach, turquoise water lapping gently on the shore, a bottle of the local brew chilling in an ice bucket at your side, and a staff of young men in uniform off in the distance, ready to cater to your every wish. (I know what you're thinking: *Hey, if this is economics, I'm going to like this.*) I visited a place like this once on the Caribbean island of Anguilla, and let me say that luxury on this scale is every bit what it's cracked up to be.

I've also vacationed on a park bench, or a series of park benches to be exact. It was a lovely day, I needed a break, so I spent a day off with a library book, bottled water, and a rotating cast of city characters.

Why do we take vacations? Frankly it doesn't matter whether it's Anguilla or Central Park, vacations give us an escape from the daily routine. The annoying boss, the bump and grind of the daily commute, the pressure to do the right thing—everyone has something he wants to leave behind.

And yet as great as vacations are, there is one thing that can't be left behind: the need to make choices. I may have been brain-dead in Anguilla, but I still had to choose between spiny lobster and filet mignon for dinner; whether to tan with SPF 15 or 30; to nap in the hammock or on the balcony of my cottage. Even on vacation, life is filled with really tough choices.

Of course, when we're not on vacation, the number of choices we encounter virtually explodes in our faces. There are all those decisions related to work, to be sure, but on top of that there are the decisions that allow our everyday lives to take shape: decisions regarding our families and friends, our health, our homes and cars, our finances and our time. Life in modern-day America is an often overwhelming stream of decision-making. No wonder we look so tired!

If there were anything I could do to get you a ticket to that ritzy resort in Anguilla, I would. Unfortunately, wishing ain't enough. I can't stop the never-ending barrage of decisions you face, either. But I can promise you that by the end of this chapter, you'll relax more, wherever you are, because you'll understand better the decisions you're forced to make each day. You see, economics is the study of human choice. There are many definitions of economics out there, and you've probably never thought of economics as the study of choice. But this is the definition I like best, the one I think best fits our lives. To understand our decisions of consequence, their parameters and implications, that's what economics—and life—is really all about.

A Day in the Life of Me

As my kids will attest, I have a habit of springing "grand experiments" on my family and friends every so often, just to keep things interesting. There was the year we vacationed on an island in Lake Winnipesaukee and rented a motorboat for transportation. The house was inhabited by roughly forty thousand spiders, a conservative estimate, of which I managed to kill only ten thousand; I bruised my back falling down the house's narrow circular steps; and I scraped the bottom of the boat and its propeller repeatedly while trying to dock in shallow waters. The trip cost me a fortune and my lower back still hurts when I climb out of bed in the morning.

Another of my grand ideas was that we finish off our basement ourselves. Let me just say that the sheetrock still shows random trapezoidal holes that were cut in error. . . . Truth is, as hard as it is for me to admit, most of my grand experiments are flops.

On a recent Friday in May, I sprang another experiment on my family, this time a relatively small one involving nothing more dangerous than dinner. Over the previous few days, I had seen numerous articles, ads, even a banner across my Yahoo homepage, promoting the "new potato." It turns out the new potato wasn't a potato at all, but rather a larger and rather ugly vegetable called a rutabaga. According to the articles, rutabagas could be made to taste like potatoes, but they offered many benefits over the lowly spud, namely more vitamins and fewer carbs. I decided to give it a shot (a quick look at the author photo on the jacket flap, if you haven't been there already, will explain my interest in food that packs fewer calories). As I picked up a few things at the grocery store that Thursday after work, I passed by the heaping display of the small potatoes that I usually buy, and instead grabbed one of the few remaining rutabagas on display in an out-of-the-way corner of the produce aisle.

I called my sister, who's a terrific cook, and told her of my intention to serve rutabagas for dinner instead of potatoes. She offered to devise a recipe for me that would make me forget potatoes forever—or at least one meal. Lo and behold, my family loved Gingered Rutabagas & Carrots. Wow! Needless to say, the rutabaga was even invited back for a repeat appearance. Over the next few weeks, I even tried other new recipes: Some worked; others didn't. On the whole, though, we became rutabaga eaters.

Gingered Rutabagas & Carrots

From Martha Moore

2–3   rutabagas, peeled and diced into 1" (2.54 cm) cubes (about 2 cups)

2   carrots, diced into 1" (2.54 cm) cubes (about 1 cup)

½   teaspoon freshly minced ginger

1   clove garlic

3   tablespoons (30 ml) olive oil

Preheat oven to 450 degrees Fahrenheit (232 C).

Place rutabagas and carrots on baking sheet in a single layer. Mix with 2 tablespoons oil. Salt and pepper to taste. Roast for 45 minutes or until vegetables are tender.

Place remaining tablespoon of oil, garlic, ginger, and vegetables in a frying pan and cook over medium heat for 5 minutes.

Serves four as a side course.

Now, let's deal with the economics of my decision. I hope you noticed my comment that at my market, rutabagas were in rather short supply when I went shopping that Thursday, while the supply of potatoes was more than ample. I shopped at different markets in the ensuing weeks, and the same was true at all of them. Obviously, I wasn't the only cook who had read the positive spin about the 'baga, and mine wasn't the only family who found the rutabaga a yummy yet sophisticated alternative to potatoes. Increased demand had depleted the shelves of rutabagas and reduced the amount of potatoes being bought.

What follows is a re-creation, for I did not talk with the produce manager of my store, or with Ned, my favorite potato farmer. But I'm sure the following series of events transpired as a result of my decision, and those of other consumers, to buy more rutabagas.

Scene 1: Day 1: The produce aisle. The high school kid who stocks the shelves complains to his boss that there is no more room "out there" for the new shipment of potatoes they just received. The store's produce manager reviews the situation, realizes the kid's not wrong, for once, and calls the head office to let them know that they'd better cut back on their potato order for the next few weeks. And while they're at it, could they ship more rutabagas. What the heck is going on?

Scene 2: Day 2: Head office. The produce buyer gets similar calls from many of the chain's stores, which leads to a call to Farmer Ned up in Putney, Vermont. As perplexed as the produce buyer is by this strange turn of events, he relates to Ned the switch in shoppers' buying habits and he cuts back on his order for Ned's taters.

Scene 3: Day 2: Ned's Potato Farm, Putney, Vermont. Ned walks from his small office to the kitchen to tell his wife that the produce man from my store's home office just called to reduce his order. Ned is truly perplexed. That's the fifth call he's gotten that day. Were some of his potatoes bad? Are these guys hiking his price without telling him, or cutting the price of Idahos? Ned's wife calms him down, says she'll do some research.

Scene 4: Day 3: Ned's Potato Farm, Putney, Vermont. As the sun sets, Ned's wife walks out to the fields to report to her husband on what New England potato farmers are starting to call the "rutabaga phenomenon." Ned and his wife discuss what it means for them, with their fields already sown with this year's potato crop. And they talk about the adjustments they could make to next year's plantings if it turns out that this thing lasts. Ned and his wife agree to keep close track of orders and shipments over the next few weeks, and to investigate fully what it would take to switch over some of their fields to rutabaga farming. In the meantime, Ned's wife suggests a nice Sauvignon Blanc to ease the pain, so the two walk arm-in-arm toward their vintage farmhouse.

My decision to put rutabagas on my kitchen table in place of potatoes, when combined with a similar decision by other consumers in my area, had a pronounced effect on our friend Ned. The harm we caused him was not intentional or personal, of course. Nevertheless, Ned's business felt the effects of reduced sales. In the long run, that is, over the course of the next few growing seasons, Ned would have important decisions of his own to make: to continue growing the same kind and amount of potatoes; to diversify into other crops like rutabagas or squash; to spend more on marketing, perhaps in an effort to win back customers like myself who may not realize the nutritional bargain that potatoes represent. In the short run, it's fair to say that Ned has more immediate problems to resolve. Should he lower his price to ensure that he sells out his entire crop? Should he begin selling to wholesalers, or kick up efforts to sell directly to a few of the high-end restaurants that he'd been keeping at bay? One thing's for sure: If demand doesn't change and Ned doesn't change, Ned's income is going to fall.

Who Can Resist That New Car Smell?

Let's switch gears. Another one of the choices I made that Friday in May, arguably with a lot more riding on it than what I put on the table for dinner, was my decision to ditch my son's old car and replace it with a new, safer vehicle. Obviously, this is not a decision I make every day, although each day in the United States thousands do reach a similar conclusion. The effect on car companies and their employees of such decisions should be pretty obvious. When more of us choose to buy a new car, car companies sell more cars, employment in the auto industry rises, and the general well-being of communities around the nation's auto manufacturing plants improves. Conversely, when fewer of us choose to replace our old cars, the industry—and the neighboring communities—suffers.

Got that? Good, because I have another point I want to make with this example, and that is that I was free to do what was right for me with regard to my son's old car. Oh sure, my son had a lot to say about it, but my congressman did not. Think back to the late lamented Soviet Union. Thirty years ago, you had to be an Olympic pole vaulter, and a damn good one at that, to get a voucher for a car in the USSR. Even today in a relatively open economy like Singapore, the government influences the people's choice of cars by imposing astronomical taxes on older cars that are more likely to break down and clog traffic. Here in the United States, I am proud to say the decision was mine and mine alone.

Once my decision was made, I should add, I had no trouble finding cars to buy. Within a ten-mile (16 km) radius of my home in the suburbs of Boston are ten new car dealers and fifteen used car dealers selling over twenty different brands of cars. Inventory was not an issue for me. By contrast, the physically fit Russian thirty years ago had the choice between a Volga and a Volga.

Now, when I say that no one else affected my decision, I do not mean that there were no other influences on my car purchase. After all, I had to be able to afford the car I picked out with and for my son. My income acted as a very real constraint on my decision. Indeed, it was my income that prevented my son from getting the car of his dreams. (What do you expect? He's eighteen—he wanted a Corvette.)

My income was a constraint that day, and virtually every economic decision I make every day.* Our lives may be filled with

---

*Let me say that as frustrating as this may be on a personal level, it's this constant struggle that makes the whole shooting match so interesting when seen from a distance. Faced with very real budget constraints, I make one decision while my neighbor makes another. Understanding the decisions we all make and being able to predict what the aggregate of our decisions will be is, in large part, what economists do. It's challenging and interesting work, and if we economists do that work well and communicate it to you effectively, we'll find our rightful place in heaven for having enriched your lives. That's my goal, at least.

choices, in other words, but those choices are hardly unconstrained. We are constantly weighing our desires against the reality of our checking and savings account balances. That's life as 99.9 percent of us know it!

One-Half of the Equation: Demand

OK, in just a few short pages, I've laid the groundwork for understanding *demand*, one of the major building blocks of economics. What I've illustrated is that in our open and free economy, demand arises from a consumer doing what's best for her and/or her family within the constraints imposed by her financial situation. As a result of those constraints, consumers typically buy more of something when it's cheaper and less of the same product when its price is high. Common sense? You betcha! Good economics usually is.

I should add here that I could make this explanation of demand more complicated, but also more realistic, by introducing the notion of time. When we borrow, we spread out payments over a longer period of time. When we take out a mortgage to buy a house, for example, or a loan to buy a car, we spread the cost of the house or car over years; this allows us to buy something bigger than we could afford if we had only our monthly income to spend. Likewise, when we save, we give ourselves the option of spending our income over a longer period of time, which also lets us make major purchases that require more cash. Saving and borrowing—transactions that by their very nature involve time—are a good, if complicating, addition to our story, one that we'll fudge for the moment. Even when the explanation of demand is complicated in this way, however, the essentials are still the same. We are, after all, rational human beings who make decisions pretty much the same way, day after day, year after year.

The American Businessperson: A Wonder to Behold

So far we've been looking at things from the perspective of the American consumer, that is, me. Let's jump to the other side of the cash register and contemplate life as a small business owner. Small businesses are the lifeblood of the U.S. economy. They account for most of the new jobs that are created each year, and obviously the vast majority of startups. Without the adventure- and profit-seeking mind-set of small business owners, our economy would be a faint shadow of itself.

I've been close to both small and big businesses in my time, and I have to tell you the decisions made by each of them are much the same. Bigger numbers, of course, with bigger businesses, but still the same decisions regarding hiring, cutbacks, new products, customer service, and the like. Oh, one more thing. I've noticed that the bigger the company, the bigger the mistakes!

If I weren't a bit tired of potato farming, I would look at Ned's business. Instead, let's consider the local garden center where I bought two rosebushes one Friday night in May to replace those that had died in the harsh winter we New Englanders so love to hate. That the garden center had the variety of climbing roses I was looking for was no mean feat of business acumen. When the garden center owners finalized their orders for plants during the dead of winter, they had no way of knowing how bad or how long winter would end up being. They had no way of knowing how many people would choose to shop in their nursery instead of the new Home Depot down the road. Nor could they tell whether rose buyers like myself would want pink or yellow roses. They had to make an educated guess about these things and much, much more.

For the nursery owners, as for Ned the potato farmer, the stakes were high for getting it right. Have too much inventory on hand and it goes bad. Even if the goods don't perish (cars, for instance), the business owner has to carry the excess stock on the firm's books, which usually means absorbing the cost of financing.* Of course, just as awful as having too much inventory on hand is not having enough inventory. That means lost sales—ouch! I was satisfied with the selection and prices at the garden center, but I noticed that the store had run out of lilacs and had just a few straggly looking philodendrons left. The owners didn't lose money, per se, from not making those sales, but they lost out on the opportunity to grow their profits. Ever meet a small business owner who wanted to stay poor? I rest my case.

If the consumer has a big cloud hanging over her head when she's shopping—that being the waning balance in her checkbook—the business owner has a cloud over her head, too: risk. Because no one can predict the future with 100 percent accuracy, business owners live and work with niggling doubts about having made the right decisions with respect to ordering, pricing, hiring, advertising, hours—you name it. Risk is what takes the fun out of running a business.

Depending on your own experiences in life, you may realize that it is possible for businesses to share some of the risk they face. For example, a restaurant owner can purchase an insurance policy on his head chef to compensate the business if something awful were to happen to the cook (ptomaine poisoning, for example). Most retail stores will routinely buy property insurance to protect their shops from natural disasters and theft. In fact, there are many ways for business owners to share some types of risk.

Try as they might to mitigate risk, however, they can't totally get rid of it. Nor do we want them to! I'm not being sadistic here (plenty of time for that later on). Risk may be the spoiler at the party, but it is also the reason why successful business owners

---

* Typically a car dealer does not pay for all the cars on the lot out of his own pocket. Rather he takes out *car* loans (or should I say cars loans) to finance the purchase from the manufacturer. Those loans cost the dealer money (interest) every day that a car sits on the lot. Dealers get such loans from the car manufacturer, or sometimes from a local bank.

make out so well financially. They've faced risk head-on and made good choices in the face of uncertainty. These folks deserve to be properly rewarded for having made good decisions. The body shop mechanic who correctly estimates how long and which parts it will take to fix the dent; the ticket scalper—oh, forgive me, ticket *agent*—who correctly estimates demand for the summer's concerts; the football team that chose wisely at the draft. All these business people faced down uncertainty and they now drive BMWs to prove it. More power to 'em.

Of course, most business owners aren't satisfied to take their just rewards for dealing successfully with risk. Most entrepreneurs and business executives dream of wealth on the scale of Bill Gates and Michael Dell. Again, this is a good thing. It's plain that very few people in our day will be as wildly successful as Gates or Dell. But it is important for corporate presidents and CEOs to try their best to be as successful as these two. The profit motive is an integral part of the American economy. Without it, the economy simply wouldn't function nearly as well.

The Other Half of the Equation: Supply

And so this brings us to the second building block of our economic system. As I explained earlier, economists use the word *demand* to represent the buying done by consumers, and I hope you understand that demand is the result of consumers doing what's best for their families and for themselves in the face of very real financial constraints. Demand is only half the equation, however. To fill in the picture, I want you to envision a transaction for . . . anything, really. Roses, cars, rutabagas? Let's make it simple: A bag of charcoal will do us fine. The consumer picks up a bag of charcoal at the store and goes to the cash register to pay for it. Watch it now: The consumer hands over the cash to the sales clerk who takes the cash and stores it in the register. Ever see a transaction where the consumer's left hanging with his cash in hand? Not bloody likely, as the Brits would say. Transactions always have two sides: the buyer *and* the seller. There is always someone to fork over the dough and someone else to grab it off his sweaty palm.

Economists use the word *supply* to represent the actions of the seller in a transaction. And like consumers, sellers conduct transactions that are in their best interests. In most cases, this means they sell goods and services in order to make the highest profits they can, all while juggling the risks that are inherent in doing business. And because they want to earn the highest profit, suppliers prefer high prices to low prices. Just another example of good ol' common sense, I hope you'll agree.

Where Buyers and Sellers Meet: The Market

The U.S. economy, like most Western economies, is a *market-based system*. I'm sure you've read this somewhere, and it's mostly true. So to truly understand economics, it is crucial for you to understand how markets work. Now, had this been three hundred years ago, the task of describing markets and their inner workings would have been relatively easy: Picture the town square on Saturday morning. Everyone in the town who has something to sell has arrived with their goods and wares, and all the townspeople have arrived to make their weekly purchases. They bargain, they haggle, they sell, they buy, and by midafternoon everyone's done the business they came to do and the only folks left in the square are the teenagers flirting with one another while the street sweepers clean up the mess.

Well, needless to say, markets have changed. In most neighborhoods in America, your goods and wares can now come to you, instead of the other way around. In fact, you might very well have ordered a pizza to be delivered to your home when you sat down to read this chapter and you might be chomping on the crust of the last slice by now. (That is a good idea: Put down the crust, out of the dog's reach, and go check on your teenager.)

As much as markets have obviously changed—the what, the who, the when, the where—amazingly enough, markets still function in much the same way they have for not just three hundred years but three thousand. The *how*, in other words, is much the same as it's always been. For this reason, I'm going to begin this explanation of markets with a description of the Haymarket in Boston. If you've never been to the Haymarket, held near Fanueil Hall on Friday and Saturday mornings, no worries. Have you been to the Union Square Greenmarket in New York? The Dallas Farmers' Market? The Hollywood Farmers' Market in LA? No? Well, have you been to any kind of farmers' market? Any such market will do.

What happens in the open at these farmers' markets is something that sets my heart aflutter: Sellers and buyers meet face to face and trade at will. Let me describe it for you. The first to arrive, as a rule, are the sellers. As they set up their stands first thing in the morning, they covertly check out each other's stalls, assessing both the quality and quantity of what's been brought to market that day. After doing so, each farmer decides on the prices that work for him, that is, the prices that will land him the most money at the end of the day. Depending on the quality of his produce relative to that of the other sellers in the market, he may decide to price his peaches—which he's mighty proud of—at the high end of the range he's seeing in the market and his tomatoes—which he may have picked too early—at the low end of the range. Odds are, though, that he'll stick within the range of prices he sees posted at the start of the market day.*

---

* If there were no differences in quality, then there would be no price range, but rather a single price for each good, e.g., $1.95 per pound for peaches, $2.25 for a pint of blueberries, and so on. Every farmer would adopt those prices unless he wanted either to go home with less money than he could have earned or go home with his van full of unsold goods. This type of market, where there's uniform quality and a single price for each good, is a perfect example of a competitive market. Farmers' markets, like the real world, are slightly less perfect.

After the buyers arrive, the farmers will very soon get a good indication of whether the demand for their product is stronger or weaker than they had expected, and they will adjust their prices up or down to ensure a good day's profits. In fact, good sellers will take stock of the market many times during the day and adjust their prices accordingly.

Most consumers arrive after the stalls are set up so that they don't waste time. Upon arrival, savvy consumers will take a stroll around before buying, just to check on the quality and prices of the goods being offered. And then they'll get down to business, searching out the best product at the cheapest price. Throughout the day, buyers will stream in and out of the market, resetting the conditions for sale.

Nothing is fixed in these markets. On the contrary, the market is in a constant state of flux. During the course of a day, the price of the average tomato or a banana might fluctuate by a penny, a nickel, or a dime, all depending on the appetite of buyers and the volume of produce that was brought to market by the sellers. Farmers have to monitor these price fluctuations carefully; otherwise, they may find themselves selling excellent quality produce for the price of lesser quality goods, or, equally bad, not selling their produce because the market price has decreased. Each minute in the market is different; each trade may be different. For me, the action of the marketplace is better than watching the Red Sox rip the Yankees, which is saying a lot.

By the end of market day, there's very little left. Unless a seller posts a price that's out of whack with either the quality of his goods or the going prices in the market, he's likely to sell what he brought. And unless a buyer is especially cheap, refusing to pay the going price for a particular item, she's unlikely to go home empty-handed. The reason these markets work well is that there are few or no restrictions on the action, and prices are free to rise and fall, as need be. No one's there to tell a seller what his produce should sell for; the market itself—that is, the interaction of buyers and sellers—decides the value of his goods. Should the seller want to set a higher price than the guy at the next stand, he's free to do so, knowing that if his goods don't justify the higher price, his return trip might be a bit heavier than planned. If he wants to set a lower price and sell out quickly, that's also his decision. Likewise, no one tells a buyer what she should pay for a basket of mushrooms; she offers what she wants and the seller is free to refuse. The price listed on the chalkboard is a suggested price, the price the seller thinks is fair for the market that day, but there's nothing to stop a bloke from haggling.

In open-air markets like the Haymarket, we all do what we want and, amazingly enough, it all works out pretty darn well. This notion—that each of us acting in our own best interests will, if prices are flexible, result in the best-case scenario—is at the core of modern-day economic thinking. When consumers act in their own best interests and sellers individually strive to generate the most profits, then the result is a set of prices in the economy that best allocates scarce resources. It's what the eighteenth-century philosopher Adam Smith called the *invisible hand*. If everybody does what's in his best interest—the consumer and business owner alike—then, as if an invisible hand were guiding us, our economy will reach optimal levels of production, income, employment, and well-being.

By what miracle does this happen? The key is flexible prices. It's prices going up and down, being rejected and accepted by the participants in the market, that does this.* Prices tell consumers

---

* To be perfectly correct about this, flexible prices are necessary, but a truly optimal situation also requires—in addition to flexible prices—that everyone has the same information, that people are free to enter and leave markets at will, that there are many players on both sides who, therefore, possess no special power over prices, and finally, that the goods sold are of similar quality. Now, these conditions rarely exist, if only because most products we buy are slightly different from the others on sale, whether they be ripe, juicy peaches or laundry detergent. Our economy does not produce truly "optimal" results, then, but rather near-optimal results. I've used the term *best possible* because I don't think there's an economic system in the modern age that can do better.

what a good or service is worth in the economy, and then the consumer determines whether it's worth it or not for *her*. Prices tell companies what consumers are willing to pay for an item, and then the company's managers determine whether *they* are willing to produce the item to sell at that price. No master planner. No Politburo chief. Each of us makes up our own mind, acts in our own self-interest, and the result is the best possible allocation of goods and resources. Pretty neat, huh?

One More Time

The role that prices play in a free market economy is so crucial that it's worth another example to drive the point home. This will also give us the opportunity to focus in on the way free markets allocate resources. Let's consider a modern market of interest to many, many people: college prep tutoring.

Any of you who have children in high school or college know that getting a kid into college today is awfully hard work. Competition is stiff at the most competitive schools, as it has always been, but it's even hard getting kids into the large state universities these days.

Thirty years ago, as a senior in high school, I took an SAT prep course from Kaplan that promised to improve my scores (it did, by the way). Most of my friends did not take the course. Today, it's just the opposite. It's the rare kid who doesn't take a course, work through practice tests, or get private tutoring for this potentially life-changing event.

There are a number of outfits out there to prepare kids for the SATs. Kaplan is still around, bigger than ever, but today it's joined by Princeton Review and a host of smaller mom-and-pop operations. Obviously, parents are willing to spend big bucks to help their kids secure a place at the right college.

How did SAT prep get to be a billion-dollar industry? Organically. As Kaplan's classes filled and sold out, the company expanded its locations and course times. Kaplan could have charged more and kept the number of seats in its classes unchanged, but the owners reasoned correctly that they'd take in more money by making a reasonable profit on an ever larger chunk of America's one million graduating seniors each year. Kaplan's success spurred firms like Princeton Review to expand from book production to class instruction. To staff its centers, Kaplan and Princeton Review hired more and more educators. (Interestingly, many more secondary teachers today take a second job as tutors or college prep teachers.) And then the inevitable happened: The strongest and most profit-minded of these teachers started their own firms, drawing on local name recognition and strong word-of-mouth referrals. The end result is an industry today that has a few big players and many small ones.

The college prep industry is a good example of consumers sending out a message of interest that was correctly interpreted by "manufacturers," who then created more "product" for sale. If Kaplan's courses had not sold out, if Kaplan had not made a profit thirty years ago, then the industry would never have grown. But Kaplan's profits enticed Princeton Review and others to get in the game, and now they are all profitably sharing in the industry's growth. We might say that the drive for profit led to an increase in the nation's resources being allocated for this purpose, correctly so.

All this goes back to Adam Smith's invisible hand. If consumers do what's in their best interests and companies act to maximize profits, then in a free market prices will send the right signals and resources will be allocated well. Look, it may not always be enough to ensure everyone a good night's sleep, but let me assure you, optimal resource use is as good as an economy can get—and right here, right now, we're pretty darn close.

Profit Is Not a Four-Letter Word

As easy as it is for me to write about a healthy profit motive, I know there are many of you out there who distrust my point about the importance of profits to the smooth functioning of our economy. Well, read my lips: You're wrong.

Why did my local grocery chain start carrying gourmet salads and organic chicken? To improve the health of my family? No. They did so to compete with the new organic market in town. Profit motivated their decision, and I am the beneficiary, because now I can buy bubble gum–flavored toothpaste for my daughter and healthier chicken for dinner at the same store.

Why did the Yankees offer $67 million to buy out the remainder of A-Rod's contract with the Texas Rangers before the start of the 2004 season? Was it to bust the chops of the Red Sox owners? Well, yeah, maybe. But mostly it was for a few more exciting years. That, the Yankees knew, would translate into sold-out games and higher ad revenues. Who knows, maybe A-Rod will deliver the pennant back to New York, in which case the Yankees will reap even greater rewards. The decision was motivated by profits (it is the Steinbrenners we're talking about here), and Yankees fans are the beneficiaries as well as the team's owners. Come to think of it, why did the Red Sox pay $51 million for the right just to talk to Daisuke Matsuzaka in late 2006? Was it to bust the chops of the Yankees? You betcha! That and another title.

Why did Texaco/Shell decide to stop funding the Saturday afternoon radio broadcasts of the Metropolitan Opera from New York? Clearly, the company couldn't trace enough benefit from the roughly $6 million it was donating each year to keep the program on the air. Now, this was bad news for opera fans in Toledo, Ohio, and indeed for anyone who relied on the broadcast to hear first-rate opera live (all ten of them). But it was good news for share-holders of Texaco/Shell who invested in the company with the expectation that their firm would strive to generate the highest profits possible in their line of business. Since Texaco/Shell is an energy company, not an opera or broadcasting company, their decision made good business sense.

Is it a good thing that I should have to make two or three stops just to feed my family a healthy meal? Of course not. Should Texaco/Shell betray shareholder interest simply to carry on a tradition that benefits the highest-income audience of any musical or theatrical genre? Of course not. Should A-Rod have played for the Montreal Expos who couldn't even fill the box seats along the baselines? I won't even deign to answer that!

When money/profit is the motivating force behind business decisions, then valuable resources like my time, A-Rod's bat, and Texaco/Shell's charitable contributions will be allocated to their best use. That's capitalism. And that, my dear friends, is a very good thing because it means our economy is operating efficiently. Economies that use resources inefficiently (think Cuba or Venezuela) simply aren't as strong as ours.

And yet, it's also clear from my examples that American business today generates winners and losers. I think this is what turns many people off about capitalism. Yes, capitalism does create losers. But in all fairness, every economic system creates losers. We can't all have everything we want, after all. *The key is how the system chooses between winners and losers.* In the American economy today, no one loses because the authorities decree that they should lose, or because one person or company wields unfair advantage over another, or because the losers are prevented from entering into a business transaction. In the American economy today, the losers lose because they are either unwilling or unable to meet the price set by the free market. Ultimately, price is the least damaging way to allocate resources. Any other way is more arbitrary, deceitful, and far more damaging. I feel so strongly about this that I challenge you to find an economic system at any point in history that allocated resources (e.g., chose winners and losers) in a more fair or efficient manner. Go ahead, think. I'll wait.

I'm waiting.

I'm still waiting.

A Note to the Morally Offended

I don't want to gloss over a very real issue for many of us, namely that in America today many people cannot afford things they need, and therefore go without. Major challenges like health care, education, and inner-city poverty stem from the unfairness that capitalism leaves in its wake. The fast-rising cost of diagnostic tests, hospitalization, and prescription drugs is making it impossible for a growing number of Americans to get adequate health care. As much as a college degree is becoming required for employment, there are still large numbers of teenagers who can't afford to attend college on anything but a very part-time basis. Many older citizens don't have enough to live on; many, many young families are finding it hard to scrape by. Our dirty little secret is that not only are the poor in this country losing ground, but the number of poor people is growing. So, no, capitalism is *not* perfect.

More than any other economic system known to woman or man, capitalism does the best job of allocating resources in an economy. But it's no hop, skip, or jump from there to the fairest economic system in the world, if by fair you mean an absence of poverty, or access to health care and education, or any number of other excellent measures of a nation's standard of living. To say that we have a near-optimal usage of the resources at our disposal—and we do—is not to say that our system doesn't hurt some people some of the time. As good economists, as good Americans, our job is to work on solutions to the problems our systems cause unintentionally. Luckily, there are many good people doing just that. You'll see.

2

Time Is on Our Side: Money, Credit, and Wealth

If you were stranded on a desert island, you'd look to the sky and ask for . . . what? Food, shelter, clothing, company, beer, aspirin? You'd probably ask for at least some, if not all, of the above.

If you were stranded in the middle of Manhattan or Los Angeles, you'd look to the sky and pray for . . . money! It can't be eaten, it can't be worn, it won't talk to you or back at you, it won't cure a headache, and it hardly hits the spot on a hot day. Still, you'd want money. So would I.

Money is an incredible invention. We all agree to use it when we buy and sell things to each other. It doesn't rot or go stale. And we can use it to describe the value of things, everything from chocolate bars to space stations.

In the United States, our money is called dollars. So the value of everything here is described in terms of dollars. That watch cost $100; your father-in-law's estate is worth $3 million (you wish!). Outside the United States, people call their money different things: euros or pounds or shekels or yen. No matter—that's their choice. We call our money dollars—and the more the better!

There comes a point, when someone has the good fortune of acquiring too many dollars, when it's simply inconvenient to walk around with all of them tucked into pants pockets. Let's pretend this has happened to you. You could leave your money at home, but that might be unsafe—what if a burglar came while you were out buying lunch? The better choice is to let someone else safeguard those dollars so you have some freedom. That's what banks do: They take your dollars and store them for you. Anytime you want your money back, just come inside and they'll give it to you—that's part of the agreement you make with a bank when you drop off your cash. I should add, just so you know, that the bank doesn't actually keep the dollars you drop off, but hands them over to its bank for safekeeping. That's OK with you, isn't it?

Of course, you don't always have to hit the bank before you make a purchase. The bank has given you little permission slips, called checks, that you can write on. When properly filled out and signed by you, these slips give the owner the right to get an exact amount of dollars from your account at the bank. Checks make life much easier: Instead of handing over cash, you simply write a check.

Or nowadays, you don't even have to do that. Most banks offer their clients ATM or debit cards. These are plastic cards, with a magnetic strip and often a silicone chip, that serve the same purpose as checks. Just give someone your card or card number, authorize the amount of dollars in the transaction, and you're done. You're no longer required to carry dollars to a store. You can even sit at your computer and move millions of dollars with a single click.

There's one more thing you should know about money. As much as a lot of money is a good thing for an individual, too much money spread across the country is a bad thing. If you were to win the lottery, dropping let's say a cool $4 million into your account at the bank, you would be a lot richer than you are now. That's because everything else stayed the same except your bank account. But what if everyone in the country—man, woman, and child (sorry, no pets)—got a $4 million infusion into their accounts at the bank? Would we all be richer? Not at all. Oh sure, everyone's bank balance would be four million bucks higher, but everything we buy would be commensurately more expensive. In fact, such an across-the-board rise in prices would pretty much wipe out the benefit from the extra dough.

The moral of this story is that what's really important to us is not the amount of money we might have in the bank or under the mattress, but its purchasing power. When prices rise for everything we buy—a phenomenon called *inflation*—it detracts from our wealth by reducing the purchasing power of our money.* If there were no reason for the extra dough to appear—that is, no work done or risk taken to justify the windfall—then you can bet inflation would arise and negate any and all benefit, down to the last dollar.

There you have it: the story of money.

What's that? There's a whole world of things I should have explained, like savings, investments, loans, interest rates, and the Fed?

No problem, I'm happy to oblige. Just as long as you realize that all these things are about credit, not money. Not only are money and credit not the same thing; they have almost entirely different stories. And where the story of money was a quick hop from point A to point B, the story of *credit* is a long, twisting road through dense forests. However, at the end of the road there are spectacular views and great riches. Let's start our journey.

The Story of Credit

Do you know what a drudge is? A drudge is an animal, or alien, that does repetitive, menial tasks. A modern-day drudge wakes up

---

* That's another definition of inflation: a reduction in the purchasing power of a nation's currency.

in the morning, goes to work, gets paid, spends his earnings, and goes to sleep, only to repeat the same things the next day, and the day after that, and the day after that. . . . Thankfully, our lives are richer than that. We have dreams and aspirations; we plan and we take precautions.

Can you recognize what it is that sets us above the drudge? It is that we recognize time. Time—the past and future—gives our lives meaning. We can look forward to the future in the form of a long-overdue vacation or the birth of a child. We can prepare for a home of our own. We can plan for our child's medical school costs. Likewise, we can use some of our past income to tide us over when things get tight, such as when an unexpected illness sends us home from work or legal bills stare us in the face. It's our ability to embrace time that enriches our material lives.

When we look at transactions that take place over a period of time (such as the building of a house), instead of a single instant (such as the purchase of your morning coffee), we are in the world of credit. Because to spread a transaction over time, there usually has to be some allowance made for the payments to come in pieces over time. And that allowance is what we call credit.

This admittedly squishy definition of credit will become clearer if we take a concrete example—literally. Let's talk about Kyle's parking lot over near the new sports stadium. When Kyle's dad was young, he had an empty lot next to his garage where he used to store cars. Back then, the sports arena was over on the other side of town, and nobody had any interest in the empty lot. Then the city came up with a new redevelopment plan that included moving the sports arena to his dad's part of town. Bingo! Kyle's dad became an instant millionaire; when his dad died, Kyle inherited the now-valuable property.

Kyle has decided he wants to improve his lot: He wants to build a multilevel garage that will protect cars from the hot summer sun (did I mention that Kyle lives in the Southwest?).

Everyone he knows thinks it's a good idea, but Kyle doesn't have
the ready cash to finance the operation himself. So Kyle heads
down to his bank to talk about the project. He and a small business loan officer spend a few hours kicking around the idea. Since
Kyle's done his homework, and the sports arena is under construction, the banker likes his proposal. The two of them sketch out a
series of payments that will be necessary to get the job done on
time, paying off the various contractors as they finish their work
on the garage. And then they sketch out a series of payments that
Kyle will make to the bank, when the garage is up and running, to
pay back the bank. It's a win-win, as far as Kyle and the bank are
concerned. When it's all over, Kyle will have used very little of his
own cash—just enough to set the cornerstone. He'll be using his
take from the garage to pay the bank back the money it advanced
him, as well as to cover the bank's fees, for a few years. Then the
extra profit from a bigger parking garage will be all his.

The building of Kyle's Garage took time. Planning, construction, building inspections—they all took time. Naturally, Kyle and
the banker wanted to spend the money they set aside for the
project over time. You don't pay the plumber, after all, when the
foundation's being dug. When money is paid out or received over
time, it becomes credit. Credit is money enhanced by the fourth
dimension of time.

Now the dictionary lists the definition of credit as a loan or the
creation of a debt. We're not far off. Kyle did take a loan out from
the bank to pay his contractors; since a loan is a form of debt, debt
was created. But *credit* has a deeper meaning that *loan* doesn't completely capture. When the construction workers on Kyle's site went
to the Home Depot for supplies, they bought them on credit, which
is to say that the Home Depot advanced Kyle credit. The contractors themselves also advanced Kyle credit, so to speak, because
they didn't insist on being paid at the end of the each workday.
Notice how the word *advanced* crept into each of the two previous

sentences. Money delayed, money advanced—money enhanced by the fourth dimension of time—that's my definition of credit.

Turn your attention to the bank for a moment. Where do you think the bank got the money to loan Kyle? Easy. From people who have been saving up for something themselves, but are not yet ready to use the money. Your Uncle Harry and Aunt Sally, who are saving for a new apartment in Manhattan. My Cousin Vinny, who is saving up to get married. Your next-door neighbor Tracy, who is saving for the prom, and then college. Virtually everyone you know, fictional or real, is wittingly or unwittingly a source of funds for the bank, which is to say credit for the economy.

Supply and Demand, Credit-Style

Most descriptions of credit take a left turn right about now into a discussion of the types of credit that exist and the details of those credit contracts. It's the easy way out, and unfortunately for the people who take it, not the road to enlightenment. We're headed straight ahead. (Go ahead, get yourself a cool drink. This is going to take some time [pun intended].)

If credit is something that is transacted, and it is, then surely it is subject to the same analysis to which we've been subjecting every other good and service, that is, the laws of supply and demand. You read right: supply and demand. Just because the good in question isn't a concrete one, like concrete or rutabagas, doesn't mean it's not subject to the laws of supply and demand. I am going to make one adjustment, however, to make this discussion simpler. I want to introduce the word *funds*. Funds is a curious word: We all know what it refers to instinctively, yet what does it mean? Sometimes it means money or cash—when my son asks for funds, that's exactly what he has in mind. Sometimes it means savings, like when you deposit money into your mutual funds. Other times it means credit, as when Kyle went to the bank to secure funding for his new garage. Let's agree that funds is a nonspecific term for financial resources. Sometimes it's nice to have a word that doesn't mean exactly money, credit, savings, or cash, and that word is funds.

My analysis, then, is going to be in terms of the supply and demand for funds. Actually, since you're now an expert on supply and demand, you probably don't need me to analyze the market for funds. But for those who skipped chapter 1 (shame on you) . . . anyone who needs funds (to make a purchase that she can't cover out of her current income) is a demander of funds. Examples include Kyle and everyone else who's ever taken out a loan from a bank; the U.S. Treasury when it borrows to pay for a war; the local school authority when it borrows to build the new high school; your Aunt Sarah when she buys her third condo unit in South Beach. Anyone who *has* funds (that they don't need right now) is a supplier of funds. Examples include Bill Gates; the Japanese Postal Service (which is the main savings bank for the Japanese); your Aunt Sarah who doesn't want to tie up all her money in her third condo unit in South Beach.

Quick aside: Most of us are like Aunt Sarah, both suppliers and demanders of funds. Modern life is complicated.

Supply meets demand in the market for funds. Now, given the sizable volume of funds that exists in the world, it's not surprising that there is no single market for funds. Not only couldn't it fit into a single space, but there are so many small variations that it would be foolhardy to lump them together. No, the market for funds is a very amorphous thing, existing in accounts at banks, inside mattresses and piggy banks, in traders' computers all over the world. By the way, I've learned from my years of teaching and lecturing that one of the things many people have a hard time grasping is that the market for funds exists even without a phys-ical space to call its own. If you're having this difficulty, let it go. Remember, ours is not a controlled-from-the-top economy but a freewheeling amalgamation of transactions that individuals enter into of their own free will. The market for funds fits that description to a tee.

Any one of us has the potential, theoretically, of directly engaging in the funds market. Big companies, Uncle Sam, Sam Walton and his ultrarich buddies do just that. You and I, on the other hand, would easily get lost in the hubbub—trampled is more like it. So how do individuals, even small governments, companies, and the very but not ultrarich get into the market successfully? We get help from our friends. Friends who have clout and presence because at the same time that they represent our needs, they also handle the needs of others like us. You know these friends by the names on their doors—Merrill Lynch, Citi, Wachovia, Fidelity. I'm going to give them all a different name: *financial intermediaries*. Financial intermediaries pass on our requests to the market and come back with those requests either filled or not. On occasion, they may fulfill our requests or deny them on their own accord. The important point is that they neither represent the final demand for funds nor its final supply, but rather stand as the runner in between the two groups.

OK, a quick recap. We've defined *funds,* sort of. We know there is a market for funds that exists somewhere, everywhere. We know how different types of people and institutions enter the market—some go it alone; most of us don't. The next step is to look at the functioning of the market, the place where supply meets demand to determine price.

The Price of Funds

Every second that the market for funds is up and running, suppliers are duking it out with demanders to establish a fair price for funds—just like the action at a lively cattle auction. When there's a relatively large volume of funds available on the market, the price of funds is likely to fall. When demanders are packed in, well, like cattle, then the price of funds is likely to rise.

You may be scratching your head at this point and wondering why you've never heard of the price of funds, or if it has a special name that I've failed to mention. It has. The price of funds is called the *interest rate*. The important thing to note right off the bat about this two-word name is the second word: *rate*. Rate signifies that the interest is going to vary and be measured against a benchmark of one sort or another. A marathon runner's mile rate is the minutes and seconds he runs a specific mile (1.6 km) of the race, which gets compared either to his rate at other stages of the course or to the rate other runners are posting. If it were tax rates we were talking about, the tax would vary based on our income— that is, rich people pay a higher rate of tax. But we're talking funds, not taxes or marathons, so the relevant benchmark isn't income or miles. The price of funds, or the interest rate, is going to vary based on time, that is, the length of time for which the funds are being exchanged.* (It all fits, doesn't it? Time is the benchmark for the interest rate; time is what differentiates money from credit.)

Let's restate the market's results in terms of the interest rate, then. When demand pushes hard on supply, it will result in a higher interest rate (that is, a higher price for funds) being set in the market. Alternatively, when the supply of funds is relatively plentiful compared to the demand for funds, the interest rate will fall (making for a lower price for funds). All of this is true and eminently straightforward. But because the interest rate is a *rate,* because there is the element of time to factor in, the market's determination of the interest rate is also more complex than I've just described. To put it bluntly, what works for cattle works for the interest rate. But there are other things that affect the funds market and interest rates that you just don't see in the cattle market.

---

* Loans can be made for any length of time to which two parties agree. To make things simple, the interest rate is always expressed as the interest for a single year.

You should know that interest is expressed as a percentage of the funds borrowed, usually for one year. Also, before I spin the interest rate yarn any further, it's time that I came clean on one other thing: There are hundreds of different interest rates, not just one. In fact, if you consider all the countries in the world, there are probably more than a thousand different interest rates being quoted on any given day. Each and every one of them reflects a slice of the global credit markets. Here are some you probably recognize:

- **Thirty-Year Mortgage Rate:** Loans made for people to buy a house or condo unit are called *mortgages*. The most common mortgage is the *thirty-year loan*. Over the course of the next thirty years, the new homeowner will pay back the amount borrowed (the principal) as well as interest. The interest rate on that loan is called the *thirty-year mortgage rate*. It will differ slightly from lender to lender, borrower to borrower, location to location, but competition between lenders keeps the differences small (except when the borrower's financial health is way below the norm; then the differences can be huge). The average interest rate on thirty-year mortgages is what you read about or hear referred to as the *current mortgage rate*.

- **Ninety-Day Treasury Bill Rate:** Uncle Sam is a voracious borrower, as we'll see in chapter 5 on government finance. He borrows for the long term; he borrows for the short term. One of the constants in the credit markets is a weekly borrowing for just ninety days. The interest rate on that loan, adjusted so that it reflects the rate that would be paid if the loan were for a full year, is the ninety-day Treasury bill rate.

- **Ten-Year Treasury Rate:** Hop, skip, and a jump to the ten-year Treasury rate. Yup, it's the annual rate on money borrowed by the U.S. Treasury for ten years.

- **Prime Rate:** This rate, announced by banks themselves, is the interest rate that they supposedly charge their best business customers. Or, once upon a time it was, but this is hardly the case anymore. Nowadays the rate is mostly used as a benchmark for consumer loans.

- **Federal Funds Rate:** Banks borrow from and lend to each other all the time. These loans are very short-term, some for no longer than a day. The federal funds rate, or the *funds rate* as it's commonly called, is the rate that banks pay for overnight borrowing (again adjusted so that it's an annualized figure).

The credit section of a financial newspaper like the *Wall Street Journal* or the *New York Times* will list these and a bunch of other interest rates every day—and I mean every day. All these rates will change from minute to minute or day to day. One thing you'll notice if you track these rates, though, is that they are all loosely linked to one another. The ninety-day Treasury rate, for instance, is not far off the funds rate. And the thirty-year mortgage rate isn't far off the ten-year Treasury rate. The reason this is so is that all interest rates have one thing in common: They result from the interplay of the supply and demand for funds. Since funds are what economists call *fungible*—that is, they flow effortlessly from one market to another, always searching out the best return for a given amount of risk—interest rates never get too far out of line from each other.

Everything but the Kitchen Sink

Have you noticed that hotel rooms in different parts of the country don't cost the same? I've done my fair share of business travel over the years, and I'm always floored by how much a room costs in San Francisco or New York, compared to Memphis or Spokane. Obviously, location matters a great deal when booking a hotel room.

Well, interestingly enough, location is one of the few things that *doesn't* matter much to interest rates. If you want to lend Uncle Sam money for ninety days, he's going to pay you the same amount of interest whether you live in Spokane, Wichita, or Las Vegas. Likewise, a bank in Portland lending money overnight is going to ask for the same rate as a bank headquartered in New York or Charlotte. As long as we're talking about a single country, and a single currency (dollars, in our case), money's constant search for the best home ensures that location has a very minor effect on most interest rates, if at all.*

But if location doesn't matter, trust me, almost everything else does. Cash is near and dear to our hearts, and no one lets go of it without first assuring herself that (1) it will eventually return, and (2) she will be well and fairly compensated in the interim for her sacrifice. So let's return to the interest-rate story where we left it a few minutes ago, talking about the many things that lie behind the supply and demand for funds and thus influence interest rates.

Time Brings Uncertainty, Which Means Risk

The best way to explain an interest rate is to break it down into three (easy) pieces. The first piece is what we'll call the *real interest rate*. It's the rate of interest—the payment, the bribe—that a lender needs to receive in order to part with his money. You might be willing to lend money to a friend without asking for some kind of payment, but you're bloody well not going to lend money to a perfect stranger without getting some sort of compensation, are you? Of course not.

The real interest rate moves around a bit, but it's actually pretty constant compared to the other components of interest

---

* The only exception, you no doubt realize, is the mortgage rate. More about this later.

rates. It's usually thought to be between 2.5 percent and 3 percent. You should know that real interest rates have been trending near the lower end of the spectrum since the 1990s. There are a variety of reasons why this has been the case; certainly it's no accident that lower real rates of interest have coincided with the technology revolution, the end of communism, and the integration of developing nations (like Korea and China) into the global financial marketplace. All these changes have delivered a bigger supply of funds to the U.S. market, which has naturally translated into lower real interest rates.

The second component of interest rates is the *expectation of inflation*. A few paragraphs ago, I linked the notion of inflation with purchasing power. I knew what was coming. Inflation, which you'll remember is a general rise in prices, means that we have to pay more for goods that used to cost less. That's exactly what we mean by a decline in the purchasing power of the dollar. When inflation sets in, dollars don't buy as much as they used to.

If I answer two questions, you will understand why the expectation of inflation is a component of interest rates. The first question is this: Why does inflation matter to a lender? The answer is that the lender is lending funds *over time,* and there's no guarantee that tomorrow's dollars will be worth the same—in other words, buy as much—as today's dollars. Indeed, in a period of inflation, dollars lose their value, so getting the same number of dollars back won't work. A lender has to get more dollars back in the future so she can buy what today's dollars will buy. Put more formally, to compensate for inflation, a lender will insist that the inflation rate—the rate at which prices are rising—be built into the interest rate she receives. Thus, if inflation is 5 percent, and the real interest rate is 3 percent, she'll demand an interest rate of 8 percent. The first 3 percent will compensate her for the lost use of her money over the term of the loan. The second 5 percent will compensate her for the reduced purchasing power of the dollars she'll get back.

The second question I have to answer is why interest rates incorporate the expected rate of inflation rather than the actual rate of inflation. The answer is that the loan runs from now into the future, so the relevant inflation rate is the future inflation rate, not the current rate, which is really nothing more than the rate at which prices have risen in the past twelve months. Got that? Good, because there's one more twist. Because the interest rate on a loan incorporates the inflation rate expected over the term of the loan, loans of differing terms will have different interest rates. In normal circumstances, short-term interest rates incorporate an expected rate of inflation that is close to the current rate, because over the short term we assume that not much will happen to the rate of inflation. Conversely, in normal circumstances we'd expect long-term interest rates to incorporate a higher inflation premium because over a long period of time the risk of rising inflation is much higher—that is, there's more time for something to go horribly wrong.* What this boils down to is that, under normal circumstances, long-term interest rates are higher than short-term interest rates. In fact, rates can be charted along a continuum from one day to thirty years.

Not many loans are considered risk free, which basically means there is no risk associated with the borrower himself. Here in the United States, the only risk-free borrower is the U.S. Treasury. Interest rates on U.S. Treasury borrowing have just the two components listed above: the real rate and the expected infla-

---

* A diagram showing interest rates plotted against the term of the loan is called the *yield curve*. I'd show it in a graphic, but I promised no charts. The yield curve is usually an upward-sloping line. Occasionally, the curve becomes inverted and short-term interest rates are higher than long-term rates. This usually occurs when inflation is expected to drop in the future from its current level.

tion rate. For every other type of loan, there's a third component to interest rates: credit risk.

Risky Business

When you buy a muffin and coffee in the morning, the last thing you worry about is whether the fellow who takes your money is going to die before he can hand you your breakfast. That's not even on your radar (I hope). However, when the bank set up the loan for our friend Kyle (remember him?), that is something they factored into their thinking. It wasn't an issue, given Kyle's age and apparent health, but the bank officers did consider it. They also considered the possibility that his business might fail. What if the pro team went through a prolonged slump and the stands stood empty? Demand for Kyle's parking spaces would fall, as would his income and his ability to repay the bank. The team had posted winning seasons the past few years, but that could change with injuries to one or two key players.

Kyle would be in default if he didn't repay the loan; he'd be delinquent if he didn't pay the interest on time. Either way, the banker who supplied the funds to Kyle would be quite upset. To manage this risk, suppliers of funds make an assessment of the demander's likelihood of defaulting.* Now, here's a wrench in the works: Lenders call default and delinquency risk credit risk. (Yes, a different name would have been helpful.)

When a prospective borrower comes into a financial intermediary like a bank, he will fill out lots of forms about his financial situation and the bank will run a credit check on him. Based on these forms and his previous experience with loans, referred to as his *credit history*, the bank will assign the potential customer a

---

* This is one way that financial intermediaries help out the medium- and small-size supplier. It would be well nigh impossible for suppliers to effectively inspect their trading partners quickly and cheaply on their own.

credit-risk ranking. The bank does the same for businesses that want to borrow money. Were you to ask your bank for your ranking, the odds are the banker would tell you. Or better yet, walk into a car dealership that's offering 2.9 percent financing to "qualified borrowers." If they offer you 2.9 percent, then you have an excellent credit rating. If they offer you 7.9 percent, you might want to take another look at your finances!

3

Bonds and Stocks and Interest, Oh My!

You have been extraordinarily patient. You've been reading about money and credit and interest and car parks, all the while wondering when I would finally get around to talking about something you're interested in. Eureka! Your time has come. I promise: No rutabagas in this chapter.

What you will find in this chapter is an introduction to bonds and stocks. Got that? Don't expect a heartfelt debate over the relative merits of utility stocks as opposed to convertible bonds (say what?). Do expect a concise and clear explanation of bonds and bond yields, on the one hand, and stocks and stock prices, on the other.

Anatomically Impaired: Bonds

Assuming that you read the last chapter, you now know that the interest rate is the price established in the funds market: It is the cost of borrowing money, the price of credit. You know that there are actually lots of different interest rates, depending on the length of time for which credit is being advanced, the purpose of the loan, and so on. And you know that interest rates (other than Treasury rates) have three components: the *real interest rate*, which reflects the interaction between the supply and demand for funds; the *expected inflation rate,* which varies depending on the length of the loan; and a *risk premium* that reflects the credit risk of the borrower. (As I've already mentioned, Treasury rates lack this last element because the U.S. government isn't ever expected to fail.) Pat yourself on the back. You know quite a bit already, and I admit it wasn't always easy going. By contrast to what comes next, however, that was Apple Pie 101. Now we're going to talk about bonds.

No, not Barry Bonds, although he, too, is complicated. Bonds, you know, debt. Well, so maybe you don't know debt from a home run. No time like the present to learn.

When a bank makes a loan—heck, when I make a loan—the person borrowing the money signs a loan agreement that lays out how much money was borrowed, how long the loan will last, and when and how the money will be paid back. Assuming it's all been done on the up and up, that piece of paper is good in court to prove the lender's right to be paid back the money she lent, plus interest.

When the loan is between two parties, like Kyle and the bank, or me and my neighbor, a loan agreement on this order is enough. But what if there are more than two parties involved? What if there's a chance that the lender may want to sell the loan to someone else down the road? Then it helps to formalize the agreement into a standard contract. That contract is called a *bond.* Or to be absolutely correct, it's a note or bill if the loan is a short one; it's a bond if the loan is to last more than ten years. I'll use the word *bond* for all of 'em to make life easier. Bonds are one type of *security,* which is an umbrella term for contracts with financial value.

Bonds can have one of a few first names. U.S. Treasury bonds are bonds issued by the U.S. Treasury. Agency bonds are bonds issued by agencies of the U.S. government, for example, FHLMC (Freddie Mac) or FNMA (Fannie Mae). Corporate bonds are bonds issued by corporations. Municipal bonds are bonds issued by state and local governments. Foreign bonds are bonds issued by foreigners, either foreign governments or foreign companies.

Bonds have a few attributes that also get special names. The length of the loan is the bond's *maturity*. That's when it comes due; that is, when the loan ends and the borrower repays. The *face value* of the bond is the amount that's written on its front side (cute, huh?). That's the dollar amount the owner of the bond will get back when the thing matures. The coupon is the amount of dollars (*interest*) that the borrower will pay the owner of the bond at specified intervals, like four or two times a year. It's called a *coupon* because in the old days, before electronic filings, the bond actually had these coupons attached to the paper security that the bond owner clipped and submitted for cash, just like at the supermarket.

So, to put it all together, if GM borrows $400 million for ten years, and promises to pay $10 million in interest twice a year in each of those ten years, then the bond has a face value of $400 million, a coupon of $10 million, and a maturity of ten years. For what comes next, let's assume that GM issues a single bond for $400 million with these characteristics. In the real world, GM may find a single buyer for a single bond, but it's more likely that GM will issue, say, forty bonds, each with a face value of $10 million. That's what makes bonds so much better than bank loans—it's easier for GM to rope in many lenders, each supplying a small amount, than it is to find a single lender who will fork over the full $400 million.

Now comes the hard part. Take a close look at that $10 million coupon. Since GM is paying $10 million twice a year, that's $20 million a year on a loan of $400 million. That works out to approximately 5 percent.* When the loan was made—that is, when the

---

* No, it's not exactly 5 percent because half the money is paid halfway through the year. Do you really want to go here?

bond was first sold—5 percent was the going rate in the markets for a borrower like GM. (That's why GM agreed to pay $10 million—trust me, they tried to pay less but no one came forward with the $400 million when the coupon was any less.) Assuming that whoever bought the bond was willing to hold onto it for the full ten years, then the owner would get his $400 million back at maturity. The return earned on the bond would be the very same 5 percent.

It's not always the case, however, that a bond buyer wants to hold onto the bond until maturity. For whatever reason, the owner of the bond may choose to sell the bond before it matures. No problem: GM is a well-known corporation with known credit. Yes, but. The question is this: What's the fair price for a bond that's sold before maturity? The answer depends on what's happened to interest rates in the time since the bond was issued. If the going interest rate in the market for a borrower like GM is still 5 percent, then the price of the bond will be the same—the bond will sell for its face value of $400 million. But what if interest rates have since gone up? What if GM was lucky when it arranged the loan because, soon after, companies with similar credit stories were paying 7 percent interest? This could happen for a variety of reasons; after all, the price of credit rises either because there's been a rise in demand or a drop in supply, right? So, how much can a bond owner expect to get for the GM bond that has a coupon equivalent of 5 percent when new bonds in the market are paying 7 percent? How can she unload this thing?

Well, the owner of the bond does the same thing the owner of a used car does: She lowers the price. It's clear that no one's going to buy the bond for its face value of $400 million, so the owner lowers the price. Now a new buyer can buy the bond *at a discount,* which is good because the new owner wants a 7 percent return. To get 7 percent from a $20 million a year payment, the price of the bond has to fall to $286 million ($20 divided by $286 is 7 percent). That's how much that bond now sells for: $286 million, or $715 per $1,000 face value.

So the new owner of the bond is all set. The "used" bond he's bought at a substantial discount from face value offers a return that's comparable to the going rate in the market. The original owner of the bond lost out, though, didn't she? She loaned GM $400 million, and now she's clear of the transaction but with only $286 million in her pocket. Hardly the investment she planned!

There's no law that says that bonds have to trade at their original price, and if even there were, it wouldn't work. Bond prices can't be stagnant because interest rates aren't stagnant. As interest rates go up and down, bond prices have to go down and up. That's right: The prices of existing bonds *have* to change to bring the coupons attached to the bonds into line with the current price of credit. If interest rates have gone up since the bond was issued, then the price of the bond has to fall and the original owner will lose out. On the other hand, if interest rates have fallen since the bond was first issued, then the price of the bond has to rise. The only way a bond can stay at the same price is if nothing has changed since it was issued; that's hardly likely, is it?

The fact that bond prices go up and down, just like the wholesale price of Iowa corn, means that the amount of money one earns from holding a bond—the rate of return, or total return—varies. Total return has two components, you see. The fixed coupon payment is only part of what you earn when you own a bond. The other part is the amount of appreciation or depreciation that takes place in the price of the bond. For example: If you were to buy a bond at face value, you'd be forking over $1,000 per $1,000 face value. If the price of the bond ends up unchanged after a year, the coupon payment is your *return*. If the coupon had been set at $50 per $1,000, you earned 5 percent. But suppose instead that the price of the bond fell over the year to $960 per $1,000 face value. Your total return in this case is the $50 coupon payment added to the $40 depreciation in its price, for a grand sum of $10. That $10 represents a 1 percent return on the initial $1,000 investment. In bond-speak, you earned 5 percent interest and experienced a 4 percent capital loss (i.e., a 4 percent decline in your capital or investment), leaving you with a 1 percent total rate of return.

At this point, you're probably scratching your head and thinking: Gee wiz, bonds seem kinda risky. Thank you for that. It leads directly to my next point: Bonds are securities, yes, but that doesn't mean your money is secure. In the case of a bond, the interest payments and the final payoff at maturity are "secured" by the assets and future profits of the borrower, but that simply means that if the issuer of the bond ends up in bankruptcy court, you stand near the front of the line of people looking to get their money back. To say a piece of paper is a security is not the same thing as saying it's secure.

Unless a bond is formally secured, it's backed only by the promise that the borrower will do their best to pay the money back. By contrast, when a prospective homeowner borrows $400,000 to buy a house, the mortgage company insists that the mortgage bond be secured by the house (i.e., the lender gets his hands on the value in the house in a bankruptcy). It's the same scenario when a prospective car buyer takes a loan for a new $20,000 car. When my town issues a municipal bond to pay for a new school, even that bond is secured by the town's tax revenues. When GM issues a $400 million corporate bond, however, no such binds exist.

One last word about bonds: I've neglected to tell you about the tax consequences of bonds. You'll be happy to know that on your federal tax return, the interest you earn on municipal bonds is excluded; that is, the interest is not taxed. On your state return, the interest you earn on U.S. Treasury, Agency, and your state's bonds is not taxed. And for large-city dwellers, the interest on federal, state, and city bonds may not be taxed on your local tax returns (triple tax free!). These are general rules, by the way, and there are exceptions, so please be sure to check on the tax status of any bond you buy. If you are considering a tax-free bond, make sure you figure this into your calculation of returns. Depending on your tax bracket, a U.S. Treasury bond offering a 4.5 percent return might actually yield more after taxes than a corporate bond offering a 5 percent return.

Renting versus Owning

We're going to take a left turn at this point to talk about another way that companies raise funds for their operations. Since this alternative funding source is not a loan, and no debt is created, it's not a credit instrument. But since it's the first word that comes to every investor's lips every morning, I expect you'll forgive me this detour.

As I said earlier, with many types of bonds there is some secured property or stream of income to raise the odds that the bondholder will recoup the original loan amount and receive interest along the way. The owner may have to wait until the bond matures to get it all back, but in most cases it will happen eventually. There's another type of security that doesn't have even that protection. In fact, the paper it's written on is pretty worthless if the issuer goes bust, because owners of this particular security come in last in the long line of people with their hands outstretched (otherwise known as *lenders* or *creditors*) who line up at the door of the bankrupt. I am speaking, of course, about stocks, also called *equities*.

Equities are ownership. When you buy equity, you do just that—you become an owner of the company. You have a right to a portion of the profits it decides to pay out (these are called *dividends*), and if the company is sold, a portion of the sale.* How

---

* Not all profits are paid out as dividends. Companies like to reinvest their dividends to enhance future earnings.

much your share of the company is worth on any given day is based on—want to take a guess?—the supply of and demand for the stock. If the stock market—the market where equities are traded—is efficient and sane, then the price of the stock will reflect the company's prospective earnings. Stock markets aren't always without emotion, however, so stock prices can, and will frequently, deviate from what the experts think is a fair price.

You should know that here in the United States, there are two types of stock. *Common stock* is pretty common (sorry, cheap joke). It represents the most common form of ownership: usually one vote per share to elect the company's board of directors; a percentage of the company's profits paid out (called *dividends*), and a place that's last in line when things go horribly wrong. *Preferred stock* is a better security in some respects, but worse in others. Owners of preferred stocks get their dividends, which are fixed, before any profits are paid out to common shareholders. And if the company goes belly up, preferred shareholders stand in line ahead of the common shareholders (although both come after bondholders). On the other hand, owners of preferred stock don't get to vote for the company's directors, as do the owners of common stock. As with most things cooked up by Wall Street, there's no obvious winner—it's impossible to say one type of stock is better than the other under *all* circumstances.

How much do you earn when you buy stock? While it's impossible to predict the future, or even make sense of the present, it is actually easy to calculate one's return looking back. Your annual return on the purchase of a stock has two components: what the company paid you in the way of dividends over the course of the past year added to the amount of appreciation (hopefully) or depreciation that took place in the price of the stock you own.

A quick example should help to nail this down. Suppose you bought stock in NJK Associates for $12 a share. Say you bought 100 shares on January 2, 2007. NJK Associates had a pretty good year in 2007 and paid out dividends of $0.30 per share. Since you own 100 shares, the check that came in the mail to you was written for $30.00. Sensing that NJK Associates was in for a big year in 2008, investors bid up the price of NJK to $18 by the end of 2007. So your initial investment of $1,200 (100 times $12) became worth $1,800 (100 times $18). The value of your stock appreciated by $600—nice job. In sum, you earned $630 in 2007 on your investment of $1,200. In percentage terms, that amounts to a 53 percent return. Nice job, indeed.

There's one hitch to that return, however. It's not that the return isn't real—it's real all right. What it isn't is *realized*. Unless you actually sell the stock and get $18 a share for it, the appreciation of the stock is a paper profit, not a realized profit. The dividend is realized—the check came in the mail and you cashed it. The profit is not realized until you turn that into cash, too. Did your mother ever teach you not to count your chickens before they hatched? That's a mother's way of explaining paper versus realized profits!

Why make a big deal about realized versus paper profits? For the simple reason that stock prices don't stand still. One day the price of NJK Associates is at $18; the next day it may be down to $11. One day you have a nice fat paper profit; the next day your investment's a loser. If buying stocks is a tricky business, believe me, selling them is worse by far. Do you sell when NJK gets to $18? Not if you think it's going to $25. Do you sell if it dips two bucks to $16—you've still got a profit at that point, right? Not if you think it's going to go back up. How do you know if you're being greedy? Or too cautious? Yes, this is hard. At least we can all agree on that.

Stocks versus Bonds

Stocks and bonds are the two most common forms of securities. To some extent, they are interchangeable. To some extent, they are not. Let's look at this from two perspectives: the borrower's and the investor's.

Why might a company (the borrower) sell stock rather than issue a bond or borrow from a bank when it needs to raise cash? To that $64 billion question there is no simple answer. Bonds are a clear-cut loan. Sometimes that's just what a company needs: money with all the attached strings painted in incandescent colors. However, there are circumstances when a loan doesn't work well. When a company is about to undertake a massive initiative that brings with it loads of uncertainty, for example, bonds may not be the best choice. The company may not want to commit to a hefty quarterly interest payment just as it's embarking on a risky venture. Bonds may not make sense, either, when the need for cash is greater than the company thinks it can borrow at a reasonable cost.

With stocks, there's no firm commitment to make cash payments on a regular basis, starting almost immediately, as there is with debt. That's a big plus. But there is a downside: When a company issues new stock, each of the original shareholders ends up owning less of the company. We say their stock has been diluted—it's like adding more club soda to the punch bowl! New money doesn't come without a cost, in other words. In the case of stock, the cost is a smaller piece of the pie for existing shareholders. In the case of bonds, the cost is the interest payment that has to be maintained on a steady basis until the bond matures.

In point of fact, most companies have issued stock, most have borrowed from banks or other private lenders, and most big companies have issued debt as well. Since there is no right answer to the question each time it's raised, different answers are given at different points in time (making the job of an industry analyst on Wall Street interesting, to say the least!).

How about investors—people with savings? Why might an investor buy stocks rather than bonds? What are the advantages of one over another? Another good question, another case where there's no single answer for all circumstances, and where a really good explanation of all the different considerations worth noting would take volumes, not paragraphs. Obviously, this is not the place to embark on that journey. But I do want to raise one issue that fits in here: volatility. Given our discussion about supply and demand, you should realize that both bond and stock prices go up and down virtually every minute of every day, weekends and holidays excepted. You may only hear about the stock market's gyrations on the evening news, but that's only because most news people don't know from bonds (even though they probably own some). No, both bond and stock prices are volatile—meaning they fluctuate a lot—and money is earned and lost in both markets each and every day. Also, depending on what's going on in the world, bond prices may move in the opposite direction as stock prices—or not. Because markets are volatile and unpredictable, smart investors diversify. Hedging your bets—that is, not putting all your eggs in one basket—makes good sense. That's another thing I'll bet your mother taught you.

4

Here Comes da Fed

About a hundred years ago, a deep financial crisis crippled the U.S. economy, causing thousands to lose their savings and forcing banks to close their doors in the face of hordes of angry customers. Financial panics are as old as humanity, I imagine, but the United States panic of 1907 was particularly nasty. Stock prices had been cut in half, a dangerously large number of banks were about to declare themselves insolvent, and the hub of the country's financial dealings, New York City, was on the verge of bankruptcy. (And to think, it was all started by two men in their lust to corner the copper market!)*

Thankfully, a full-blown collapse of the U.S. economic and financial system was averted that year. Most of the credit for stanching the bleeding goes to J.P. Morgan, the indomitable head of the bank that carried his name, J.P. Morgan & Co. With the help (read: *money*) of a few Wall Street financiers, stock exchange officers, and high-ranking Treasury officials, J.P. Morgan raised enough cash to prop up the exchanges and stop the runs on banks.**

---

* According to Montana historian Sarah McNelis, financier Augustus Heinze made a loan to his brothers so they could corner the copper market on the stock exchange. Their failed attempt to do so led to a run on Knickerbocker Trust, which spread like wildfire to other trust companies and banks. Source: *The (Minneapolis) Region* (August 1989).

** A bank run is when many of the bank's depositors show up at its doors, demanding that their deposits be paid back immediately.

It was both the speed and efficacy of Morgan's actions in 1907 that led Congress to deduce that the United States might well benefit from a strong central bank that could help to steady the banking and financial systems going forward. In 1908, Congress created a National Monetary Commission to study banking and currency reform in detail. After much debate, haggling, and politicking, Congress finally passed the Federal Reserve Act of 1913, creating the very same Federal Reserve System that exists today. (Well, maybe not the *very same* Federal Reserve we know today. I'd like to think that today's Federal Reserve would not have made the mistakes it made in 1929 when, in response to a crash in the bond and stock markets, the Fed took actions that led to the Great Depression!)

The *Federal Reserve System*—or the *Fed*, as it's commonly called—has one ominous-sounding name, so let's break it down. *Federal* suggests that it is a U.S. government institution, as it is. Its middle name, *Reserve*, will become clear in the next chapter when we look at the inner workings of banks. Meanwhile, *System* implies that there's more to the Fed than a single office block in Washington. Indeed, there is. The Fed consists of a Board of Governors that is located in Washington, between the White House and the Potomac River. In addition, there are twelve regional Federal Reserve Banks scattered across the country (Boston, New York, Philadelphia, Richmond, Atlanta, Cleveland, Chicago, Minneapolis, St. Louis, Kansas City, Dallas, and San Francisco). Only thing is, the Fed was established in 1913, when most of the population of the United States was near the East Coast. Thus, as you look at the list of the so-called District Banks, few are far west of the Mississippi. Not to worry: The Fed is a not a representative system like the House of Representatives or even the Senate for that matter.

The chairman of the Board of Governors of the Federal Reserve System is commonly referred to as the second-most powerful man in the world—second only to the president of the United States.* That should give you some indication of the power that the Fed wields—and explain why we're going to spend the rest of this chapter talking about what the Fed does. Unlike most groups in Washington, however, the Fed's power is not dictated from above, although it's all legal and above board. Rather, it's a bottom-up affair. The Fed derives its true power from the work that it does.

There's a nifty little book (well, at 146 pages, maybe not that little) that the Fed gives out for free that describes the Fed's work in great, but readable, detail.** I recommend it if this stuff interests you. According to its own PR professionals, the Fed operates in four major areas: (1) The Fed provides financial services to commercial and foreign banks; (2) the Fed is the preeminent regulator of the U.S. banking system; (3) the Fed is charged with maintaining a stable financial system and "containing" financial market risk; and (4) the Fed is charged with conducting monetary policy that leads to stable prices and economic growth. That's some portfolio. I can't think of a Cabinet-level post that has as much in its inbox. That's why I say that no one needs to confer power on the Fed or its chairman; it's natural given what they do.

These are the Fed's four roles. However, I think these roles will be a bit easier to explain to you if I break them down even further.

The Banker's Bank: Early on in chapter 2, when we were defining money, I snuck in the fact that the banks you and I deal with have a bank that they themselves use for deposits, loans, and the like. That bankers' bank is the Fed. Virtually every bank in the United States (including all nationally chartered banks) has an

---

* When the Fed chairman was Alan Greenspan, he was affectionately referred to as "Uncle Al" by participants in the financial markets. Now that Ben Bernanke has taken over the helm, you don't hear much use of the title "Uncle"—Uncle Ben is rice, not power!

** You can download it from the Fed's Web site, http://www.federalreserve.gov/pf/pdf/pf_complete.pdf.

account at the Fed, and it is to this account that the bank makes deposits, or taps into, zillions of times each day as it conducts transactions with the likes of you, me, and GM.

If only because it is the central bank, the bankers' bank, the Fed has a dominant position in the U.S. financial system. But there's more.

The U.S. Government's Bank: The U.S. government churns through trillions of dollars each year, which makes the federal government's banking business one hot commodity. Problem is, can a private bank be trusted to handle all that money without the slightest temptation to fleece Uncle Sam? Rather than figure out the answer to that question the hard way, Uncle Sam uses the central bank, the Fed, as its bank. This isn't to say that normal banks don't have some U.S. government accounts—they do. But these are minor affairs. The big money of Uncle Sam's is at the Fed.

The U.S.'s International Bank: Being the U.S. central bank, the Fed also gets to look over the flow of money to and from foreign countries. Many foreign central banks have accounts at the Fed, and the Fed itself safeguards a hoard of foreign currency in its vault in New York.*

The Bank Regulator: In addition to providing normal, everyday financial services to the global banking system, the Fed is also there as good cop/bad cop for U.S. banks. This means that the Fed has primary responsibility for ensuring that banks in this country are financially sound and behaving responsibly. Congress has long been concerned that the wealth of the nation courses through the banking system each day; thus it has passed laws to ensure the safety of that money. The Fed enforces those rules— and lays down a pack of rules of its own—to ensure a stable, efficient, and fair banking system.

---

* With advance reservations, you can get a glimpse of the New York Fed and the bank's U.S. and foreign money and gold reserves.

I've made it sound like the Fed's nothing but the bad cop, and that's not true. When necessary—and it doesn't happen all that often, thankfully—the Fed will provide emergency loans to help a bank (or the banking system as a whole or even a financial institution that's not a bank) stay on its feet. The Fed's engineered a few notable bailouts in its history, even recently. One example came immediately after 9/11. After direct hits to the financial system on September 11, 2001, the Fed announced that its loan office was open and available for any institution that needed help to remain open for business as usual. Largely because the Fed took this uncompromising stance, the U.S. financial system was not brought down when the twin towers collapsed.

An even more recent example of the Fed's stabilizing presence came with the crisis in the mortgage market in 2007–2008. In the spring and summer of 2007, the financial markets as a whole were negatively affected by homeowners defaulting on their mortgages because either the interest rate on their mortgage went up (not all mortgages have a fixed rate; some vary) or their property value went down so much that it made sense for them to walk away. Big mortgage lenders, to be sure, were hurting, but the aftershocks were felt by many, many financial institutions, as well as by the markets themselves. Indeed, in the spring of 2008, a large investment house, Bear Stearns, came within minutes of bankruptcy due to its shaky mortgage portfolio. Luckily, the Fed was responsive, and the problem was contained as well as could be expected. The Fed can't prevent everything from hitting the fan, after all, but it can redirect the blades. . . .

The Clearing Bank: Because every bank either has an account at the Fed or is at most just one step away, when a bank needs to send money to another bank, the sending bank uses the Fed to make the transfer. The first bank simply instructs the Fed to make the transfer between the two banks' accounts there. Look at it this way: When my daughter borrows money from a friend at school, the cash changes hands right there on the spot, in front of the cafeteria checkout. But what if my dentist in Boston borrows money to buy a home from a bank in Seattle? Is he supposed to fly out there and pick up the cash himself? Of course not. The Seattle bank "sends" the money to my dentist's bank via the Fed. First, the Seattle bank sends instructions to the Fed to transfer, say, $500,000 to the Boston bank's account at the Fed (remember, real estate is expensive in Boston). The Boston bank then transfers the money to my dentist's checking account. To finish the story, my dentist writes a check on his bank account at the real estate closing.

The Fed is the central clearinghouse for all financial transactions, not just loans. Checks, cards, electronic transfers—everything that passes from one financial intermediary to another—passes through the Fed at some point. Even when interbank transactions are lumped together, that's still zillions of transactions each day! This beehive of activity is what is called in Fed-speak the *payments system*. And the Fed is in the center of it all.*

Actually, to say that the Fed is at the center of the payments system hardly does it justice. Grab a dollar bill out of your wallet. What does it say? Yes, it's legal tender in the United States. Yes, it was printed by the Bureau of Engraving. But who issued the piece of paper you're looking at? The Fed. That note allows you to go to the nearest Fed bank and get, well, $1 in return (did you expect gold?). Silly, really, the idea of exchanging one note for another, but the fact remains that the Fed is the maker of U.S. money. Remember that fact: We're going to use it in a less than a minute.

When the Fed, by its own admission, says that it is charged with maintaining financial market stability and "containing" risk, it means that it exercises with great care its responsibilities toward

---

* Just for the heck of it, take a quick look at the back of a check that cleared and was returned to you (if you can; if your statements are delivered electronically, you may no longer have that option). On the back of the check, you'll see the stamps of which Fed district bank handled your transaction.

making money, facilitating the payments system, and watching over banks. Not that occasional lapses don't occur—they do—but all in all the Fed deserves high marks for its work in this area.

The Maker of Monetary Policy: From its dealings with all the U.S. banks and many foreigners, the Fed is in the unique position of being able to influence the financial system from the ground up. This ability to influence the outcome of financial transactions — the level of prices, interest rates, and exchange rates—is called *monetary policy.**

Let's deal with the obvious first: Why? What does the Fed hope to accomplish through monetary policy? The quick and dirty answer, which is not an untruth, is that the Fed wants to influence prices, interest rates, and exchange rates so that Americans lead more productive lives and enjoy an ever-rising standard of living. When prices, interest rates, and exchange rates are stable and predictable, it's easier for all of us to plan and execute the thousands of transactions that we conduct each year. Also, when the economy is growing slowly but surely, so job losses are at a manageable level and undue upward pressures on prices are being contained, then the odds are good that growth will continue. We can't deny that shocks will occur that derail the financial markets and the economy. As the saying goes, %$#^ happens. But if the underlying conditions of the economy are strong, our ability to weather these shocks is much improved.

OK, then, how does the Fed make monetary policy? This question can be answered on two levels: first, by considering the actual mechanics of how it affects the level of interest rates and exchange rates, and second, by assessing the thought process that goes into

---

* An exchange rate is the rate at which one can exchange one currency, say, the dollar, for another, say, the euro. It is, in essence, the foreign price of the dollar. Or the purchasing power of the dollar in terms of other currencies. This last definition makes clear the connection between exchange rates and inflation: When the dollar buys fewer goods at home, it usually buys fewer euros and yen abroad.

decisions to change policy. Needless to say, the former topic is something of a bore, the latter immensely fascinating (really).

Money was defined earlier in this book as the cash, checking account, and checking account-like deposits that we all use every day to transact business. The Fed's control over money is thus pretty direct. For one, the Fed is responsible for printing those dollar bills. (I said we'd be using in short order the fact that the Fed was the maker of money; this is where that comes in.) For another, the money in the checking and checking-like accounts that we hold at banks is passed on by our banks to the Fed; that's where the money is stored. Still, the Fed can't print money willy-nilly or make random adjustments to the banks' books—people go to jail for that sort of thing!

In theory, the Fed has three ways in which it changes the amount of money in the economy to influence interest rates. Only one way is used consistently.* This strategy is called *open-market operations,* and it works like this: The Fed and commercial banks all own quantities of U.S. Treasury bonds. Why? Other than cash, which earns no interest, this is the only way that the Fed can hold its assets because it's a government body. Banks have a good part of their assets in the loans they write (because they are owed money, loans are considered a bank's assets), but they also hold a considerable amount of U.S. Treasury bonds to help manage the risk in their portfolios.** To put money into the banking system, all the Fed has to do is convince some banks to sell it some of their Treasury bonds. This reduces the dollar amount of bonds on the banks' books and increases their cash deposits at the Fed. The

---

* The other two are changes in the rate at which the Fed loans commercial banks money in a crisis—the so-called *discount rate*—and changes in the amount of reserves that banks are required to hold at the Fed. In the spring of 2008, the Fed expanded its repertoire, but as of this writing it's too soon to tell if these additional tools will become routine, so I hesitate to include them here.
** Remember, U.S. Treasury bonds are considered the best risk in the world. By contrast, loans are risky business. Banks don't want a portfolio full of risk!

banks will put that extra cash to work because sitting on it would earn no interest. The bank may make a loan to you, me, or Kyle. Or maybe make a loan to Microsoft or Novartis. Whatever. The point is that as long as the bank does something with the extra money, the money flows into the economy, meaning that the supply of money is increased.*

All things being equal, when the Fed puts more money and credit into the economy, interest rates fall, which means it's cheaper for people to borrow money for big-ticket items. Bottom line: The economy expands. Of course, if the Fed were to carry these actions to excess, or undertake them when the economy didn't need the extra push, inflation would occur. So the Fed governors and reserve bank presidents together think long and hard before taking action.

Just to reinforce the lesson, consider how the Fed drains money from the economy. Since the Fed wants some of the money it holds for banks to disappear, it contrives to sell U.S. Treasury bonds to the banks. The banks end up with more of their assets tied up in Treasury bonds and they have smaller cash accounts at the Fed. With smaller accounts at the Fed, they have less money at their disposal for loans. Fewer loans and more expensive credit, all things being equal, will lead to a reduction in the economy's rate of growth. This isn't something the Fed wants, obviously. It's just that sometimes it's necessary to reduce the risk of inflation.

Not So Fast

Executing open-market operations is the least cumbersome part of making monetary policy. The really big decision is how much. In other words, how does the Fed know how many bonds to buy or sell?

Will I shock you if I say that not only do they not know at the time they order the operations, but they won't know if they

---

* When the cash sits in the Fed's account, it's not money because it's not in the private sector. But when the cash from the Fed is transferred to the bank's account at the Fed, it comes into the domain of the private sector and thus gets counted as money.

picked the right amount until months, if not years, have passed? It's fine-tuning with a sledgehammer!

The reason it takes the Fed so long to find out the end result of its monetary actions is that what it's most interested in affecting is the economy itself—sales, prices, employment, and so on. In between money and the economy, there are lots of ways that the Fed's well-intentioned policies can and do get pushed off-course. And there are lags: It takes time for the reverberations from the Fed's actions to work their way through the economy.

Economists hold differing opinions about how to handle this problem. Many economists used to think the best solution was to follow the cash. Since money is used in every transaction, money would be the Fed's best way to track whether its policies are going to lead to the desired level of economic activity. Unfortunately, this didn't work so well in practice. Other economists prefer to track the level of credit in the economy, since the availability of credit is also a factor in the economy's growth. This is a hard one to track, though, since credit figures aren't available in real time. Arguably the majority of economists think the best way to track the Fed's actions is through the federal funds rate. This has the advantage of being instantly available. And as we know, an interest rate is ultimately a reflection of both the supply of credit and the economy's demand for it, which gives the Fed a leg up.*

What a System!

So ends our "theoretical" discussion of the financial system. Definitions of money and credit, the determination of interest rates, the forms debt takes (and equity), and the Fed's central role in keeping it all together—all this is water under the bridge. It's time now to take a closer look at the institutions that play the game, and the products and tools they've given us.

---

* It's not done here in the United States, but in some other countries the government's bank targets foreign exchange rates in lieu of interest rates or money.

5

Order from Chaos: The U.S. Financial System and Its Institutions

Walk into a bank anywhere in the United States, big city or small town, and the odds are good that you've walked in to one of the nicest offices around. Banks are not foolish with money: I know firsthand that bank employees behind the scenes toil away in dark, dreary cubicles and windowless offices. So why do banks outfit their branches in Italian marble, plush carpets, and cushy sofas?

Answering this question constitutes the first step toward understanding the financial system. The answer is trust. Bank customers—all of us, in other words—feel more comfortable dropping off our hard-earned cash in banks that appear financially sound and firmly entrenched. Tellers in trailers could take the transactions just as well, but would they take in as many transactions as tellers treading imported tile? Probably not. A nice-looking branch office is a bank's most powerful marketing tool. Besides, how does the saying go? If you've got it, flaunt it!

Getting customers to bring in their deposits is the first order of business for banks. It's the equivalent of a tailor buying cloth and thread or a phone company buying fiber optic cable. Money is the raw material with which banks ply their trade. And their

trade is simple enough: They lend the money back out to customers who hold their credit cards, borrow for a new car, or need
financing for a major business expansion across town or halfway
around the world. Some of the bank's customers are consumers
like you and me. Some of the bank's customers are businesses large
and small. Some of the bank's customers are local or state governments. And this goes both ways: Many customers both deposit
and borrow from the bank, or, if not the same bank, then *some*
bank (which for our purposes is one and the same, since we're
interested in the banking system, not Citi or Bank of America
specifically).

You might well be wondering how banks earn a profit if they
simply lend out the money they "acquire" from our checking
accounts, savings accounts, and CDs.* Here's the trick: Banks only
keep on hand a fraction of the money they show on their books as
deposits. And a small fraction, at that! So consider the $100 my
son deposited into his checking account this morning. The bank
will probably hold onto about 10 percent of that $100, or $10. The
rest ($90) bank officers will recycle into a loan for another cus-
tomer who comes through the door with a new mortgage application, for instance, or one who's on a shopping spree on Fifth
Avenue with a credit card issued by the bank. The interest on the
mortgage loan, say, 7 percent, is a pretty good return on the bank's
money. The interest on the credit card could be as high as 30 percent—that's a whopping good return on the bank's money.

And that's not all! Think about what happens when the seller
of the home goes to the closing. She gets a big check for the house

---

* *CD* stands for certificate of deposit. It is a savings account at a bank or thrift, but
it's different from the normal savings account, called the *passbook*, in that it has a
specific fixed term (usually three months, six months, or from one to six years). A
penalty is imposed if the owner of a CD redeems it before its maturity. The interest
on a CD is fixed as well, but thanks to the more limited redemption options, that rate
is higher than the rate on passbook or statement savings.

she's sold and deposits that into the bank. Part of my son's $100 was included in that deposit. Or think about what happens when a fellow pays for his new home theater system at Best Buy. Best Buy takes the day's cash receipts and deposits them in the bank. Part of my son's $100 might have been in that deposit as well. (For simplicity's sake, it makes sense to pretend there's only one bank in the area. In truth, there are many, but, again, from our industry perspective, it makes no difference.)

The money the bank lends out, in other words, comes right back to it. It comes right back as a new deposit that, you guessed it, the bank then lends out again. My son's initial $100 deposit can feed loans totaling $1,000, with the bank earning anywhere from, at present, 5 percent to 30 percent on each dollar lent out.* Let's do the math. The initial $100 deposit cost the bank nothing, because it didn't pay my son any interest on the money in his checking account (had he deposited the cash in his savings account, they would have paid him a bit of interest, say, 2 percent per year). Let's say, on average, the bank earned 10 percent per year on all the money it lent out, all $1,000 of it. Ten percent of $1,000 is $100. So, the bank earned a return of $100 from an initial $100 deposit that cost nothing to acquire.

Explains the marble, doesn't it?

Banks are good business, about that there's little doubt. Yet the number of banks is shrinking. Why? Well, the simple answer is that there are too many of them (7,303 at last count).** If you think about the banking choices you have in your own neighborhood, it's likely to be ten to fifteen companies, taking into consideration the small local banks as well as the big national banks. Those kinds of numbers make for a lot of competition, and a lot of

---

* $100 + $90 + $81 + $72.90 + . . . = $1,000
** As of September 2007. This is the number of commercial banks insured by the Federal Deposit Insurance Corporation (FDIC).

opportunity for mergers and acquisitions.* Bankers are always looking for a chance to acquire a bigger deposit base—for the reasons explained above. Of course, when a business transaction like a merger or acquisition is going on, the deposits don't come for free. The acquiring bank has to pay a price, after all, for the bank it's acquiring. Even so, bankers haven't flinched.

Industry shrinkage isn't simply a matter of takeovers, though. As we'll see later in this chapter, the banking industry is coming under pressure from other types of financial institutions that offer consumers and businesses many products and services that banks have not, and, in many cases, cannot deliver. You see, the U.S. banking system is probably the most heavily regulated industry in the country, nay the world. Bankers' hands are tied not just by national regulations and international agreements but by state regulations as well. In fact, banking is one of the rare industries in this country where interstate business is highly regulated, even today. Banks still make a good profit; don't get me wrong. But there's been even bigger money made in the financial industry away from banks in recent years.

Bank Wannabes

Not every institution that you might think is a bank is actually a full-fledged commercial bank. The bank at the office or factory may well be a credit union, not a bank. The savings bank in town is probably a savings and loan association or a mutual savings bank, not the commercial bank that I've just described. A brokerage firm (e.g., Charles Schwab or Merrill Lynch) may take your money and give you checks, but it's a brokerage company or

---

* In a merger, two firms agree to merge their businesses and, typically, the new management includes members of both companies. In an acquisition, one company buys out the other, and the buyout can be either friendly or hostile. Either way, management at the new company is likely to be lopsided in favor of the acquiring company, and if there are layoffs, they are likely to be from the ranks of the acquired firm.

investment manager, not a bank. A mutual fund company may also set you up with deposits and give you checks, but it's not a bank either.

These financial institutions make money on your checking and savings deposits the same way a bank does. For them, the percentage they hold as reserves, what was 10 percent for the bank, may be more or less. This changes the math, but not much else. More importantly, many of these nonbanks have other ways of earning money, too. So don't go off thinking that to make the big bucks you must be a banker. The financial industry offers many well-paid career options, some far more lucrative than banking. (I say this without facetiousness. Whenever I give this explanation of how banks work, someone always asks, be it a sixty-five-year old retiree or a twenty-year old student, "How can I become a banker?")

A *savings and loan association* (S&L) is the closest relative of a bank. The big difference between a bank and an S&L is that most S&Ls don't make loans to businesses, concentrating their efforts instead on consumers and local construction. S&Ls got a bad name in the 1980s when many of them went bust—a feat that was only partly their fault.* The S&L crisis dominated the headlines for years. And for good reason: The problem was severe enough to warrant a federal government bailout to the tune of $150 billion. As you might expect, that much money bought the industry a long-lasting stigma that to this day discourages new deposits. As a result, there aren't as many S&Ls around these days, and many now call themselves thrift institutions instead. I would be

---

* A full explanation of the S&L crisis can be found on many Web sites. Essentially here's what happened: S&Ls made too many loans that were not prudent. They got caught by a rise in inflation and interest rates. They faced increasing competition from aggressive mutual funds and brokerage houses. And because they were S&Ls and not banks, their operations came under scrutiny by a different regulator from those that oversee banks. Oh, and did I mention fraud?

misleading you, by the way, if I didn't mention that commercial banks suffered a similar crisis in the 1980s, for many of the same reasons. The banks weathered the crisis more successfully, however, because they are more diversified in their dealings and less tied down to certain locales. But back to S&Ls: Fewer than nine hundred exist today, half as many as ten years ago and a quarter of their number twenty years back.

Another type of thrift institution, or nonbank, is the *mutual savings bank*. Mutual savings banks, found mostly in the Northeast, also don't write loans to businesses as a general rule. On the contrary, the owners of mutual savings banks are the depositors themselves, and they tend to invest very cautiously. If this sounds like the place for your money, just be aware that such cooperative ownership makes for more difficult oversight. Think coop board, condo association, or dorm council. *Dysfunctional* is the word that comes to my mind, although almost all of them run flawlessly nonetheless. The profit motive, I guess, keeps the crazies in line.

Credit unions are the last of the thrifts. Like mutual savings banks, the credit union's own depositors own the institution. Credit unions are definitely a class unto themselves, however. For one thing, members have some connection to one another—they may work for the same company or be part of the same trade union, for example. Secondly, reflecting and respecting the tie that connects its members, credit unions are nonprofit organizations; they do not try to earn a profit from the services they provide and thus pay no taxes on the earnings they may generate. This allows the credit union to offer its members lower interest rates on loans and higher interest rates on deposits.*

---

* Credit unions have a slightly different legal structure; depositors are shareholders in the company. Thus, the interest on deposits is technically a dividend on a share account.

With all of that going for them, you might think that credit unions, at least, would be a growing industry. You'd be wrong. The number of credit unions in the country is shrinking, just like the number of S&Ls and mutual savings banks. The issue facing all thrifts is that they tend to be local while both consumerism and business are increasingly becoming national and global. That puts them all at a comparative disadvantage in relation to commercial banks. Thrifts are also vulnerable to takeovers. Does it really make sense for there to be five separate mortgage departments within a block of each another in a small community? Or five safes? Or five branch managers? Truth is, the potential for cost savings in the banking and thrift industries remains huge, even today, even after the massive number of mergers and buyouts that have already taken place.

Inflation Changed Everything

When your great-grandparents and grandparents banked, they probably had a long-standing relationship with a particular bank in the neighborhood where the banker knew their name, where they deposited their paychecks, where they used a checking account for day-to-day bill paying, and where they had a savings account or two that held their investment dollars.* Life was simpler back then. Banking was simpler back then. We can look for many reasons why the world changed, and there are many we could cite, but the biggest catalyst for change was one thing and one thing only: inflation.

When there was no inflation to speak of—it truly wasn't even a word people knew—the interest rate that your ancestors earned on their savings was low. We're talking a percentage point or two. The rate rarely changed, and no one really cared much when it did

---

* Actually, there's a good chance they held their savings in an S&L because these could offer a slightly higher interest rate by law than commercial banks.

because the change was so small. Remember, many workers knew their retirement would be covered by the company pension plan, and fewer children attended college, so their savings, while important, didn't have the same weight as they do today. The creation of the social security system, as part of President Franklin D. Roosevelt's New Deal, also kept a lid on savings, as it provided a safety net in old age for American workers.

Interest rates in the good ol' days weren't even of the bank's own choosing, really. National and state regulators decided what the rates on savings accounts could be (and checking accounts paid no interest at all). They were careful to recognize that longer-term deposits deserved higher returns, that is, higher interest rates. And the regulators worked together to set standard differences between the different types of institutions—commercial banks, S&Ls, and the like. Heck, they even instituted laws, still on the books today, that effectively limited the size of an individual's single savings deposit at a bank, thereby encouraging more banks to open in growing towns.

On the flip side, banks priced their loans back then a standard amount above the rate they paid to depositors. The regulators watched that pretty closely to make sure that the banks didn't rip off borrowers. Again, the regulators were careful to recognize that not every borrower was of the same quality; some people were better credit risks than others and earned preferential rates, while those with worse credit histories were made to pay more to borrow.

Everything having to do with a bank or thrift was well defined, all well executed back in the days before inflation. Probably the biggest risk these guys (and make no mistake about it, there were no gals) faced back then was robbery. Indeed, the combination of low inflation and regulated rates made banking pretty much a part-time job, which explains why, to this day, golf is the favorite pastime of bankers. Bank managers became infamous for the martini lunch and/or the afternoon eighteen holes (plus #19 back at the clubhouse).

Life was good, but as it does so often when things are good, the world quickly came apart. Starting in the 1960s, inflation crashed onto the scene with a loud bang. And it screwed up the banking/thrift industry but good.

There's a long story here, I'm sure you can feel it coming, but I'm going to cut it short because, at its heart, the problem inflation caused the banking and thrift industry was a simple one. (I'm going to make the story even shorter by using the term *banks* to refer to both banks and thrifts.)

Stage 1: Banks realized that, due to inflation, they had to raise the interest rates they charged on loans. Borrowers weren't happy, but they realized that the price of everything was going up, so why not credit. In other words, if they had to pay more for a mortgage, big deal, since the price of the house they were buying was going up, too. The first stage didn't hurt banks and thrifts; in fact, the effect was just the opposite. Since banks were not allowed by law to raise the rates they paid on deposits, banks earned an even bigger spread (read: *profit*) on the loans they made during this period. The two-martini lunch was born.

Stage 2: The proverbial *&#%$* hit the fan. Depositors rose up in arms that they were being had (that's the polite term, of course). The price of everything was going up, including the price of credit, yet their bank deposits were paying the same measly percent or two in interest per year. "Are we going to be driven like sheep to slaughter?" they called out. Not on their life, your life, or mine.

Stage 3: With consumers up in arms, the free market did what it always does to solve a problem: It innovated. In a few short years, the U.S. financial system, dragging the UK and European financial systems right behind it, went through enormous structural change. To an outsider looking in, most of the changes appeared to benefit consumers. There was plenty of that, but it wasn't all. The structural changes forced by inflation had just as large an impact on business finance. I think it's fair to say that most of what you see in the world today by way of financial institutions, policies, and investment/borrowing choices were put in place in the 1960s and 1970s in response to inflation.

Consumers Break Out

The first thing that had to go was the ridiculously low interest rates that banks and thrifts were paying on savings accounts. Laws were adapted to allow these rates to rise, but the adjustments were neither quick enough nor large enough to make consumers happy. Thankfully, mutual fund managers stepped in to offer consumers a way out.

The mutual fund industry had been around for years, offering consumers and other investors a vehicle to invest in stocks and bonds without necessarily having the expertise to do so (more about mutual funds later). But mutual fund investments had always been of a long-term nature; there were restrictions, and costs, associated with withdrawing money from these funds. The traditional mutual fund product was no answer to the consumer's frustration over low savings deposit rates at banks.

End of story? Hardly. Eager to make money on the billions of dollars in consumer deposits, mutual fund companies devised and delivered a completely different product to woo consumer savings away from banks and thrifts: the *money market mutual fund*. Money market funds represent capitalism at its best, which is to say that they are innovative, responsive to the customer's needs—and profitable!

First off, money market funds give consumers a better interest rate than savings accounts at banks. Mutual fund companies, you see, are not subject to the same restrictions as banks; they're not even regulated by the same government bodies. The mutual fund company is free to pay a higher rate of return to savers because it has the ability to lend cash to corporate borrowers who are willing and able to pay higher rates to borrow. Pretty smart, huh? Are money market funds more risky than a bank deposit? Yes, indeed, they are. Do they pay better than a bank deposit? Yes, indeed, they do.

Money market mutual funds aren't quite as easy to use as a savings account at a bank. You can't roll up to a local drive-in window and withdraw cash—no lollipops for the kiddies or bones for the dog. Sometimes there are restrictions on how many withdrawals you can make in a month. But money market funds give you checks that you can use just like bank checks. Indeed, they are bank checks with your name on them.

Banks didn't take the money market mutual fund lying down. Bankers swigged their martinis quickly and hit the drawing boards themselves. The result was the Money Market Deposit Account, or MMDA. It's a different animal from the money market mutual fund, but it shares one crucial trait: Like a money market mutual fund, it offers savers higher short-term rates of return than banks pay out on their regular savings deposits. Another example of capitalism at work!

Driver's Ed

It's time to take a step to the side in this discussion of financial institutions and address the question of regulators. I've referred a few times already to the federal and state government officials that oversee the actions of banks, thrifts, and other financial companies. Who are these gals (bank regulators are often women), why do they exist, and how do they work?

OK, OK, not the burning questions you want this book to answer. However, since you won't understand the financial system unless you know about these folks, I'm going to plow ahead—quickly and quirkily.

Do you remember what a driver's ed car looks like? If not, go ask a teenager. It's a regular car with one major adaptation: It sports a second foot brake for use by the front-seat passenger, that is, the instructor. Anyone who's followed a student driver down the road knows exactly why that brake is there: to protect the passengers in the car, other drivers on the road, and hapless pedestrians, animals, and small children who might be within reach of the car's fender. The instructor's job is to let the student learn how to drive on her own, but sometimes a hard brake is in everyone's best interest.

There you have the philosophy behind banking regulation. Bank regulators don't want to stop banks from running successfully, and they don't want to interfere with the free markets, but they are there to protect the bank's customers (savers and borrowers) from decisions that break the law or put people in unexpected jeopardy. Regulators also have the responsibility to ensure that banks don't damage the communities they serve.

Unfortunately, it's not always clear exactly what kind of intervention regulators should arrange, nor is it always obvious when they should stick their necks out and when they should schedule their own round of golf. More so than many other activities in the financial industry, regulation is art as much as science. (Another reason it's sometimes lax: Many regulators take up management positions in banks after a short stint regulating them. Since they don't want to ruin their chances with a potential employer, bank and thrift regulators are often a bit less aggressive than many in Congress might like.)

Banks in the United States are regulated for the most part by the Fed and the Federal Deposit Insurance Corporation, or FDIC.*

---

* The Office of the Comptroller of the Currency, which regulates about three thousand somewhat smaller banks, is now out to get me for not mentioning its role (but its influence is less than that of the FDIC or the Fed).

Congress and state governments have passed laws that limit what banks can and can't do, and it is the job of these two government entities to make sure banks follow the law to the letter. The Fed and the FDIC also make their own rules for banks to follow, and banks must abide by these rules just as carefully. If it sounds to you like the Fed and the FDIC are powerful forces in the banking industry, you've got it right.

The FDIC has the more limited role, so let me quickly dispose of it (only figuratively). The FDIC provides a safety net so that people feel more comfortable trusting their money to banks (for some, Italian marble and plush carpeting just aren't enough). They do this by guaranteeing the safety of an individual's money in the bank up to $100,000. So, if a bank were to fail, for lending too much to a big-time crook, for instance, the FDIC would make up the loss for depositors, up to the $100,000 ceiling. When individuals, small nonprofits like churches and private schools, and others have more than $100,000 that they want to store in a bank or thrift, they typically spread their money around at different banks/thrifts in the area so that all their money comes under the protection of the FDIC guarantee.*

If the FDIC's role sounds like it's a good one, from the perspective of the consumer/saver, it is. Not much in economics is 100 percent pure, however, as you've learned. For one thing, the banks must pay the FDIC for the insurance it provides. Needless to say, the bank passes that cost on to its customers by way of lower interest rates. Much more important, however, is the effect the insurance sometimes has on bankers and even the FDIC itself. Because the insurance is there as a safety net for savers, some bankers may feel free to make foolish investments in the hope of

---

* Some institutions expand insurance coverage beyond the $100,000 FDIC maximum. They do so with private insurance, however, which means it's backed by the owners of the insurer, not the U.S. government.

earning just a tad more return for the bank.* That's not what the program is there for, obviously. And then there's the problem that the FDIC creates for itself: It never wants to pay out on those insurance policies because it certainly isn't sitting on enough cash to handle more than a few bankrupt banks at any one time. Therefore, the FDIC jumps through all sorts of hoops, with the Fed by its side, to prevent banks from failing, especially big ones that would set the FDIC back billions.

Lucky That the Fed Can Print Money, Eh?

Of course, I'm kidding. These are not exactly the circumstances when the Fed powers up the printing presses, although, as we've seen, the Fed does react to financial turmoil with an infusion of extra cash. Let's now move on to the Fed, for the Fed's regulatory influence on banks is unquestionably more significant than that of the FDIC.

Although the Fed would deny it, bankers would swear to this fact: Just about anything new a bank wants to do has to get approval from the Fed. Want to branch out? Better call the Fed. Want to close branches? Better call the Fed. Want to offer financial advice to customers? Call the Fed. Want to investigate a new line of lending, say, to casinos? Better call the chairman of the Fed. The first act of the Fed is indeed to oversee the banks' branch system. Until 1999 there were some very long-standing laws on the books in Washington that limited how and where banks could open up branches. These laws were finally repealed in 1999—is there any state where Bank of America or Citi doesn't have a branch or an ATM?—but the Fed still oversees branch networks.

The second act of the Fed is to watch over the bank's books like a hawk to ensure that there's no funny business. Remember those reserves that the bank had to put aside from my son's deposit? The Fed watches to make sure the bank does it. The Fed

* The tendency to take on too much risk carries the delightful name of *moral hazard*.

takes note of the rates the bank is offering on its different types of accounts, and makes sure that all the rules and regulations of those accounts are being followed. The Fed also makes sure that banks aren't lending money out incorrectly. Banks face very strict limits on what kinds of investments (loans) they can make. For instance, banks can't buy stock or bonds issued by corporations. The Fed gets real-time reports on bank holdings so Fed officials can sniff out anything that smells illegal. And they conduct on-site audits periodically.

The Fed also worries about the health of the bank, even when the bank's been proven to be following all the rules. Just because a bank is buying Uncle Sam's debt, you see, doesn't mean the bank can't screw up. Rest easy that the Fed has joined with other central banks around the world to monitor a whole variety of very technical measurements of bank solvency. One part of this effort has been to devise methods of assessing the riskiness of a bank's transactions. Trust me, banking regulation is well into the twenty-first century in terms of market sophistication and mathematical prowess. But, then, bank regulators have to be financially savvy: Banks have been stealing math PhDs out of graduate schools for the past forty years!

That's all I'm going to say here on banking regulation. Between the last chapter on the Fed and this section on regulation, I think most of the important stuff has been covered. Any remaining questions can be answered by the public relations office of your local FDIC or Fed office, or by checking their Web sites (www.fdic.gov or www.federalreserve.gov). Let's turn back to the financial system, where we pick up the saga of Great-Grandpa Joe already in progress. . . .

Great-Grandpa Joe's Pension Fund

The odds are that neither you nor the person to your right or left is covered by a traditional company pension plan. There's a good chance, I hope, that you have a 401(k) retirement or similar plan through work to which—with even more luck—your employer contributes. The reality is that an old-fashioned pension plan is not run-of-the-mill anymore. Great-Grandpa Joe had one. You and your cousins probably don't.

Retirement savings are something we're going to tackle in chapter 7, but right here, it's appropriate to take a look at pension plans from, say, thirty thousand feet up. Why bother? Only because private and government pension plans control roughly $13 trillion of assets in the U.S. financial system. If money talks, then pension plans scream!

What is a pension plan? It sounds a bit silly to me even to ask this question, but then I'm over fifty and I can remember the days when pensions were commonplace. You may very well not be familiar with this retirement-income tool. Basically, a pension is a savings plan that is designed to allow workers to rest easy about their retirement. The company contributes so many bucks each year you work into the pension fund, and the money is "saved" for you until retirement. When you retire from the company, the cash is either paid out to you or your family in monthly installments, or in some cases in one big, big sum (called a *lump-sum payment*). Since the monthly benefits of the pension plan run straight through to death, Great-Grandpa Joe planned to live to a ripe old age to get the most out of his years with the company.

So right there you can see why pensions don't really make much sense any more. How many people do you know who have held a job at the same company their whole lives? Very, very few, I imagine, if any. But let's not get ahead of ourselves. Before we look at the innovation that has taken place in this area, let's stick with the traditional plan a minute more. There's a great story of lies, deception, sex, and everything else to be told (well, maybe not sex).

The pension plan I've just described is what is called a *defined-benefit plan*. Now, you don't need to remember that; I say it because the name explains the benefit and the pitfalls of the plan. You see, it provides a defined, specific benefit to the retiree; let's say 60 percent of his average monthly income during his last five years at work. The manager of the pension has to invest the contributions in such a way that there's enough cash in the pension to pay out retirement benefits to the company's retired workers every month for as long as these guys and gals live. That's no sweat when things are good and everyone's earning lots of money in the markets; it's a darn-sight harder when the markets are losing ground.

In principle, the pension fund should take the extra bucks it earns in the good years and put them away for the rainy days, that is, the lean years. Then the pension would be all set. Unfortunately, the laws have been written in this country for something else to happen (which is why I put the word *saved* in quotes above). The laws governing pension plans in the United States allow a company to put its hands on the extra dollars earned when the markets are good—and to use those dollars for whatever it chooses. Naturally, then, when the markets are running strong, and there's excess money in the pension fund (money above and beyond what the accountants project is needed for retiree benefits), the company will strip the pension fund of the excess. But wasn't the excess from the good years supposed to cover the lean years? Yup. So this means that when the markets run lean, the retirees get fleeced? Yup. Great system, huh?

In reality, then, there are two major problems with the defined-benefit pension: It no longer fits the modern lifestyle of many jobs over a lifetime, and it's essentially without protection against senior management raiding the plan for a new office tower in midtown Manhattan.

Enter the *defined-contribution plan*—a pension plan for the ages. For one, it's portable. Leave one job; take it with you to the next. Or roll it into one of the new retirement savings plans out there like an IRA. Also, with a defined-contribution plan, the money in the plan is mostly coming from you, which is not so hot, but on the upside you have much more control over the assets accumulating in your name. You have choices about how much to contribute, how to invest, and how much to withdraw in retirement. And like the pension money, the cash going into the plans is not taxed up to a certain limit. Best of all, the company you work for can't raid the funds that are deposited into defined-contribution plans. All in all, it's a big improvement over the old system.*

Didn't think pensions still existed, did you? Well, they do, but you may not even recognize them as such. You certainly wouldn't see the connection with Great-Grandpa Joe's plan unless you looked really hard.

Bricks and Mortar

Let's go back and look at your great grandparents' finances one last time. Yes, they had their checking and savings accounts at banks. Yes, they may have had a pension for their old age. What other financial stuff did they buy?

Here's the likely answer: They bought a life insurance policy, in case Great-Grandpa Joe died from a heart attack after the Brooklyn Dodgers announced their move to LA.

One of my all-time favorite bits of trivia is that life insurance policies were originally called death insurance because, after all, they paid off when the insured died. Problem is, the inventor

---

* Regulation of pension plans is more hit-and-miss than it is for banks and thrifts. Congress passed major legislation in 1974 specific to pensions (ERISA), but still the safety net is loose.

couldn't sell policies called death insurance so he changed the name to life insurance. The rest, as they say, is history.

You may not think about a life insurance policy as a financial investment, but it very much is. Unlike the premiums you pay for car insurance, which beef up the insurance company's profits if you never get into an accident, the premiums you pay for life insurance are, to some extent, yours. A good chunk of the annual premiums is kept "in trust" for the day when you, the insured, will die. Or if death takes too long in coming and you'd prefer to cash out the policy and enjoy life, the death benefit can be paid early. Either way, it marks a distinct difference between car insurance and life insurance. A car can avoid being hit; a person always ages and dies. Sooner or later they gotta pay up!*

Life insurance policies are the ultimate long-term investment. As I've explained, the money can be retrieved before death, but if the policyholder tries to do that too far in advance of when the insured is scheduled to die (from the insurance company's perspective, not God's), the penalties are huge. When a life insurance company receives an annual premium, believe me they're not thinking of investing it for thirty days. Thirty years is more like it. This is why life insurance companies are very big lenders for long-term investments like a new car factory, a new power plant, ships, offices, and shopping malls.

The life insurance policy I've been describing has a first name: It's a *whole life policy*. As I've explained, it's sort of a Big Meal combo—part insurance in case the insured croaks early, part savings account for the later years of one's life. Unlike the deals you get at McDonald's or Burger King, however, the value of the Big

* Companies that insure property (property and casualty insurance) are not covered in this book's discussion of the insurance industry because the types of insurance they offer are considered less as "financial" instruments and more like "goods and services."

77

Meal combo can be invisible. Most policies were drafted back in the good old days (c'mon, c'mon, when were the good old days?) . . . before inflation. The savings portion of insurance policies written before the 1970s accumulated savings at a whopping 2–3 percent interest per year, by contract for the life of the policy, because that's all that inflation near zero justified back then. Now, the insurance company's 2–3 percent was actually better than the bank's 2–3 percent because the insurance policy had a good kicker—the money was accumulating tax-free. That's right: The insurance companies were smart enough to negotiate a deal with the IRS that made banks drool.

So, what happened when inflation picked up? The %$#& hit the fan again, this time in the insurance industry. Now insurance salesmen were more beer drinkers and hot dog eaters, so the crisis was easier on them than on the martini-swilling bankers. Even so, the insurance industry came in for its share of lumps when inflation changed the ball game.

You know that the story doesn't end here, don't you? Faced with products that were out of date, policyholders who were up in arms, and prospects who crossed the street rather than look an insurance salesman in the face, what happened? The insurance companies innovated. The simple solution to keep the industry afloat was to refocus on *term life policies*. Different first name, different product. Essentially term life insurance is car insurance on your life. If you don't die during the term of the loan, the premiums go straight to the insurance company's profits.

With term life, there's no savings component at all, so the offensive thorn of low interest rates was removed. But that very fact made it an incomplete answer to the insurance company's woes since the insurance industry had traditionally been investors as well as salespeople. (That's a fancy way of saying that whole life policies bring in more cash than term life policies, so the insurance company's profits were greatly reduced when they were no longer selling whole life policies.) The solution was simple, if somewhat difficult to formulate: Allow the rate of return on the whole life policy to vary, depending on the rate of returns that are available in the market. Thus was born the universal life policy.* The industry hit it big with universal life for two reasons. First, it suited the customer's needs. That's always important. Second, the industry was able to get Washington to again allow the interest inside the policy to remain free of taxes until the final payout.

Wait, wait, we're not done. Another product soon rolled off the drawing boards to join universal life. *Variable life* is the ultimate expression of free choice for the policyholder because he gets to direct where his investments go. Stocks, bonds, foreign oil—it's all open to the buyer of a variable life policy. And, of course, the interest and dividends inside the policy accumulate tax-free (the insurance industry has gotten quite good at lobbying, don't you think?). In truth, this nifty little product was specifically designed to be marketed as a tax dodge for the rich, which is exactly what a variable life policy is today.

One last note on insurance companies: In some respects, their business is easier to manage than that of other financial institutions. Because the majority of the investments insurance companies make are long term, there's plenty of time for them to wipe out mistakes. But it's not perfect. Remember when I said that the FDIC insurance program sometimes led bankers to take undue risks because their depositors were covered if something went wrong? Well, the same principle applies with life insurance.

---

* A universal life policy is a cross between a term life and a whole life policy, with elements of both. The amount of cash that goes toward the life insurance part of a universal life policy can vary, and even the amount of the premium (the amount contributed each month or quarter) can change. And, as noted in the text, the amount earned on the savings component of the policy is based on the returns actually earned in the market—the return on the policy's assets is transparent, in other words.

When people take out a life insurance policy, they often live a more risky lifestyle, making the predictions of who will die when that much less precise. Since getting that single question right is the biggest bet insurance companies make, life isn't always a bowl of cherries for the insurance industry. One way some companies have tried to manage this risk is by adopting a different corporate structure. There are plenty of firms out there that try to make a profit, to be sure, but there are also mutual insurance companies whose aim is to reduce risk, rather than maximize profit. That's something to keep in mind when it's time for you to insure your death (oops! I mean life).

Let's quickly regroup. This chapter started out by talking about banks and institutions that look and feel like banks. Then we addressed the problems that the inflation of the 1960s and 1970s caused the banks and thrifts. After a quick detour through the world of bank regulation, we got back on track with a discussion of the other two traditional financial institutions that ordinary people typically save with: insurance companies and pensions.

Now it's time to throw the net wider and farther to catch all those fish that were driven away from the family nesting areas by the inflation of the 1960s and 1970s. Prior to 1960, few people had contact with securities firms and few held stock that they chose themselves. Not so today.

6

Rediscovering Markets: The Big Bang of Finance

The Brits are a funny people. On the one hand, they revere the queen and the royals; they revel in a colonial past that's filled the British Museum with stolen antiquities and their tummies with takeout curry; and they warm to old-time favorites like bangers and mash or toad in the hole (even if washed down with a pint, these foods are a horrific affront to the digestive system).

On the other hand, the British have given us Monty Python, Princess Di, the Beatles, and, at least the staging for, James Bond.

Is it any wonder, then, that when the time neared for the Brits to revamp their financial system to bring it up to the twentieth century, the name they chose for the process was the Big Bang? The *big bang* is, of course, the term astronomers use to describe the creation of the universe in a massive fireball. It marks the beginning of the beginning. Well, no one ever claimed that British financial types aren't modest. To them, no doubt, it was the beginning of the beginning, all over again.

I use the example of the Brits only because their revolution had a name. It didn't have one on this side of the pond, and, truth be told, it was far less of a revolution here in the United States, where business practices have always been a bit more free-wheeling. Named or not, however, the changes were significant in the UK, here in the United States, and around the world.

What we saw begin in the 1960s—in response to inflation—was a massive change in the way people handled their financial decisions. Individuals, businesses, and governments learned to rely on their own knowledge, skills, contacts, and information to research, decide, and execute financial transactions, rather than let others do the work for them. Of course, they really had no choice but to become more independent: The financial companies that they had been dealing with proved to be far more interested in their own profits than those of their clients, leaving many investors and borrowers without an anchor in turbulent financial seas. Even when some institutions tried to be more responsive and responsible, they were bound by old rules that prevented them from providing the products and services that would have helped consumers and businesses survive the storm. So kicking and screaming, passive and complacent, or totally lost at sea—it didn't matter. People started handling their own finances to an extent never before seen, beginning in the 1960s. Fortunately, the dawn of the information and computer age was at hand; information was coming in by the bucket, and technology was rapidly changing the back-office operations of financial institutions and financial markets. Technology was the enabling force, often the driving force, behind change in the financial industry; new technology meant that the process of assuming ownership of one's finances was now technically feasible.

As individuals, businesses, and governments became more independent, they naturally sought to cut the costs associated with their financial transactions. The obvious choice was to cut out the middleman—in the same way that a company might resort to just-in-time inventory control or a chef might buy direct from the grower.* In the financial industry, the middlemen were the established financial institutions, like banks, thrifts, and insurance companies—remember we even called them "intermediaries." These guys got the old heave-ho, and in their place emerged a new brand of financial intermediary, one who would work on contract. The "new" financial institution would provide the customer with exactly the pieces the customer demanded, and price each piece separately, to better accommodate the customer's needs. Not much different from buying a granite countertop.

But there was even more to this revolution than cost cutting. The bigger change was that ordinary people and companies, and ordinary governments big and small, gained direct access to the financial markets themselves.

I think it's fair to say that the latter half of the twentieth century was a period in which markets displaced institutions as both the source of funds and the depository for funds for ordinary people and businesses. What this means is that ordinary people began trading actual securities, and, with the help of specialists like mortgage brokers and auto finance companies, ordinary people actually tapped into the financial markets to finance their major purchases. Also, ordinary businesses got the funds they needed directly from the stock and bond markets, and ordinary businesses invested their cash directly in the markets. Financial institutions became order takers rather than decision makers.

Of course, the markets had to adjust to accommodate the trades of more, and often smaller, players. It's all very well for me, a small investor by any measure, to want to invest in mortgages, but how do I go about doing this? At last look, my local Wal-Mart

---

* Just-in-time inventory management is the better example. Companies contract for the goods they need for production to be delivered by the factory on the day they're going to be used, thereby knocking out the wholesaler and the wholesaler's charges. Chefs will buy direct from growers, but it's often as much a question of freshness and quality as it is one of cost.

was not selling mortgages. No, the market had to change so that I could make a mortgage investment. In many cases, the actual securities had to be recast so they could be more easily sold as well-defined "solutions" for savers like myself. Indeed, the most notable achievement on this score was the creation of a mortgage securities market where mortgage pools are sliced and diced to provide investors with the specific term, interest rate, and risk characteristics they have in mind.* Based on the success of mortgage securities, the industry created similar securities based on auto loans, student loans, and even boat loans.

I should also mention that we saw the disintegration of geographical boundaries between markets and institutions during these years as well. Starting in earnest in the 1970s, large and aggressive Japanese, German, U.S., Asian, and Canadian financial companies began to grab business miles and miles away from home. Building skyrocketed on Wall Street and in the City of London; cranes dotted the skylines of Tokyo, Hong Kong, and Chicago (where a lot of innovative securities were created and traded). By the end of the twentieth century, there existed a few financial hubs in the world, at least one for each time zone, where "face time" could be had with the now-global movers and shakers of the industry. Meanwhile, smaller financial centers, like San Francisco and LA here in the States, Paris in Europe, and Singapore in Asia, woke up to find that much of their business had moved elsewhere.

Without any doubt, the 1970s and 1980s were heady times in the global financial markets. There were lots of ideas floating around, some incredibly good, some notoriously bad, and some downright dangerous. There were lots of people coming and going from the major hubs—lots of dinners out and badly ended affairs.

---

* A mortgage pool is a bunch of mortgages put together, so investors can lessen their risk by holding a piece of a geographically diverse portfolio of mortgages.

And there were lots and lots of plump bonuses handed out at the end of the year. Oh, the good old days!

The Advisor

None of the massive changes of the latter half of the twentieth century could have come off without the hard work of some very intelligent and very hungry entrepreneurial companies. We call these *securities firms*. After all, they're in the securities industry, not banking, not insurance, not kitchen appliances.

Who are they? We'll talk about four types. You've got your *investment house,* your *brokerage house,* your *mutual fund,* and then your *hedge fund*. There's also your venture capital fund, but that's not for the likes of you or me; venture capitalists provide financing for startup companies for the benefit of the überrich.

Investment houses have been active in the securities business for centuries.* Back in the early 1900s, when Ford wanted to issue stock, or the state of Ohio wanted to borrow money to build a bridge, they sought the services of an investment house. They still do so today. You probably have heard of many of the investment houses that dominate the industry. They have names like Goldman Sachs, Lehman Brothers, and JPMorgan.

The *investment house* researches the client and feels out the market to see if there would be interest in the client's securities, and if so, at what price. They advise the client of their research conclusions, and if the client (that is, a firm or government) still wants to go ahead, the investment bankers put together all the documentation for the sale of securities, get things properly registered with the authorities, and finally execute the sale.

Investment houses can organize the sale in two ways. If they like the company, the project, and the securities themselves, they

---

* I don't want to confuse you, but these investment houses are also called investment banks, and their employees are referred to as *investment bankers*. I'll try to avoid doing so.

can underwrite the deal. This means that the investment house itself buys the securities it sells for the client (Ford or Ohio, in this example). That's right: If the investment house underwrites the sale, then the first leg of these securities' journey is from the desk of one employee to that of another at the same investment firm. Why might the investment house do this? Money (that's always the safe answer, isn't it?). Investment bankers pick up a better fee from the client if the client knows, really knows, that all his financing is secure. The investment house also figures that it can probably sell the securities for a higher price (i.e., a tidy profit) if they don't dump all of them on the market all at once. So it works out well for both the client and the investment house when the investment house underwrites the sale of securities. Most new securities sold today are underwritten by an investment house or, more often, a syndicate of investment houses.*

The investment house doesn't have to underwrite the deal, however, if it doesn't want to. The alternative is to act as the agent for the client (again, Ford or Ohio). In this case, the investment house does all the same things in preparation for the sale of securities, but when the time comes, the investment bankers sell them all in the market, retaining little or none for themselves. Sounds like far less demanding work for the investment house, doesn't it? It is. That's why the profitability of such deals is far more limited. Investment houses are built to assess and manage the risk of selling securities in the open market. It's how they earn their daily bread. It's why most new securities sales are underwritten.

By the way, before we move on, I would be remiss if I didn't mention what many of the other people do who work for investment houses: They advise companies on mergers and acquisi-

---

* Syndicate is a fancy term for a group. A group of investment houses gets together for this deal, and this deal only, and does the work together. P.S. Bonds are underwritten in the same way.

tions. Think about it: These firms have the research staffs, they have the market knowledge, and they have the financial savvy. It's a no-brainer.

The Trader

Once securities are sold in the open market, there is often a vibrant, active market in the security, what's called the secondary or after-market. If the security is a stock, then the odds are it is listed on a stock exchange or two. Stocks sell on the exchanges in big lots, more than the small orders everyday people place. (The exchanges would be utterly clogged with business if they didn't limit the size of transactions.) Enter the *brokerage house*. Brokers handle the small transactions of people and other financial institutions, lump them together into big trades, and then execute the trades on the exchanges. The broker earns a commission on each trade she executes on behalf of a client, whether the order was to buy or sell. In other words, they got you coming and going.

Brokers have been around as long as investment houses, and again the names on their doors are familiar ones: Merrill Lynch, Smith Barney, A. G. Edwards. Ah, but they also have names these days like e*Trade, Schwab, Scottrade, TD Waterhouse, and Ameritrade. Technology, and the overall trend toward people managing their own finances, has really changed this segment of the financial industry. Brokers used to, and many still do, provide research for their clients. But since many people do their own research—thank you, Internet—they prefer to trade securities more cheaply without the benefit of their broker's research. That's how companies like Ameritrade and Schwab got started—offering to trade securities at a deep discount from what the traditional brokers were charging. They still hold that ground today.

Two things to add: (1) Thanks to lively cross-fertilization, with the government's blessing, there is basically no distinction anymore between an investment house and a brokerage house. To wit, Merrill Lynch does both, as does Citi. The two functions within the institution are not merged, but they are under the same ownership. (2) The regulator that gets to figure all this out, and somehow take the side of the consumer, is the Securities and Exchange Commission, or the SEC. The SEC has its hands full.

The Pooler

Take heart: We're in the home stretch here. The third kind of securities firm is the *mutual fund*—you know, the folks we talked about in the previous chapter who came to the rescue of ordinary people being ravaged by inflation. A mutual fund is a company that pools the savings of lots of people and then invests the money for them. Some funds have a very wide mandate, allowing them to invest in short- and long-term debt, stocks, foreign stocks, oil, and other commodities. The majority of funds, though, are pretty specific in what they invest in. You'll see everything from a foreign government bond fund (which invests in bonds issued by the likes of the UK or Singapore) to an emerging markets stock fund (which invests in stocks issued by companies in developing countries).

Why invest with a mutual fund rather than go it alone? There are several reasons, including information, skill, time, access, discipline, and size. Most mutual funds hire financial professionals to invest your money. They presumably have the time and skill to interpret a preposterously large amount of information on each and every company and security. Because their trades are very large, they presumably have access to company officials and other experts that the likes of you and I don't. And because they do this for a living, they presumably have the discipline to invest wisely, take profits appropriately, and bail out without regret when the rest of us would be drowning our sorrows in scotch whiskey.

You did notice that each of the previous three sentences included the word *presumably*. Why? For the simple reason that as much as ordinary people should do better with mutual funds than on their own, there is no evidence that this is the case. Let me be more explicit. Yes, there is evidence that a mutual fund's portfolio managers will occasionally win, that is to say, do better than the market as a whole, but there is no evidence that they will do so on a regular basis. Ordinary people will make out much better if they stop trying to pick stocks or pick mutual funds and simply invest in the market as a whole. Unless you're a natural, you're actually better off owning a slice of the New York Stock Exchange, with a chaser of the NASDAQ, than owning a single fund or a group of funds. Picking winners is that hard!

This truth, which the industry has been grappling with for years, is not in its best interest, of course. The industry would like you to think that its pros can deliver. Well, some of them can, and some can't, and few, if any, can string together years outperforming the markets. Enter the index mutual fund. It's just what you think: a mutual fund that doesn't try to pick winners but rather copies the makeup of the market it corresponds to. If Google is 5 percent of the NASDAQ, then the index mutual fund's "NASDAQ fund" will have 5 percent of its money tied up in Google. Simple as that.

A few mutual fund companies are renowned for their index funds, including Vanguard. Since everyday people like you and me have been figuring out this fact, however, most mutual fund companies have come up with their own index funds. The benefits for the consumer are obvious: Your portfolio does just what the market does, which research shows is the best way to earn money over the long run. And because the index fund isn't actively managed, the costs associated with it are lower. Computers run these funds, you see, not people.

The Übertrader

The *hedge fund* manager doesn't look like you or me. He rarely sleeps. He eats extremely poorly and then extremely well. His clothes are Eddie Bauer and Armani. He may live in a small dive or a mansion along the coast; he vacations on yachts in the Mediterranean.

The hedge fund manager lives this lifestyle because his job is to manage the money of the incredibly rich, and, as we all know, the überrich are different from you and me. Specifically, when it comes to investing, what these gazillionaire investors want is the right to do what they want with their money without government interference. Well, they made their case to the powers that be and they prevailed. Thus, hedge fund managers pretty much do what they want.

What is it that they do exactly? If I could tell you, I'd be one. I know that they have a sixth sense, and superfast computer programs, to take advantage of market prices that don't quite match with their information or understanding. I can tell you that when they decide something is a good or bad investment, they just don't jump in or out with their two feet—they borrow the body parts of many others. They produce huge positives and negatives. They work for high fees. They work without a lot of supervision. The only thing, and I mean the only thing, that matters to them is results.

Does the formula work? Pretty much. Hedge funds have nicely contributed to the growing gap between the rich and poor throughout most of the world. Which is why the new trend in this field is to lower the entrance requirements. Nowadays you can find hedge funds that require no more than a $100,000 investment. Since that's within the reach of people who are not überrich, it's not at all clear that hedge funds are on the right track. While it's good that less wealthy people have the opportunity to earn incredible rates of return, what's going to happen when they lose what is to them incredible amounts of money? Remember, high returns come from assuming high risk. There ain't no free lunch—return and risk go hand in hand.

Taking in the View

There, you've done it! You've slogged through I can't tell you how many chapters on the financial system. It's an accomplishment equal to climbing Mt. McKinley, or Mt. Hood at least.

In case you missed the scenery because of all the fun you were having, you actually learned a heck of a lot about money and banking and finance. You now know exactly how your local banker can afford to vacation in the Caribbean each winter. You know why the nameplates on financial institutions are changed more frequently than my son's sheets at college. You know that money does indeed make the world go 'round, because it never, ever stands still.

Seriously, your initiation into the world of finance included a lot of really important stuff: the difference between money and credit, what determines interest rates, how bonds work, what stocks are and how they're priced, what makes a bank a bank and what makes everything else something else, and last but hardly least, the difference between financial institutions that act on your behalf and those that act on your orders. Did you know these things two weeks ago? I thought not.

Now that you're ready for it, here comes the fun stuff. The next chapter is about personal finance. All this stuff about money and banking and investments—it's time to put these concepts into the context of your life. In other words, it's time to think about *numero uno*.

7

Doing Without: The Basics of Middle-Class Finance

I have always gone to bed every night between 9 and 10 p.m., even in college (there goes the last shred of respect you had for me). As doctors will tell you, an early bedtime has its benefits. As teenagers will tell you, an early bedtime has its costs. I have never seen David Letterman, nor Jay Leno, Conan O'Brien, Craig Ferguson, or Jimmy Kimmel (despite a conviction that we share some ancestry). Luckily, the CBS Web site provides a daily recap of Letterman's Top 10 lists for those of us snoring away when he signs on.

Clearly, my bedtime makes me an unlikely candidate to write a Letterman-style Top 10. I was therefore hoping that Letterman's writers might help with this chapter, but they declined my request for assistance. So I had to do it myself. Here is my *Top 10 Things You Need to Know about Personal Finance.*

Before you get on me, let me say that I know it's not perfect. My list is not as funny as Letterman's would have been because I don't have Letterman's sense of humor. And don't expect my list to run from ten to one; I can't write backward, either.

1. Three Simple Words: Earn, Spend, Save

When an economist looks at consumers—at us, in other words—what she sees are people who do three things over and over again:

- We work so that we can earn money. There are variations on the theme, to be sure. Some of us work at home, some of us go to an office, some of us work at a factory, some of us work by smiling into a camera. It's all work. We do it for the cash. (OK, so there are some folks who don't need the money. Do you know lots of these people? I don't.)

- We spend most of the money we earn. On groceries, mortgage payments, shoes, heating. . . . You don't need me to tick off my list; you've got your own.

- We save some of the money we earn. In a perfect world, we would all save 10 percent of every check that we cash. Some of us do this; some save more; many save less.

Personal finance is all about the last two items. It's about the percentage of our income we spend and the percentage we save. It's about making good spending decisions. It's about doing the right thing with our savings.

Personal finance is also *personal*. Just like your PDA or the personal pan pizza you get at Pizza Hut, it's yours and yours alone. For this reason, I can't write down what's right for you. What I can do, and what I've tried to do here, is to lay out some things you ought to know.

2. There Is No Substitute for the Truth

Now is no time for self-deception. If you want to pretend you're someone else, then head down to Rosie's on Saturday night. Heck, I'll even meet you there—I'll be the one in the pink feather boa. In the meantime, let's get down to business.

The fact of the matter is that personal finance requires a degree of honesty that makes most of us feel uncomfortable. Answer these three questions for me:

- Does the road from Pittsburgh to Dallas pass through Atlanta?

- Can you get a good night's sleep in a house with an infant?

- Can you retire comfortably at age forty, after working for the USPS for twenty years?

The answer to all three questions is a simple no. I don't want to hear about interstates and traffic, the Faber system of getting babies to sleep through the night, or retirement costs in Mexico. If you didn't answer no to all three questions, then grab a pen and paper and write the following sentence one hundred times: "When it involves my finances, there is no substitute for the truth." Everyone else, let's get a cup of coffee while those who were hoping to indulge in some "harmless" self-deception learn this lesson.

OK, we're back. Are we all onboard?

Personal finance requires completely honest answers to three important questions (you'll see why we practiced with the softball questions first):

- Where are you financially right now?

- Where do you want to go?

- And do you have the willingness to do what it takes to get there?

Let's tackle the first question first: Where are you financially right now? In many respects, this is the easiest of the three to answer, although it requires a bit of elbow grease. Pull out your bank statement from the cupboard drawer; find your savings account statements; get whatever quarterly or annual reports you can find on your 401(k) or mutual funds; if you have stocks or other financial investments that you've made on your own, grab the latest accounting statements from your broker. If the list isn't too long, get new prices for these assets from yesterday's newspaper. If I missed anything, ignore my mistake and add it to the pile. Now tally it all up. These are your financial assets.

What about your tangibles? Do you own jewelry—a diamond ring or an expensive watch perhaps? Do you own your car? You probably own some of it, that is, the amount the car is worth minus what you still owe on the car loan. Do you own your house? Again, subtract the balance of your mortgage from the current market value of your home. Anything else? A timeshare? A portion of your grandfather's house at the shore? Try to put a dollar value on all these; they are your tangible assets.*

Do you have any debts, aside from the mortgage and the car loan? Your credit cards, for instance. Here's where it gets really painful: Add up the outstanding balances on your credit cards. Owe mom and dad some money, or Aunt Sarah? Count that. By the way, if you borrowed money from a 401(k) plan, make sure you subtract that from the number you came up with earlier.

You're now ready to calculate your net worth. Please, we're not in church! Nobody is implying that this is what you're worth as a human being. *Net worth* is a technical accounting term: It means your assets minus your liabilities (what you owe). So add up your assets—financial and tangible—and subtract your liabilities. The worst is over; take a deep breath.

We're not done yet, though. Where you're at financially isn't only about money. How many more years can you work? Is your health good? What skills/experience/education do you have that are valuable in the job market? How established are you in your career? Who else are you responsible for now or may need to care for in the future? In other words, take stock.

On to the second question: What are your goals? Remember, total honesty. If you want to retire at the age of fifty, say so. If you

---

* Is there such a thing as *intangibles*? Yeah, but it's not usually helpful to include them in this kind of analysis.

want to be able to send your kid to Harvard or somewhere else equally expensive (this describes more schools than you can imagine), then say so. If you have your heart set on a house overlooking Laguna Beach or a remote lake in Minnesota, say so. If you're worried about your health and need to guarantee good medical care down the road, say so. If all you really want is to raise your kids in a good neighborhood and retire in the same house, then say so. There are no right or wrong answers to this question. Each of us is different. But be honest about your goals. Goals are not dreams. Goals are not what you'd do if you won the lottery. Goals are what you expect to achieve in this lifetime.

It's also worth stating the obvious: Goals are not static. As a single mom with three kids, Diane doesn't want to work two jobs. My friend Julie has both parents in a nursing home; she cut back her hours at work to find time to check in on her folks. George likes to take long vacations with his family because he's worried that diabetes will soon impair his mobility. At college, Julie, George, and Diane shared the same goal: to retire at age fifty-five with a million in the bank and a house by the sea. They each had to adjust that goal to reflect changes in marital status, health, and family.

Ordinarily, when people ask you to define your goals and tote up your net worth, their real purpose is to get you to whittle down your expectations. Well, some of this is probably necessary. (George, Julie, and Diane all aimed perhaps a tad high.) But I also look at things from a different angle. Are you willing to do what it takes to achieve your goals? Don't answer yes so quickly. Many of us are not.

The biggest hurdle for most people is saving. Spending is a whole lot more fun because the gratification is instant. Even if you get a chill down your back from reading your brokerage statements, saving is a long-term affair. Many of us don't want to sacrifice the present for the future. Is that immature? Is it shortsighted? Is it self-defeating? Yes, yes, and yes. And we do it anyway. Day in and day out we prove ourselves unwilling to do what it takes to achieve our goals.

3. Are You into Instant Gratification or Leaving a Legacy?

Over twenty years ago an author named Gail Sheehy wrote a book titled *Passages*. The premise of this landmark work was that adults inevitably pass through well-defined stages of life as we go through our twenties, thirties, forties, and on into old age (by her reckoning, I think I'm dead). Sheehy addressed the psychological and sexual changes that characterize each stage of life (which is why she sold more books than I ever will), but we can identify clear-cut stages of adults' financial lives, too. Part of the process of being honest with yourself about your financial goals and abilities is identifying the stage(s) you're in now and recognizing the stages you've yet to pass through. The cases below are not exhaustive, but illustrative, of the lives many Americans can expect to lead. Let me make it clear that my examples parallel Sheehy's approach. The details, and the mistakes, are all mine.

When we first start working, be it after high school, college, or grad school, all we can think about is what we're going to buy with the next paycheck. Hopefully, we've been implored by our employer to join the company's 401(k) program. And hopefully we've listened to our parents and friends and maxed out our contribution to these plans. Otherwise, this is the period of instant gratification. About the only discretionary "saving" that most of us will do is pay off our student loans. A few serious-minded kids will start to save, which is a very, very good thing, but the need for instant gratification is hard to shake.

As we reach our late twenties or thirties and start to marry, our attitudes toward savings change, thankfully. Even those of us who are single start thinking about buying a condo or a house, splurging on good furniture or taking an exotic vacation with friends. But this is a dangerous time because many of us don't realize that we need savings destined for the long haul. It's fine to save for a vacation or furniture, as long as we put aside money above and beyond our target percentage. All too often we don't make the distinction between short- and long-term savings, so we get started off on the wrong foot. On a positive note, most of us in our twenties and thirties have an iron stomach when it comes to risk, so our investment portfolios are growing rapidly.

The next twenty to forty years are years of heavy-duty saving. We're enjoying our peak earnings, and thus are socking away cash not just for our retirement, but for our kids' education and all the other goals we've set for ourselves. Statistically, this is also the time when the lucky among us inherit, if not the earth, then a large portfolio of investments or a big house. Depending on when we had kids, college expenses can come early on or later in this period. This is also the time when our health starts to factor into our plans. Reflecting our maturity, we display less interest in risky investments.

In retirement, most of us are drawing down our savings since few of us receive a monthly pension check. At this point, our retirement income is pretty well fixed, and most of our investments are geared toward retaining the money we've saved. As we age, we start to think more seriously about the legacy we will leave our children and our community.

You are probably wondering where you stand. Let me say that for every person I know who fits neatly into one of these categories, I know at least two who do not. Don't fret if you're a misfit. Knowing that you don't fit neat characterizations is exactly why benchmarks like this are useful.

4. *Off-the-Rack* Is an Adjective for Clothes

Some 99.9 percent of women buy clothes off the rack. Whether it's Neiman Marcus or Wal-Mart, we buy clothes already finished. Oh sure, a few wealthy women have their clothes made for them. And more, but clearly not many, will take the clothes they've bought at the store to a tailor for alterations, or even sew a hem themselves. The vast majority of women, however, buy a garment, bring it home, and wear it. Men are different. They buy their casual clothes off the rack, just as women do. When it comes to suits, however, men get better treatment. Their suits are finished but for the cuffs, and they usually get free or low-cost alterations right at the store to make the jacket and pants fit better.

Off-the-rack clothing is fine; I have no problem with it. But off-the-rack financial planning is a disaster. You're not going to care whether your pants are a little wide at the knees. You *will* care if your investments don't fit your goals, and right you are. You have to live with your financial plan for a long, long time. More to the point, you're counting on your investments to allow you to live well long after you've stopped saving. A missed sale here, the wrong mutual fund there, and your goals could easily be in jeopardy.

You've already taken the first step to prevent this from happening. You've made an honest appraisal of your financial situation, and you've set realistic goals. The next step is facing your idiosyncrasies. C'mon, you know you have some. You think not? Are you willing to invest in bonds issued by the Singapore government? How about tobacco stocks? And how do you feel about De Beers, the African-based diamond mining company? (Did you see the movie *Blood Diamond*?) Face it: You have opinions. This isn't a problem; you just need to get them out in the open.

There are a couple of components of a financial strategy that require you to think long and hard about your preferences. Your task here is to recognize these preferences, communicate them to your financial partners (whether yours is a spouse or a bank manager), and then tailor your strategy so that it respects and reflects these preferences.

First up, *risk*. Risk is defined as the possibility of a loss. Except for sure things—such as lending money to the U.S. Treasury for a short period—everything entails risk. Your house can depreciate (go down) in value if the real estate market goes bust. Your bonds will depreciate in value if interest rates rise. Your stocks may depreciate in value if the economy slumps. Since it's impossible to prevent all real estate busts, inflation, and recessions, nothing is 100 percent safe. Still, some investments are safer than others. The long-term trend in an investment's price is a good, if imperfect, indicator of whether you're likely to experience a loss. By the way, risk also exists when you borrow money. If you borrow at a high point in interest rates, you may be stuck paying a high rate for the life of the loan (this is usually not the case with mortgages and car loans, however; these can generally be refinanced). In this case, your "loss" is the difference between the interest you're paying and the current rate being offered in the credit market.

Investment risk is often measured by *volatility*. High volatility means large and frequent swings in price. Low volatility means small and infrequent changes in price. Obviously, a volatile investment carries an increased chance of loss because at the time you want to sell, its price may be down.

I prefer a slightly different measure of volatility. To me, high volatility means large and frequent swings in price around its trend line. Conversely, low volatility means small and infrequent changes in price around its trend line. Defining volatility in this way, let's differentiate between two different questions that investors often answer differently:

- Can you handle losses?
- Can you handle a roller coaster?

In the next section we come back to risk, so this discussion is not done. My point here is that you need to communicate your tolerances for risk and volatility and integrate them into your financial strategy. A good financial strategy is one that let's you sleep well at night.

Second up, *taxes*. I know people who don't like to pay taxes, no matter what. They'd rather earn less and not pay taxes than earn a higher return, pay taxes, and still be left with more. That's what experts call an aversion to taxes. In a perfect world, people like this could be taught the error of their thinking. In the real world, they're not going to give in to common sense. If not paying taxes no how is your choice, then you need to be careful how you set up your financial strategy.

Tax attitudes are one thing; tax rates are something quite different. Different tax brackets mean different rates of return for investors. For example, buying a house provides a wonderful tax deduction, but only if your income isn't so high that Uncle Sam has restricted your itemized deductions. As you tailor your financial strategy to your situation, don't forget to factor in taxes. The easiest way to do this, by the way, is to look at returns and costs on an after-tax basis. You can do this yourself with just a calculator. For instance, an 8 percent return when you're in the 20 percent tax bracket means an after-tax return of 6.4 percent (20 percent of your 8 percent [or 1.6 percent] goes to Uncle Sam).

5. *Risk* Is Not a Four-Letter Word

It doesn't matter how it's spelled. *Risk* is not a dirty word. It's a fact of life.

We put up with risk because higher expected returns only come about by assuming more risk.* Why would an investor lend

---

* Note that I snuck in the work *expected*. No one can predict the future. One year down the road a very risky investment may have bombed, making the risk-free alternative the better choice. Or vice versa. All we can say at the outset is that riskier investments have to hold out the promise of higher returns or naturally risk-averse people won't buy them. Said differently, riskier investments offer higher *expected* returns.

money for a longer period, when the risk of getting paid back in dollars of equal value was less? She'd do so because the longer-term loan paid a higher amount of interest. Why would an investor buy a bond issued by a high-tech startup rather than an established firm like Google? He'd do so because the coupon attached to the startup's bond was much bigger. Why would someone buy a troubled stock like Ford when she could buy ExxonMobil? She does so because there's a chance, if Ford straightens itself out, of a higher return than she could earn with ExxonMobil.

As I said, nobody chooses risk willingly. It's something we have to put up with to reach our financial goals. If at sixty-five, Joanne is already within reach of her goals, then from here on out she doesn't need to take on much more risk. She's earned enough to play it safe. If at sixty-five, Michael isn't close to the amount he's decided he needs to retire, then he's going to have to accept some riskier investments if he hopes to reach that goal. Of course, Bobby, age thirty-five, is far from his retirement goal as well, but he's got plenty of time before he retires so he doesn't have to take on as much risk as Mikey.

Risk isn't something you walk into the store and buy. Rather, it's the measure of how far you have to go, and how fast you have to move, to reach your goals. If the amount of risk you need to assume is higher than your tolerance, as discussed above, then it's time to redraft your goals.

6. *Debt* Is Not a Four-Letter Word

Out in the American heartland there are still lots of people who own their homes outright and would rather die than use a credit card. The idea of owing somebody money is abhorrent to them. Are those folks acting rationally?

This is an interesting question to ponder because debt has almost religious connotations in our society. For some, the Bible's rejection of usury means that debt is a sin. That's perhaps an extreme position, but many, many people feel guilty about taking out a loan. Since I'm not about to deny anyone's religious beliefs, let me say that the following is a discussion about the economics of debt—the math. You are certainly free to ignore the analysis and its implications.

From an economic standpoint, then, let's proceed. *Debt* is no more a four-letter word than *risk* is. Sometimes it makes good economic sense to take out a loan. Depending on the circumstances, it might even make sense to carry forward a balance on a credit card. The best way to imagine these circumstances is to meet a few new people.

Example 1: Jane and Harvey, like many adults with young children, lived in an apartment until they couldn't stand it any longer, at which point they bought a house in the 'burbs. Now they are saddled with a huge debt in the form of a thirty-year mortgage. Moreover, they have no more stocks or bonds, no more savings accounts at the bank, no more slush funds that they can use to sneak off to Mexico without telling anyone. Everything they've got now is between those four exterior walls.

On the surface, theirs looks like a bad decision. If Jane and Harvey ran their own business, lived in an area with a volatile real estate market, or didn't have family, a judge would probably rule it suicide. But consider this: Jane's folks are loaded! Turns out that Jane's parents actually had offered to help with the down payment for the house, but Jane and Harvey decided they wanted to buy the house on their own. That Jane's parents are there as backup changes things, doesn't it? And what if real estate prices in their area have been increasing 8 percent per year for the past fifteen years— nothing wild like we've seen in Las Vegas, just a steady 8 percent per year. Isn't that a pretty good argument for getting into the real estate market sooner rather than later, and buying as much as they think they'll be able to comfortably afford over the long haul?

Maybe Jane and Harvey's new house wasn't a bad decision after all. It's a stretch for their young family right now, and the mortgage is big, but with Jane's parents in the background, and the hope for steady appreciation of their house, I don't think their decision to buy a house was too risky.

Example 2: My neighbor Christopher always buys his cars with cash. Chris isn't wealthy; he just puts aside money every month so that he can avoid having to take out a car loan. Is Chris's thrift smart or is he hung up about debt? Let's see. Being the thrifty soul he is, Chris always buys his cars in August when he can get a good deal on the previous year's models. The last time Chris went to buy a car, the dealership was offering 0.9 percent financing on last year's models. Aha! Yes, in light of this information, Chris's refusal to take out a loan is more than emotional—it's irrational. Surely Chris can earn more than 0.9 percent in interest at the bank, so he's silly to take money out of the bank to buy the car. (Unless the low interest rate has a "cash back" alternative, in which case the better course might be to take their cash and pay with your cash.)

While I'm at it, let me use Chris to teach a new term: *opportunity cost*. Opportunity cost is what you give up when you undertake a certain action. In Chris's case, the opportunity cost of paying cash for a car is the interest he'd earn at the bank. Opportunity cost can be right there on a price tag or bank statement, but it's not always expressed in dollars and cents. Sometimes it's measured in days and months, milligrams of mercury, or lives saved. And sometimes it can't be measured at all. That opportunity costs aren't always quantifiable is not important. What *is* important is the notion that no decision comes without a cost. That's an important lesson.

Example 3: Finally, I want to introduce you to Jake. Jake had a $3,000 Visa bill but no extra money in the bank to pay it off. His parents suggested that he pay the bill off by redeeming a bank deposit (a CD). But the CD didn't mature for a few more months, so the bank would have charged him a stiff penalty to redeem it early. Jake figured out that he would be better off waiting for a $4,000 tax refund, which he expected in a month's time. Jake ended up paying the minimum necessary on the credit card immediately; then he paid off the entire balance when he received the check from Uncle Sam. I don't think his decision was a bad one at all.

So tell me, do you still think *debt* is a four-letter word?

7. Uncle Sam Wants You—to Buy a House

A house is a big investment, and for most of us, it means going into debt big time. Yet about 70 percent of Americans own their own home, and most of those who don't yet own a home of their own aspire to do so in the future. So let's take a look at what makes homeownership such a compelling choice.

You've already met Jane and Harvey and know the family circumstances that led them to buy. Let's formalize their thought process by looking at the costs and benefits of homeownership. For this discussion, I'm going to skip out on Jane and Harv and talk about the person most important to you: you.

Let's first look at the negatives. When you buy a house, you need to come up with a down payment of at least 10 percent, and lenders do not want to see that it came from anyone else's bank account than your own. When you buy a house, you also have to cover closing costs and move-in expenses. When you own your own home, it's a whole lot easier to spend for new drapes and a gas grill. When you own your own home, you'll have higher monthly expenses since rentals usually include water and may include other utilities as well. When you own your own home, you pay real estate taxes (don't even get me started).

Sometimes it feels like a house is really nothing more than risk contained by four walls (à la the movie *The Money Pit*). Insurance policies will cover you for some types of risk (e.g., the mailman slipping on your sidewalk or a tree falling on your roof), but you'll still be exposed to risk. You probably won't be able to afford flood insurance. And there's no insurance against flying squirrels in the attic (I've got them, thank you), a sinkhole in your yard, a backup in the sewer lines, or a drop in your house's value in the real estate market.

Given this, why would anyone want to own her own house? Homeownership does sound formidable, but there's something inexpressible, and certainly not quantifiable, about walking into your own home. The rooms look like you want them to. The gardens are of your own making. You set the temperature inside.

The financial incentives are pretty nice, too. As you pay off your mortgage every month, you'll be paying down the amount you owe (the mortgage principal). Early on, mostly what you pay each month is interest, but within a few years you'll be earning equity in your home. Then, too, there's a good chance that over the time you own your home, the price of your house will appreciate. Now take a moment to think about this. Say your house appreciates 10 percent the first year you own it and you bought it for $300,000. That 10 percent appreciation amounts to $30,000. If you put 10 percent down when you bought the house, you earned a 100 percent return on your money in just one year! That's right: You invested $30,000 and earned another $30,000 when the house appreciated. Wowsers! This is called *leverage,* and it's a beautiful thing when prices are rising.*

And let's not forget the tax benefit, either. The interest paid on your mortgage and your real estate taxes is tax-deductible, whereas the money you spend on rent is, as they say, money down the drain.

---

* When prices are falling, it's a downer. Mortgage companies don't want you to hear this, but if the house price falls more than you have invested in the house, walking away from the mortgage is an option. It limits your immediate downside risk, although it could hurt your ability further down the road by damaging your credit scores.

To be sure, there are times when it makes sense to rent. But you turn your back on some pretty sweet financial incentives when you don't buy.

8. The Myth of Compound Interest

If you've been around the block a few times—I know that some of you young'uns may not have—there's a table or chart forced under your nose whenever someone starts talking about personal finance, investments, 401(k) plans, or even savings accounts. It's a chart showing the *Miracle of Compound Interest*. Since I've made a vow not to include charts in this book, I'll describe the "miracle" in words. It's not hard.

When an individual saves part of her income, and invests her savings in the credit markets or at a bank or thrift, she expects to earn a positive return on her money. For simplicity's sake, let's say a person has chosen to put $1,000 in a bank account that will pay 5 percent interest every year. And let's say the deposit was made on January 1, 2007 (these dates don't really matter, I'm just trying to put a stake in the ground). OK, tell me: How much will she have on January 1, 2008? The correct answer is $1050.00—the extra $50 being the 5 percent interest she earned on $1,000. You with me so far? Good.

Now, how much will our thrifty woman have on January 1, 2009? The answer is not $1,100 (which you got by assuming another $50 in interest for the year 2008). Yes, she earned 5 percent again, but she earned it on the whole amount in the bank as of January 1, 2008, which was $1,050. Since 5 percent interest on $1,050 is $52.50, she'll have $1,102.50.

The extra $2.50 earned in 2008 doesn't seem like much, but as the years go by and the interest stays in the account, the "interest on the interest" adds up. After ten years, she'll have $1,628.89. And after thirty years, she'll have $4,321.94. Just for the heck of it, I plugged in 10 percent instead of 5 percent to see how much a difference the interest earned makes. If she can earn 10 percent per year, then after ten years she'd have $2,593.74 and after thirty years that initial $1,000 would grow to be $17,449.40!

Wait, it gets even better. Let's say our woman invests an additional $1,000 every year and let's stay with the assumption that she earns 10 percent a year. After thirty years—sit down—she has $164,494.02 in the bank. There you have it ladies and gentlemen, the miracle of compound interest (i.e., interest on interest, as described above).

Seriously now, you haven't read up to this point in the book to swallow this analysis hook, line, and sinker, have you? I hope not. Let's take a closer look at the "miracle" to see why I call it a myth.

There's nothing wrong with the numbers. As long as they're used correctly, calculators don't lie. I triple-checked my calculations. Put $1,000 each year in an account that'll pay 10 percent a year, and after thirty years you'll have $164,494.02.

So what is my problem with this concept? Is it that most people can't find a 10 percent savings account? Well, it's true that we haven't seen 10 percent savings accounts in many years. But substitute mutual fund for savings account, and it's feasible (if not likely) that our saver can earn 10 percent a year for thirty years. True, 10 percent is a stretch, but that's still not my problem.

What does it mean for a bank or mutual fund investment to pay 10 percent? Do you remember the chapter on interest rates? Let me jog your memory. The real cost of borrowing money is between 2.5 and 3 percent, which is to say that the real return on an investment is between 2.5 and 3 percent. Anything above and beyond that is used to compensate the lender for inflation, that is, compensate the lender for the fact that a dollar he gets back in ten years' time will buy less than a dollar does today. A person who lends $1,000—the cost of getting a house painted in 2007— wants to get back what it's going to cost to get a house painted in 2017, plus the real rate of return. A lender has to be compensated for inflation; otherwise, nobody would make financial investments. Instead, all the money would be held in diamonds or real estate.

My beef with the "miracle of compound interest" is that it implies that the big payoff is big, when in fact it's big only because inflation will have increased the price of everything. If this still doesn't make sense to you, maybe I can explain it this way: Your first job did, or will, pay about five times more than your father's first job. Your father is, or will be, immensely proud of you for earning so much money. He shouldn't be—the only reason you have a higher salary than he did is that the price of everything in the United States has increased fivefold since he started working. Got it now? Good.

So, am I telling you not to save? No, no, no. Exactly the opposite: I'm telling you not to rely on the "miracle of compound interest" to fill your nest egg. Here's a better solution: Expect your nest egg to grow by 2.5 to 3 percent in real terms each year, and figure out what it'll take by way of an annual contribution for you to reach your investment goal. If you do it this way, the figure you eventually reach will be the figure you currently have in mind.

9. The Five Mega Decisions Every Investor Faces

As you sit down to put together an investment plan, you will face five big-picture decisions. If you are doing this alone, then it's time to buy a book on financial planning or retirement savings so that you get the answers right. If you're getting help, make sure your collaborator brings up these five decisions. Otherwise, you're closing your eyes to what's out there.

Stocks or bonds? This is the most basic decision that you'll make. We talked in an earlier chapter about the differences between stocks and bonds. Stocks are supposedly more risky than bonds, but in periods of rapid inflation, bonds can really take a dive. Stock and bond prices supposedly move in opposite directions, except they don't always.

To be honest, most people in their middle years buy roughly equal proportions of stocks and bonds to be diversified in the face of utter uncertainty. Younger investors with a greater tolerance for risk will usually overload their portfolios with stocks. There's nothing wrong with that; they have plenty of time before they need the cash. Older people generally hold more bonds, especially those that are guaranteed by the federal or state government or issued by a well-respected corporation. There are no hard and fixed rules to follow. The good news is that small differences in your allocation between bonds and stocks are far less important than how much you save.

Mutual funds or securities? While you're deciding how many stocks and bonds to buy, you're inevitably going to be deciding whether to buy mutual funds or individual securities. There are pros and cons to both.

On the stock side, buying individual stocks is straightforward because the stock market is very liquid (*liquid* means that lots of trades take place every day, making it easy and cheap to buy or sell). If you like doing research on different stocks, have enough cash to build a portfolio that's well-balanced, and want to manage a stock portfolio, then go for it—keeping in mind what I say below about indexed funds.

A mutual fund will do some of the work for you. You still have to decide what kind of fund you want to buy, but the fund manager will pick the actual stocks. I'm about to describe three big differentiations: growth versus value, passive versus active management, and domestic versus global. Funds also define themselves by industry (e.g., technology stock fund, bank stock fund); by market capitalization, which is a fancy word for the size of the company (e.g., mid-cap stock fund, small-cap stock fund); and

other characteristics that the fund manager might be able to identify (e.g., a "contrafund," which is hopefully not made up of con-
traband stocks but rather stocks that run counter to the market).

On the bond side, it may be best to own actual bonds. That
way if a bond goes down in value, you have the option of holding
onto it until maturity when you know you'll get your money
back. The bond market is also less liquid than the stock market,
so with bonds it makes sense to adopt a buy-and-hold approach.
That's the good news. The bad news is that you have to be really
careful about which bonds you buy, seeing as you're going to own
them for a long, long time. For many people, this decision is more
than they want to handle, so either they buy bonds that they're
familiar with and that offer tax advantages (U.S. Treasury bonds
and municipal bonds issued by their their state or city) or they
buy a bond fund. In truth, fund managers do a pretty good job of
offsetting losses with gains, so over time the two largely balance
out. Bond funds are not always the bad decision they appear to be.

Growth or value? Companies that are growing rapidly have an
appeal for certain kinds of investors, and these investors will pay
up to buy the stock in the expectation that the company's earnings will soar.* Such stocks are called *growth stocks*. Stocks whose
prices are more in line with the norm, or even cheap compared to
the average, are called *value stocks,* for obvious reasons.

U.S. stocks are characterized as either growth or value stocks.
Value stocks as a group do better than growth stocks over the long
haul. The reason isn't hard to fathom: With value stocks the company's earnings are being purchased somewhat cheaply, so there's
a built-in cushion for the investor. By contrast, the dot-com boom

---

* Growth companies usually have high P/E ratios. P stands for the stock price and E
stands for the company's recent earnings. A higher than average P/E ratio means that
investors have bid the price of the stock up above what the market would normally
pay for earnings of this sort.

of the 1990s was a growth stock bubble; growth stocks outperformed value stocks by a wide margin (and value stocks outperformed growth stocks in the dot-com bust).

Although individuals will sometimes express a preference for value or growth, the fact that it's impossible to predict which type will prevail argues for a diversified portfolio, that is, a mix of both.

Passive or active? Active investors pick out particular stocks to invest in. In an actively managed mutual fund, the fund manager picks the stocks for the portfolio. A passive portfolio is one that tries to replicate the universe of investments that it's benchmarked against. A passively managed stock fund, for example, may own each stock on the New York Stock Exchange in the exact proportion that it represents on the exchange. More typically, *indexed funds*, as they are also called, are benchmarked against the S&P 500 (Standard & Poor's Index of 500 stocks) or the Russell indexes. Russell produces a broad market index, called the Russell 3000. It also produces Russell 2000 and Russell 1000 indexes.

What's to be gained from a passive fund? The better question to ask is what's to be gained from an actively managed fund? Passive funds actually have a better record than the majority of actively managed funds. I know, it's not what you'd expect. You'd think that professionals who spend all their time searching the globe for good investments would be able to outperform a market average, but most years they don't. Moreover, even when an active manager does outperform the market as a whole, that doesn't increase the odds of her doing so the next year. Still, a lot of money is in actively managed funds. . . . Of course, we go to Vegas, too.

Domestic or global? Business is global. Employment is global. The credit markets are global. Religion and politics are global. Don't you want your investments to be global?

Most people consider overseas investments too risky. Some of them are. I'm not going to pretend that Philippine bonds belong in everyone's investment portfolio. But what about British government bonds (gilts) or Japanese car stocks? They hardly seem more risky than their American counterparts.

Do recognize, though, that credit risk is just one part of the equation when it comes to overseas investments. Because their securities are denominated in their local currencies, you are exposed to the risk that their currency could fall over the course of the investment. That would be a bad thing. Don't dismiss foreign investments out of hand, though, because when their currencies appreciate against the dollar, that's a good thing.

Also, you may think that your American investments, because they're denominated in dollars, carry no currency risk. That's not true. It is true that the return you earn, and the proceeds of any sale, are already in dollars, which is how you want them. But if the dollar falls relative to the British pound—a fall that the difference in interest rates did not foresee—then you lost out by not being invested in British securities. You see, when those more valuable pounds get translated back into dollars, there are going to be lots more dollars than it took to buy the British paper in the first place.

10. Why *Help* Is Often a Four-Letter Word

Help should not be a curse. Help should not make you worse off. Help should be a means of improving your decisions. Unfortunately, in the realm of personal finance, *help* is often a four-letter word.

I've seen financial planners who meet the client once and then relegate the work to the office's computer programmer. This happens more times than you can imagine now that computer software and the Internet have made financial planning tools ubiquitous.

I've seen financial planners who didn't know the first thing about the financial markets. They were awfully good salesmen, though.

I've seen financial planners who know far less about economics than you now do. Wait, let me restate this: I've seen maybe a handful of financial planners who know what you now know.

I've seen financial planners who take basic information about the client and then categorize him using the stages approach described above. They've taken the *personal* right out of personal finance.

I've seen brokerage advisors put into client portfolios whatever stock or bond their trading floor was pushing that day.

So how do you get help that's good? Don't despair: It's doable. First off, get informed before you meet an advisor. This requires a two-pronged effort.

1. You're going to want to know about the advisor herself. You'll get important information from her office before you meet, but do some research on your own. Ask around (but be wary of what you hear; people are rarely honest about their investment performance or tax liabilities). Google her.

2. If you can make the time to do so, pick up a book or read some articles on the Internet about the task in front of you. The more you know, the better your ability to gauge the advisor's potential value to you (and the better your outcome).

When you meet the advisor for the first time, ascertain his credentials. You want a financial planner who is a CFP; in other words, he has been certified by the Certified Financial Planner Board of Standards, Inc. You want an accountant who has been certified as an accountant, a CPA. And you want to see the advisor's registration with the SEC, called Form ADV (you can request this from your nearest SEC office). Among other things, this will tell you if he cut and ran from a bankrupt practice five states away. By the way, I know a lot of people use accountants as financial planners. This makes me a bit nervous, even though I'm sure the majority of them are quite good. Look for ones who specialize in personal finance rather than 1040s and the books of local small businesses.

Also, a lot of people rely on their life insurance salesperson for financial planning advice. The problem with that is the eleventh word in that sentence: *salesperson*. Although many of these people are quite savvy, I can't help thinking you're going to end up with an awful lot of insurance products in your portfolio of assets.

One of the easiest things to measure is an advisor's independence. Is she in the pocket of a large brokerage house that puts demands on her to buy certain securities for her client's accounts? Is she able to structure a portfolio for you without outside influences? I say this is the easiest thing to figure out because all it usually takes is a glance at her business card. If Merrill Lynch's name is bigger than hers, that tells you something.

Ask how your advisor will be paid. Is it through a percentage of your earnings? A percentage of your assets? A flat fee? Commission on the trades he executes for your account? I like people to have an incentive to do well, so it's OK with me if the advisor earns a fraction of what I earn (as long as it's a small fraction). Others prefer a flat fee arrangement; this way they know the advisor isn't pushing any particular securities. You absolutely don't want an advisor who earns his bread through commissions; he has every incentive to churn your account (that is, make an excessive number of trades). An advisor who gets paid on the size of your account is also not a good thing: There's not enough incentive to do well.

In conversations with your advisor, make sure she listens and takes notes. In follow-up conversations, you'll want to see or hear evidence that she heard you. If you've said you want index funds and she suggests an individualized portfolio of one hundred stocks, then you've got to wonder who's paying her. If you've told her you want a safe, short-term investment and she suggests thirty-year Treasury bonds, walk away.

8

Trying to Defy Gravity, and Failing: The Basics of Government Finance

Some people pay their bills daily; I've always done it once a month. I sit at the kitchen or dining room table (I've heard it's un-American to do this anywhere else in the house) in a really foul mood, and I write check after check until my writing hand aches. Recently, I have taken to logging onto my computer and taking care of things with a few clicks—it's quicker and just a tad less painful. Regardless of how I pay, however, I can assure you that by the time I'm done, I'm broke. Whatever cash came in that month, the bills somehow matched it. I guess I'm not alone in this.

I also know firsthand, as many of you do as well, that sometimes there isn't enough cash on hand to pay for everything. Most people don't have enough cash sloshing around their checking account to pay for a new oven (not at what seems like $2,000 a kilowatt) or a new roof (for $500 per square foot). Hey, there have been plenty of times I've held off buying new jeans or shoes for the kids until my next paycheck arrived. Making ends meet is an inevitable fact of life.

What do people do when, because of an unusual expenditure, their monthly paycheck can't cover all their expenses? This happened to my friend and neighbor Oliver, so let's talk about him instead of me for a change. Last spring Oliver got whacked with a $9,000 bill to clean up his basement when floodwaters invaded his (uninsured) basement office. At first Oliver thought he'd cut back on nonessentials to make ends meet. For a while his family spent every Saturday night at home, where a bowl of spaghetti fed four people for $4. But it didn't take long for Oliver to realize that it wouldn't be enough to live on spaghetti and watch old movies. Oliver needed serious cash, so despite the heartache it caused him, he decided to dip into his savings for the money he needed. Ollie was lucky: He had a savings account at the local bank, a money market account at a brokerage company, and the kitchen cookie jar to raid. All were good sources of funds because the cash was easily available, even if it was earmarked for other purposes. As much as he disliked tapping into his savings accounts for repair work, it did the trick. Oliver's story ends here.

Unfortunately, not everyone with a flooded basement is so fortunate. Others may not have the savings that Oliver had to lean on. Many people live too close to the bone to have much in the way of savings at all, whether it's because they've got a new baby at home, an aging parent they're caring for, their own recovery from illness to fund—you get the picture. There are lots of reasons why people don't have cash on hand in an emergency. What then? Well, obviously more draconian steps are necessary. For people with stock and bond investments, one option is to cash in some of those securities. Borrowing is another option. Small amounts of cash are available on credit cards (most likely at a whopping 30 percent annual interest rate). For bigger needs, individuals can take out a home equity loan, or perhaps take a loan from their 401(k).

Wherever the cash is found, it has to be found. Otherwise, people facing a serious gap in their monthly cash flows will be plunged into the kind of financial turmoil that's portrayed in TV advertisements for bankruptcy lawyers. And we all know that's not pretty.

Making Ends Meet, by the Trillion

This is a chapter on the federal budget, so it's time that I switched from talking about everyday people to a discussion of one person in particular, Uncle Sam.

I may have described the need to make ends meet in terms of people—you, me, and the guy next door—but I'm sure you realize that it applies to institutions as well, from corporations to nonprofit organizations to governments. Corporations face the same constraints as you or I do, which is why companies borrow money from banks, issue bonds, and sell equity to undertake projects outside their normal scope of operations, projects that can't be covered with the normal amount of cash that comes in the door each month. Foundations and nonprofit institutions face the same harsh reality, which is why they're forced to beg governments for aid and raise money from the public with a solid calendar of fundraisers. State, city, township, and town governments have to live by the same rules as well. Governments take money in largely through taxes (which come in a myriad of forms). Governments spend that tax money on the things they are charged by us to do, whether that's teaching our kids, cleaning up the beach, paving roads, or running airports. Even for governments, the same rules apply: The money they spend can't exceed the money they take in. If this starts to happen, then governments, like everyone else, have to make up the difference. Either they cut back on expenses, delve into savings, or borrow. At the end of the day, one simple rule of accounting applies to virtually all people and institutions, regardless of location: Outflows can't exceed inflows.

You're quick, aren't you? You noticed that I snuck in the word *virtually* in the last sentence of the previous paragraph. Well, I did so because there is one type of institution that does not have to live by those rules: the federal government. You, me, city hall—we all have to balance the books. Uncle Sam does not. He's got an out that no one else has (legally). Uncle Sam can print money to get the nation out of financial hot water. "A few billion short this year," the president boasts. "Not to worry. Stoke up the printing press and print more cash."

Presto, whammo! Problem solved, right? Well, not really. I swear to you that what seems at first blush to be a blessing is, in fact, a complete and utter curse on our land. Unfortunately, it's going to take the better part of this chapter to explain this to you. So, here's what we're going to do. First, we'll look at the federal budget in some detail to figure out why budget deficits happen. Then we'll tackle the hard stuff: I'll describe the mechanics of funding the federal deficit and I'll explain why the ability to print money is more curse than cure.

Spending Way beyond Our Very Ample Means

You or I may run into a month or two—OK, maybe a few months straight if we're unlucky or errant—when we're spending more than we take in. Our creditors won't let us get away with this for too long, however, so the vast majority of us are limited in how much damage we can do (i.e., how much debt we can rack up). Not so the U.S. government. For the most part, the creditors of the U.S. government have no regulatory, statutory, legal, fiduciary, moral, logical, or even illogical restrictions on how much money they can lend Uncle Sam. Thus, Uncle Sam takes advantage of this all-you-can-eat "buffet" and eats heartily at each meal.

It's not that Uncle Sam doesn't have an income of his own, mind you. The federal budget in fiscal year 2007, which covered the twelve months ending in September 2007, shows that the government took in $2.57 trillion. That tidy sum is bigger than all but five of the world's economies. *Impressive* and *depressing* are two of the words that come to mind as I write this . . . but I digress. Where did this $2.57 trillion come from? Well, the long and short of it is you and me. The revenues aren't listed by name, as they might be at your church or synagogue. That would be unwieldy on such a large scale, in any case. Instead, the revenue side of the federal budget is organized by the name of the tax that brought the money in the door. Some taxes are called just that; other taxes have fancy names, like *fees* or *duties* or *contributions*.

Of the $2.57 trillion that the U.S. government took in during the year ended September 2007, a little less than half of it, or $1.2 trillion, came through the door as individual income tax payments. Another $370 billion was paid by corporations in the form of corporate income taxes. These two income taxes make up the bulk of Uncle Sam's income. The other "taxes" Uncle Sam collects are called *estate* and *gift taxes, customs duties,* and *excise taxes.* And then there's the obligatory miscellaneous item, of course. Add it all up, and yup, you get almost $2.6 trillion bucks in a twelve-month period.

That's a lot of moolah.

5,400 Bras Size 32B, 4,300 Size 30C . . .

With over 250,000 women in the U.S. armed forces (20 percent), our Uncle Sam is the largest buyer of bras in this country, if not the world! (Yes, Wal-Mart buys more bras from wholesalers, but only to resell.) He also ranks high among the buyers of men's underwear, marching boots, leather, file cabinets, and Cheese Whiz. Not to mention tanks, bullets, and submarines. In short, the federal government is the single biggest purchasing agent on the planet. If it's out there, it's in here—here being the list of federal procurements.

Unlike the revenue side of the budget, which is organized by what, not who, the spending side of the budget is organized by who, not what. Got that? Let me say it so you can understand: Federal outlays are categorized by office and agency. So the federal budget lists the outlays of the Department of Energy, the Department of Defense, the Department of Homeland Security . . .

and so on. Within each of those sections, the budget is broken down so that anyone can see how much was spent on the different tasks the agency or department is charged with carrying out. For instance, the Department of Homeland Security budget has a line called TSA (Transportation Security Administration), which is the amount of money that was spent on transportation security—you know, the guys who run the security operations at the airport.

Close your eyes for a moment—assuming they were open— and think for a moment about the three biggest spenders in Washington. Got 'em? It's actually not that hard to guess, is it? The Defense Department. The Social Security Administration. Health and Human Services. Those three departments spend $1.8 trillion alone. Defense spends roughly $530 billion, Social Security spends $622 billion, and Health and Human Services spends $672 billion.* There's one other massive entry on the books that you might not think of too fast: interest. Because the government spends more than it takes in, the government is constantly borrowing. Which means it has to pay interest to those who lend it money. Interest took up a whopping $430 billion of our tax money in 2007—that's more than 15 percent of the budget! Imagine paying out 15 percent of your monthly paycheck in *interest* to CitiCards or American Express. Needless to say, something's seriously wrong here. Let's investigate.

Netting It All Out

The full budget for the U.S. government is released by the U.S. Treasury four times a year, with running totals before year end so the White House, the Congress, and outside analysts can tell

---

* Social Security tax receipts are an off-budget item that is set against Social Security outlays. When outlays exceed receipts, which is expected to start in 2017 due to the growing number of baby boomers who will retire, the Social Security Trust Fund will have to be tapped to make up the difference. The government's latest estimates say that the Trust Fund will be depleted in 2041. A similar fund for Medicare will go broke earlier, in 2019, since outlays here already exceed tax receipts.

whether Uncle Sam's coming in "on budget" (note that "on budget" reflects the budget shortfall that had previously been factored into the numbers). If not, if there's an even larger shortfall than expected, there may be two reasons for it: (1) the government took in less money than it had expected, or (2) the government spent more money than it had expected. The first of these is pretty simple to figure. Tax revenues can be down for any number of good reasons, like a rise in unemployment which has meant a shortfall of income at the national level; fewer importers paying import taxes; corporations earning fewer profits on the whole; or even fewer visitors to national parks. On the flip side, the government could be spending more than it had expected for a variety of reasons such as much-needed hurricane relief, a resurgence in fighting abroad, a drought that required additional assistance for farmers, or even a few extra trips for the president abroad. Like your family budget at home, the federal budget is alive with unexpected ins and outs that are perfectly unpredictable and (hardly) charming.

With the exception of a few years under Bill Clinton, the federal government has continually faced a budget shortfall. In the fiscal year ended September 2007, the shortfall was a "mere" $163 billion. The year before that, it was $248 billion. Yes, the war in Iraq was a big part of this. But the shortfall in fiscal year 2001, which ended September 30, 2002—that is, the *deficit*—was an ever-impressive $159 billion. Budget deficits are not the occasional cold or flu—they're more akin to a long-term, life-threatening condition like heart disease or diabetes that has to be carefully managed!

A Sale for All Sales

Unlike my neighbor Ollie (you remember him, right?), who had savings to rely on when his basement flooded, Uncle Sam has very little in the way of savings to fall back on when spending unexpectedly ramps up. Actually, now that I've written it, I have to admit that's pretty much a lie. The idea that Uncle Sam only runs into trouble every so often I've already shown to be untrue. Budget deficits are a year-in, year-out occurrence. It's also a lie that Uncle Sam has any savings at all to fall back on. So the point I should be making is that since the federal government has no savings to fall back on, it always has to borrow to make up any and all shortfalls.

The U.S. Treasury is the government department charged with borrowing, and as you might expect, it's a formidable task. Because the deficit is so large, that is, the government's need for extra cash is so enormous, the U.S. Treasury has formalized its borrowing into a calendar of bond sales.* The Treasury's calendar includes weekly sales of bills, monthly sales of some notes, quarterly sales of other notes, and semiannual sales of longer-term bonds. Oh, and don't forget sales of cash management bills and floating rate notes (called *TIPS* [Treasury Inflation Protected Securities]) when the need for cash arises. In the final quarter of calendar year 2007, the Treasury conducted fifty-five auctions and sold $968 billion worth of new debt. At the end of that calendar year, the amount of Treasury debt outstanding was some $8.5 trillion. No wonder the Treasury's interest payments on the debt totaled over $400 billion—you owe a lot, you pay a lot.

Now in case math is not your strong suit, let me point out that the $968 billion of new debt sold by the Treasury is much, much larger than the $87 billion that the Treasury had to raise. Why the difference? The Treasury has to auction off brand-spanking-new

---

* You'll recall from chapter 2 that bills, notes, and bonds are fancy words for government IOUs. Lenders (that is, investors) get IOUs (bonds, along with interest about twice a year) in exchange for the cash they hand over to the Treasury. At the expiration of each bond—at its maturity, that is—the lender (investor) gets the full amount of the loan back. Bills are the IOUs associated with short-term loans of one year or less; notes are IOUs for loans that last from one to ten years. Bonds are the IOUs associated with long-term loans. Finally, remember that bond sales are called auctions because the sales are run as auctions—duh!

securities to cover the shortfall in the budget deficit *and* to pay off the bills, notes, and bonds that are coming due from previous bill, note, and bond sales. It's called *rollover*—rolling over the debt that's coming due. And what it means is that even if the federal government keeps its deficit constant, the amount of money it needs to borrow will continue to increase. Hell, even if the government stops running a deficit at all, it'll still need to borrow money for years to come simply to cover the rollover of bonds that are maturing. That's why I like to say that the day the Treasury stops selling bonds will likely be the day the world stops spinning. And that's why I encourage college kids to consider Wall Street careers. . . .

Take a Breath

Let's recap. I've taken you on a long, winding road, but the distance between where we're at and where we started isn't all that far. The U.S. government raises money through taxes of various sorts and spends it on a variety of projects, including but certainly not limited to defense, social security, welfare, interest on the public debt, and fireworks for the Fourth of July. Unfortunately, our government is not particularly thrifty, so it constantly spends more than it takes in. To cover the gap, the U.S. Treasury sells IOUs (called bills, notes, and bonds) to whomever will buy them, which is to say, it borrows money. The gap itself is called the *deficit*.

Not so difficult to understand, is it? OK, then, here's the next wrinkle. Sometimes the Treasury has trouble selling all the bills, notes, and bonds it wants to sell. This often happens when the deficit is rising faster than the economy is growing. When the Treasury's been particularly active in the market, investors may already have their fill of Treasury bills, notes, and bonds (alternatively called *paper*). It will take a higher interest rate to lure new investors out of the woodwork to buy the new debt. Or, investors may worry that they've underestimated future inflation. This, too, may force interest rates up. (Time to review how bonds work? For a quick refresher, see chapter 3.) Those are just two reasons why new Treasury borrowing may cause interest rates to rise; there are others. Regardless of the reason, higher interest rates generally aren't all that good for the economy. Higher interest rates make it more expensive for the rest of us (you, me, GM) to afford the financing for a new house, a used car, or a new plant in Kalamazoo. . . .

Therein lies the big conundrum. The U.S. government has things it wants to spend money on, things it can't really afford given its current revenues. Everything looks like it comes out OK when the Treasury borrows the money to cover the deficit, but, in reality, the Treasury's borrowing could force interest rates to rise and that would mess us all up (even the Treasury; the government has to pay out a higher rate of interest, too).

But wait. I said Uncle Sam has another option that no one else has. I said Uncle Sam can print money to cover a deficit. Well, yes, he can. But as I'll now explain, "That don't work real well neither."

Daddy Warbucks

Ask a kid rummaging around the museums of Washington, D.C., who's got the best job in town, and she's likely to say the president, followed by the treasurer of the United States—you know, the guy who signs dollar bills (and fives, tens, twenties, and hundreds). Kids are smart. Being in charge of the printing presses for paper money sounds like a darn good job. Except that the guys who run the place aren't the ones who get to decide how much to print. That job rests ultimately with the Federal Reserve, which explains why a fellow named Alan Greenspan only reluctantly gave up the job of Fed chairman when he was eighty years old! (The present holder of this office is an economist from Princeton University, Ben Bernanke, which goes to show that not everyone in New Jersey acts like Tony Soprano.)

Remember the Fed? The Fed is the U.S. central bank, which means it is the government bank as well as the banks' bank. In the vaults of the Fed are zillions of dollars, zlotys, and yen, not to mention gold and Treasury bonds. Treasury bonds? You betcha! Bills, notes and bonds, to be exact. In fact, the Fed is one of the Treasury's best customers, buying up a good chunk of the debt the Treasury sells each month.

Please do not store this little fact away as quaint or at the very least convenient—sort of like a father buying up his son's IOUs. There's nothing sweet about it. Here's why. Every time the Fed buys the Treasury's debt, it injects cash into the economy. But every time the Fed adds money to the economy above and beyond what's necessary for economic growth, it raises the level of inflation.* And we know what inflation does to an economy, right? It undermines income, rewards borrowers and punishes savers, and causes everyone to pay higher interest rates on new borrowing.

So funding the federal deficit is a no-win proposition. Either the Treasury borrows money (sells bonds) to fund the gap, or the Fed buys the Treasury's debt. Great choice, huh? Either we compete with the U.S. Treasury for loanable funds and face higher interest rates if the deficit is rising faster than the economy—an action that hampers growth in the private sector—or we face inflation, which erodes the purchasing power of our income.

Still think government deficits are harmless?

---

* Remember, money at the Fed is not money for the benefit of the overall economy because it's out of circulation. Once money leaves the Fed's coffers, however, it becomes part of the economy's money supply, with all the joy and sorrow that cash infusions always create. First the new cash stokes the economy's fire, which means that at first the economy sees new spending, new jobs, and so on. This eventually gives way, however, to nothing more than a burst of inflation.

9

Multiply by a Gazillion: Tracking the Course of the U.S. Economy

Each night on the evening news, broadcasters struggle to report the latest economic figures out of Washington. Not only can they not make sense of what they're reading off the teleprompter; half the time they can't even pronounce the words. I'm not talking widgets here*—they routinely mangle simple words like *exports* and *investment*.

What are your options? Well, you could quickly press the MUTE button on the remote control so you're saved their embarrassment. That requires action on your part, which isn't always convenient, and it puts you at risk of missing the next segment of the news that might have a more immediate effect on your life (let's say, another recall of SUV tires). Alternatively, you could just tune out—that's what most people do. I'm going to give you a third option. You can read this chapter, listen to the nightly broadcast, and then congratulate yourself on having a better understanding of the financial news than many of the highly paid folks reporting it. This third option has a few advantages over the other

---

* FYI: A widget is an imaginary good that economists talk about because they don't want to use something real. I don't get it, either.

two. For one, you get a good chuckle and these are always hard to come by around dinnertime (overcooked peas and cheap beer notwithstanding). For another, you'll learn something about the economy's functioning that most people won't know unless they are in the small minority of people who read (and understand) economic news as part of their jobs. At the very least, it'll pay off the next time you have an argument with your brother-in-law. (Let me add that in my house there's a crucial third reason: It gives me an excuse to ask my off-key teenage daughter to stop singing because there's something important on the TV.)

Option three it is, then. Here's how this works. I'm going to describe in broad brushstrokes the doings of ordinary people here in the United States. Then we're going to multiply figuratively (emphasis on the word *figuratively*, meaning "not really") the actions of those ordinary people to see how economists measure and track the big picture.

Because this chapter starts off with a lot of definitions, it's probably the slowest chapter in the book to get through. If you hang in there, however, you'll gain a lot of nifty little insights that will make you a more intelligent voter and savvy consumer. You'll understand things like why politicians always rave about the *number* of jobs they've helped create. Or why honest people come up with completely different opinions about certain stocks. Or why the economy can't always grow. Or why men quote movies and women don't. (That last one is a joke—I haven't a clue.)

Ordinary People Work, or They Don't

If people work, even part-time, they are considered employed. If they do not work, but have looked for a job and can't find one, they are considered unemployed. Please note that government statisticians are very particular about the definition of employment. Someone is not considered unemployed if she's sick, lazy, or in school (even if she's in school because she couldn't find a job).

If you take the number of unemployed folks and divide it by all those people who work or want to work, you end up with a fraction, like 0.051, which is 5.1 percent. That's the unemployment rate.*

The employment figure can be a little tricky because the number keeps rising as the population grows. The unemployment rate is the better measure of labor conditions because it shows the percentage of people who want to work but can't find employment. If you want to know whether it's easy or hard to get a job, then look at the unemployment rate.**

The fact that there are two ways to measure "employment" allows for one of the nastier tricks that politicians play. Elected officials of all stripes love to brag about how many more jobs were created during their time in office—that is, how many more people are employed. However, the better measure, as explained above, is the unemployment rate. I guarantee that if you hear a politician boast about the *number* of jobs created it's because she can't boast about real improvement in labor conditions, as signaled by a decline in the unemployment *rate*.

Ordinary People Earn Income

Ordinary people work for an obvious reason: to earn money. The wages and salaries earned by ordinary people are the bulk of what is called *personal income*. Income earned by ordinary (and not so ordinary) persons, that is, personal income, also comprises the

---

* The official unemployment rate actually understates the percent of people unemployed because you'll notice it only counts those who are looking for work. Individuals who have stopped looking, say because they are discouraged by their job prospects, are called *discouraged workers*. Discouraged workers are not part of the unemployment formula.

** Still confused? Think about it this way. India has many more people employed than does Russia—467 million Indians to 69 million Russians. But the Russians have a lower unemployment rate, which is a sign of better labor conditions in Russia than in India. The reason India has a higher employment number is simply that it's a bigger country in terms of population.

money we earn through our investments in stocks and bonds (dividends and interest) and real estate (rent). Also considered income is the money that people receive from others, like pensions and social security. Did I forget anything? Oh yeah, we need to add in the money people earn from their own businesses. The woman down the street who owns her own beauty salon, or the guy who runs the snowplow in the winter, earns income that doesn't qualify as wages—but it's spent the same as money received in a paycheck.

Ordinary Corporations Earn Income, Too

Companies earn income, too, of course. It's called *profits*. I will spare you the long story about profits; believe me, it *is* long. You see, what accountants call profits is not the same as what the IRS calls profits, nor is it the same thing that government statisticians call profits. Moreover, financial analysts on Wall Street (the guys who tell you which companies are good investments and which are not) make up their own definitions of profits. Of course, many companies reject all of the above for their own spin on the numbers. And to top all this off with a bright red cherry, economists have yet a different measure, but then we're more conceptual types than the guys in New York and Washington. And you wonder why so-called experts can't agree on the value of certain stocks, or why Enron was able to get away with fraud and deception for years.

Well, in point of fact, I don't really care which measure you have in mind as you read this book, because they're all variations on a simple theme. Companies take in money for the products they sell, and their profits are what remain after they subtract the cost of making/delivering those products. It costs Christopher Jr. down the street $4 to make a pitcher of lemonade, including his time in the kitchen and at the lemonade stand (although, as an eight-year-old, his time is cheap). If he sells the pitcher of lemonade for $6 (12 cups for 50 cents each), then his profit is $2 per pitcher. If he sells four pitchers a day for five days a week for ten weeks, that's a profit of $400 for the summer (2 × 4 × 5 × 10 = 400). I wish I had made $400 when I was eight!

Ordinary People and Ordinary Companies Make for an Ordinary Nation

Governments don't usually turn a profit; neither do nonprofit agencies. So the income of the nation is the combination of personal income and corporate profits—what's called *national income*. Funny, you say, you've never heard anyone speak of national income. That's because people are generally interested in personal income and some people are very, very interested in corporate profits, but few are interested in their sum total when it's packaged as national income. With a few small adjustments, however, national income can be transformed into a measure of the nation's output, which is called *gross domestic product,* or GDP. The nation's output is of real concern to us all because it's the biggest, broadest measure of the sum total of the nation's economic activity.

Swapping GDP for national income is an easier task than you might imagine. Think of an outstretched hand, say, a teenager asking for payment after washing the dishes. You can count the five bucks as it lands in her hand, or you can count the fiver as it reluctantly leaves the parent's fingers. When we count the money crossing the teenager's palm, we're counting income (counted in national income). When we count the cash leaving the parent's hand, it's an expenditure, an outlay, spending (counted in GDP).

Here's a test. Does the example of the teenager with her palm outstretched jog your memory at all? Do you remember back when I first described supply and demand? I said then that a transaction takes place when a supplier hands over goods and receives payment from a buyer, and that the sale and cash receipt are two sides of a single transaction. Well, national income and GDP represent that same idea, only the numbers are ramped up to cover all the transactions that take place over a period of time in the country. National income and GDP are sort of like supply and demand at the national level.*

As with supply and demand, there's real value to be had from looking at things from two different perspectives. With national income, we get to see how well people and companies are faring. With GDP, we get to understand how people, companies, governments, and foreigners are spending their money. That's valuable information for people looking for a job or contemplating a career change, investors looking for the next big winner, companies deciding how and where to expand or shrink operations, and even governments deciding whether to build a new sports arena or school.

The majority of the economic indicators that follow in this chapter are in one way or another part of the calculation of GDP. Before going there, however, it's helpful to understand the mega breakdowns in GDP. The economy's zillion transactions are sorted into one of four barrels:

- *consumption,* which is spending for ordinary items by consumers, from peaches to cars

- investment, which is spending on things that are expected to last for more than a few years, such as houses, office buildings

---

* Now is as good a time as any to make it clear that GDP is the sum of all *final* goods and services. No intermediate steps are included in this figure or there would be massive double-counting. For instance, when a car is sold, it is entered into the GDP accounts under *motor vehicle sales.* The car is the sum of all its parts, however, and it would be double-counting to count the car as well as the tires, brakes, engine, and so on. Thus, when Goodyear sells tires to GM, it does *not* get counted in the GDP; Goodyear tires are an *intermediate good* when sold to the car manufacturers. If you understand this, then you'll also understand that when I buy Goodyear tires for my car, to replace a worn tire, that transaction *does* get counted in GDP.

and plants, factory machinery, and software (who're they kidding?)*

• government spending, which represents the outlays of all sorts of government bodies, from your local water board to Uncle Sam

• and *foreign trade.*

All the purchases that you, Uncle Sam, and I make are sorted into those four categories—no exceptions for the rich or the thin.

As you might imagine, a person could spend her entire life in the nooks and crannies of the GDP accounts. We won't. I'll only ask you for fifteen minutes.

Ordinary People Buy Ordinary Goods and Services

If there's one thing that defines Americans, it's that we shop. We are a nation of shoppers. So, naturally, government economists have all sorts of different measures to describe our favorite sport. And what the government doesn't collect in the way of data, trade organizations and special interest groups do. I once had a job that required me to evaluate all these different economic reports. I liked it, but then, as an economist, I'm a bit different from most people.

To cut to the chase, there are two spending measurements that deserve your attention. The first is retail sales. As you might expect, it totes up all the sales that take place at retail establishments during a month, from gasoline to handbags, groceries to cars. You might be wondering about the Internet, as online sales

---

* Businesses spend lots of money at Staples and Wal-Mart on things like paper clips and printer paper. These consumption-like purchases are not counted in GDP, because they are intermediate purchases whose value is rolled into that of the final product or service that consumers buy.

have taken a good chunk of business away from the brick-and-mortar stores themselves. Internet sales are included in retail sales, although everyone realizes that those numbers are, as my off-key daughter would say, a bit sketchy.

Somewhat broader than retail sales is personal consumption. Consumption includes retail sales but it also includes what we spend on services. In America in the twenty-first century, we spend much more money on services than we do on actual goods. Think about the bills you pay each month: electricity, gas, mortgage, rent, air and train fares, medical costs, vacations. . . . Those are all services. And since many people write a huge check each month for the mortgage or rent, services make up the bigger slice of monthly outlays.

Ordinary People Save (Just a Little)

Americans are famous worldwide for being great shoppers and lousy savers. It's true: We're notoriously and dangerously bad at saving. Some months in the United States, personal consumption actually *exceeds* personal income, meaning we draw down our savings to pay for what we want. Few nations can equal this kind of shortsightedness.

How do we get away with it? Part of the answer is that we save by investing in real estate. Since housing is a long-lasting investment whose price has been rising almost without an end in sight (that is, until the subprime mortgage meltdown that began in 2007), maybe mortgage payments should be counted as saving rather than consumption. It's something to think about. Even if you reclassify real estate as savings, however, the United States still comes up short in the personal saving contest, compared to all other developed countries. (And we are light years behind developing countries, but that's because they generally don't have the same social safety nets as the developed world. Lest you think we created this mess all on our own, however, you should know that the industrial country that comes closest to matching our miserable saving record is, you guessed it, the United Kingdom.)

Ordinary Governments Spend Our Hard-Earned Money on Underperforming Schools, Shoddy Roads, Slow Service, Fourth of July Fireworks . . .

Forgive me my rant. I'm writing this just after April 15. Can you tell?

Government spending. I won't say much since you just read chapter and verse on federal finance. Let me merely point out that, as with ordinary people, in the GDP accounts the outlays of governments are divided into those that mimic consumption (that is, the purchases of goods and services) and those that mimic individual or business investment (i.e., investment in physical plants like schools and prisons and in durable machinery like voting machines [except in Florida]).

Ordinary Foreigners

No wisecracks about the existence of ordinary foreigners. We all know lots of very ordinary people who live outside the United States.

Insofar as we are interested in the economic goings-on here in the United States, what foreigners do in their own countries is not our business. However, we do have to take into account the goods and services Americans buy that are "made" abroad. Likewise, we have to take into account the goods and services "made" here that are sold outside the United States. If we don't make these adjustments, our income and product accounts won't be in sync. (Note that *made* is in quotes here because so much of what we trade is not a physical product that is actually constructed, or made. Rather, services represent a good deal of our trade. No one uses the word *made* in the context of accounting services or IT.)

From the perspective of GDP, which again is *national product,* we want to include the goods and services produced here and sold abroad, which are called *exports*. We want to subract from our GDP accounts the goods and services that are produced elsewhere and sold here, which are called *imports*. Let me think of a good example of exports. Oh yes, chick flicks. What a contribution Hollywood makes to the world economy! And imports? Toys from China. Clothes from China. Computers from China. Appliances from China. Chinese food (tainted or clean) from China. China from China. And cars, crude oil, and natural gas from Canada. Of course, that's only a partial list.

Subtract imports from exports and you get what's called *net exports*. Were the day ever to arrive again when we sold more abroad than we imported, net exports would make a positive contribution to our GDP. Instead, GDP is brought down a notch or two to reflect the fact that we spend some of our hard-earned income on goods and services made abroad (read: *China*).

Exports and imports are really hard to measure, even more so than the variety of domestic measures we've looked at. You'd think it would be easy, what with our borders being well defined (and often protected with barbed wire). But that's not the case, mostly because a lot of what we trade is services and because American number crunchers have no stick they can swing at foreigners to induce them to report cross-border transactions accurately.

For better or for worse, then, the government still puts out figures monthly on international trade. The tables show exports and they show imports: one table with lots of small numbers and one table with lots of big numbers. The gap between the two, in our case a deficit because imports dominate exports, is the headline. In case you're wondering, it's getting bigger all the time.

Ordinary People Are Productive

One of the more interesting subjects in economics (no, I'm not kidding) is *productivity*. Productivity isn't simply a measure of how much is produced. It's a measure of how much is produced for a given amount of labor. It's one thing to say that we're producing a lot more goods; it's something else to say we're producing a lot more goods with the same number of people putting in the same number of hours.

Productivity numbers are not easy to calculate. Oh, sure, it's an easy slog if all you have to count is the hours your employees work making picture frames. How about if the output is computer software? Or computer repair? Or stock trading? The preponderance of services in the economy makes the calculation of productivity pretty darn difficult, and at times unreliable.

Even so, productivity is something you want to watch. At times in U.S. history, productivity growth has been near-stagnant. So far in the 2000s, however, productivity growth has been pretty strong. The typical driver of productivity growth is additional and upgraded machinery or tools, and this is a big reason for the recent revival of productivity growth in the United States. Robots let automobile workers focus on the jobs for which human skills are necessary. Put in the robots, and each worker can produce more.

The second reason productivity growth is on the upswing is better labor. Companies have been benefiting from the maturation of the labor force (thanks, in part, to the aging baby boomers). And they've been benefiting from a smarter workforce, as new grads bring new tools and methods to their new jobs.

But the big reason that productivity has turned the corner in recent years is technology. Computers. The Internet. Wireless communications. These technological advances have made each and every one of us more productive with our time,* both at home

---

* Companies have been known to try to increase productivity without installing better equipment or devising better methods, simply by laying off some of their workers and asking the remaining employees to work harder. We've all experienced this one way or another, and it's unpleasant. The limits of such tactics should be obvious: Unless the company had scores of workers lounging around doing unnecessary tasks, the gain would be minimal. More importantly, on a national level, such tactics can't explain the now longer-term trend toward increased productivity growth that the United States is enjoying.

and at work (indeed, thanks to technology, work is often done at home). The technology revolution has ushered in a period of lower inflation rates, lower interest rates, stronger productivity growth, and stronger income growth. Indeed, I can't say enough about the influence of technology on the economy, but I'll stop here because you need to eat at some point.

Let's get back to the productivity numbers. I told you they're something you want to watch. That's not just because productivity growth is going up. It's because productivity is a *free lunch*. You don't get many of these in life, so you should definitely appreciate them when they're offered.

What does it mean to have a free lunch, you ask? Think about what happens as Jane, a package sorter at UPS, gets more experienced. She gets faster, meaning she can sort more packages per hour. That means that in Jane's unit, UPS loaders can load more boxes onto trucks and ship more packages to their correct destinations. More boxes mean more money (translation: profits). Experience alone allowed this chain of events to happen; it didn't cost UPS an extra nickel. That's a free lunch!

What happens to the extra profits UPS was able ring up thanks to Jane? It gets divvied up, of course. Part of the extra profits goes to the owners of UPS, as it should. But given that UPS has incentives for its workers, Jane and her boss probably get a bit of the extra cash as well, maybe in the form of a year-end bonus, maybe in the form of a merit pay increase.*

My story about a new-and-improved Jane was a simple one, but the same principles apply when UPS invests in new equipment to

---

* It's my experience, and probably yours, that most of the extra cash will accrue to the shareholders, and that Jane's boss will make out better than Jane. This hardly seems fair since it's Jane who worked her butt off for the company. Whether we like it or not, however, this is entirely consistent with the underpinnings of capitalism. Capitalism says that the *owners* of capital reap its rewards. Once Jane has shown up for work, UPS owns her. Of course, Jane doesn't have to work for UPS. One of the best ways for Jane to grab her share is to talk to the HR department at FedEx.

speed the work of sorters and loaders. Or when UPS gives the people who ship with UPS the ability to track their packages over the Internet. This job used to be nearly impossible, and if a shipper demanded to know where his package was, it required the involvement of many UPS workers. Not so anymore. Productivity is actually labor productivity, you see, so extra machines and new technology are freebies. Not to worry, though; companies also monitor capital productivity to make sure that their investments in machinery and technology are yielding the benefits expected of them as well.

Here's the great news: When productivity growth lagged in the 1970s, GDP growth lagged as well. Now that productivity growth is faster, GDP growth is faster, and that means incomes are rising more quickly, as well as stock prices. No complaints.

Ordinary People Are Real

What do you say to your best friend when she calls to say that her company is handing out 5 percent raises across the board this year? Since she's a good friend, you say, "Hey, that's great!" And what do you say when she calls later in the day to say her rent was just increased 7 percent and her car insurance was jacked up 10 percent? It's OK; I won't print it.

We all know that prices sometimes rise and rarely fall. And we all know that just to keep our heads above water, we need a little more every year. A recipient of food stamps or social security knows this phenomenon as a *cost-of-living adjustment*. Income is adjusted higher to compensate for higher prices. Most companies raise their employees' wages and salaries each year to accomplish the same thing.

We've been looking at a lot of statistics in this chapter that are measured in terms of dollars. GDP, consumption, savings, and retail sales are all measured in dollars. But if the prices of goods and services are rising, then these measures will rise even without an increase in the number of units bought or sold! We easily spend more on gasoline each month, even though we drive the same car the same distance.

In order to provide a more realistic estimate of what's actually going down, statisticians convert the current dollar numbers into real numbers; that is, current dollar GDP becomes *real* GDP and current dollar consumption becomes *real* consumption.* Real spending is spending adjusted for rising prices or inflation. So, for instance, if gas prices alone are behind a rise in our outlays for gasoline, current dollar consumption will show an increase but real consumption of gasoline will not.

Real consumption, *real* GDP, *real* sales—all *real* numbers represent units sold, priced not at current prices but rather at prices as they stood on a single date in history. That's the way statisticians eliminate the price effect. At the moment, statisticians are using prices from the year 2000. Thus, current dollar GDP includes today's gasoline sales (in gallons) at today's prices while *real* GDP includes today's gasoline sales (same number of gallons) at 2000's prices.

Now before a bunch of economists come roaring down at me with jackhammers, let me say that this has been a conceptual explanation of what they do down there in Washington. The conversion between current and *real* is infinitely more complex and is therefore nothing you want bother with. The only point worth noting is that, if done right, the conversion factor for each economic concept is different. For GDP, a broad-based inflation figure is used. For consumption, the inflation number used for the conversion is an indicator of inflation at the consumer level. In other words, good statistics keeps apples with apples and away from pears.

---

* This definition of *real* has nothing to do with the real and imaginary numbers you learned about in high school.

Ordinary Inflation

There's nothing ordinary people would like better than to have prices stand still. That ain't happening. So measures of inflation are a necessary fact of life. Lucky for you, the government gives you lots of numbers to choose from. You only need one or two, though. In all likelihood, the consumer price index, or CPI, is the only number that will affect you in any way. Why? Because it's the best indictor of what inflation is like for consumers. In addition, most cost-of-living adjustments to paychecks, pensions, insurance payouts, social security, and the like are based on the CPI. And finally, many floating rate mortgages are tied to the CPI.

Another measure of consumer inflation that you'll hear about is the CPI excluding food and energy. From your standpoint, that of the consumer, this makes no sense. After all, American consumers spend an awful lot of money each month on food and energy (which includes gasoline as well as home heating oil, electricity, and gas). Why exclude them, then? It has nothing to do with what's important. It has to do with the fact that food and energy prices are more volatile than other prices, that is, they move around quite a bit more than the prices of other goods and services.* Excluding food and energy provides a more stable view of inflation, one that is less likely to be knocked about from month to month. In other words, it has analytical value. So, now that you know, fogettaboutit.

Ordinary Ups and Downs

Our lives are not static, so it should come as no surprise that economies neither stand still nor grow evenly at the same pace year after year. Just like you or me, the economy has its ups and

---

* Something is *volatile* if it has the tendency to move about sharply and quickly, that is, to be unstable. To say that food and gas prices are volatile is to say that some days they're up, others they're up even more, and others they're down. The same is true with markets. Volatility is the noun—the state of being volatile.

downs. And while it may seem to you that it's mostly down, that's your own bias you're reflecting on the economy as a whole. (Albeit for good reason: In the United States today, the small number of very rich keeps getting richer and the rest of us are losing ground. But I digress.) In point of fact, the U.S. economy as a whole has been growing over time, even adjusting for inflation, even adjusting for the larger population that has to share its income. (Don't worry: I'll deal with the growing gap between rich and poor later.)

The ups and downs of the economy are called the *business cycle*. For those of you not reading on the beach, in which case you are forgiven, the notion of a cycle should suggest to you a natural progression from up to down to up again to down again. Indeed, that is what happens, although there is much disagreement among economists about exactly what causes the cycle in the first place. Many believe, as I do, that human errors contribute mightily to the volatility of the economy.

No fancy name is associated with the boom part of the business cycle. It's simply called *growth*. Growth is, of course, a good thing. It means rising incomes, rising profits, rising employment, and a declining unemployment rate. Mind you, not just any amount of growth will do. Because the population of the country is growing, a certain minimum amount of *real* GDP growth is necessary just to keep people on the same even keel.

It used to be that economists called a declining economy a *depression*. The economy was depressed, in the sense that output and incomes were lower. Then came the Great Depression of the late 1920s and 1930s. Millions of people—roughly one in four—were out of work. Millions more were barely getting by. It took World War II for us to finally put the Great Depression behind us, and after that, no one wanted to hear the word again. So the term *recession* was born. Same idea, less baggage.

It's not a recession when the economy experiences a one-time drop in income. Terrorism, droughts, floods, and other natural and human-made disasters can cause the GDP to come up short in any one quarter. It is officially a recession when the economy experiences two back-to-back quarters of decline. These episodes are less frequent, but not out of the ordinary. Since World War I, the U.S. economy has experienced nine recessions. (As of this writing, it is not clear whether the U.S. economy slipped into its 10th recession in the first part of 2008.)

Traditionally, economists thought that recessions were like an attic clearout. (Another image comes to mind, but since it has to do with bodily functions, we'll stick to the attic metaphor.) Stuff accumulates up in the attic year after year until you can't even walk into the space. So you clear it out, all at once. You generate lots of refuse (unemployment), and lots of dust (declines in profits). But when it's all done, you have the room to start accumulating stuff all over again. That's what a recession is like. Companies eliminate unnecessary inventories; they close some operations; they lay off workers; they *rationalize,* as they say. As a result, many companies will take a one-time charge against profits, meaning they earn lower profits that quarter (or may declare a loss). An economy in recession will experience rising unemployment, declining incomes, and weaker profits.

Recessions do serve the purpose of clearing out the cobwebs, getting companies—even industries—back on the right track. But recessions aren't always caused by inventory buildup or by a stagnant workforce.* Recessions are also caused by wrongheaded government policies, specifically monetary policies. In my humble opinion, this is the biggest reason for the recessions and inflation of the last century. Of course, it's not an intentional foul-up.

---

* In fact, the slowdown in early 2008 was due to neither inventory nor workforce issues but rather a credit crunch that ensued from the subprime mortgage crisis.

No, what happened is that the central bank found itself in the unenviable position of having to crimp the supply of money in the economy to rein in inflation, and this resulted in a loss of income, that is, recession. Let me explain.

Remember that inflation is caused by there being too much money sloshing around in the economy—when there's more money than is needed to purchase existing goods with existing income at existing prices, prices will rise. To counter rising prices, or inflation, it's necessary to drain the extra money from the economy. That's exactly what a central bank like the Fed will do when confronted with inflation. In the short run, however, this has the unfortunate effect of making people feel that they're poorer, so they immediately spend less. These cutbacks can snowball into a full-fledged recession if the central bank is aggressive in its effort to stop inflation.

Of course, once a central bank like the Fed realizes that it's caused a recession, it will usually take steps to reverse course. This will entail putting more money into the economy so people no longer feel poor. That has a positive effect on the economy in the short run, but it likely will cause inflation in the long run. . . .

Any similarity here to a Three Stooges routine is not intentional, but it is real. The central bank doesn't set out to push the economy forward and back, to the right and left, but all too often in the past, that's just what happened.

The good news is that it hasn't happened much lately. Thanks to wiser central banks, and a much wiser Fed, as well as changes in the structure of the economy—namely, smaller inventories of manufactured goods, because of just-in-time inventory management, and a smaller manufacturing sector on the whole—the business cycle's ups and downs have been smaller over the last two decades. All the better.

Time to Move On

Good news: We're there. I've given you a quick and dirty run-through of the various economic terms and reports that the pros use to describe the ups and downs of the American economy. I've also given you a rough-and-ready explanation of the causes of the cycle itself. On the assumption that most of you have had enough, it's time to follow the yellow brick road to Emerald City.

Addendum to Chapter 9: The Inside Scoop

For those readers who are interested in more of the down and dirty details about the economic indicators discussed in this chapter, I offer the following embellishments and links.

Employment Reports: Take a survey of all the employers in the country. Add up all the people who are employed somewhere besides a farm. That's *nonfarm payrolls,* the best measure of employment. An alternative measure of employment comes about from a survey of households, where survey takers ask for the number of household members who are employed. However, it's the number of unemployed people that's generated from the data in the household survey that's most useful because it's the number used to calculate the *unemployment rate.* Both surveys are quite literally that, surveys. Not every household or employer is contacted, but, rather, a representative sample that produces results that are similar enough to let government statisticians sleep at night. One last thing: The surveys are conducted and the numbers crunched monthly by the Bureau of Labor Statistics (BLS), which is part of the Department of Labor. Want to see the latest release? Find it at http://www.bls.gov/news.release/empsit.toc.htm.

Personal Income: The figures on personal income are compiled each month by the Bureau of Economic Analysis (BEA), which is part of the Department of Commerce. As noted earlier, the biggest contribution to personal income comes from wages and salaries, but the figure also includes rental income, government subsidies, interest, proprietors' income, and dividend income. Along with personal income, the BEA reports on personal consumption expenditures. This is a broad-based measure of consumption, that is, it includes spending on services. Want to see the latest release? It's at http://www.bea.gov/bea/newsrel/pinewsrelease.htm.

Corporate Profits: The BEA is also responsible for calculating corporate profits. It releases its data together with its estimates of GDP (see below).

GDP: The BEA compiles GDP along with national income and corporate profits data. The data are compiled by quarter, but what with advance estimates and two rounds of revisions, the BEA ends up making monthly releases. The data are annualized, so the figures for each quarter are ramped up by, basically, a factor of four. As discussed above, GDP comprises consumption, investment, government spending, and net exports. Consumption is by far the largest of the four. GDP is also broken down into two measures that economists look at separately for clues to the economy's health: *final sales* and *inventories.* Final sales offer an indication of true demand. Inventories represent the change in inventory levels. Unfortunately, inventories can be up for a variety of reasons—some good, some bad. For example, if people stop buying, inventory levels will rise. That's a bad sign. On the other hand, if spending is strong, companies might want to have more inventory on hand to accommodate increased sales. That's a good sign. Bottom line is that interpretation of the inventory data is particularly problematic. Note that GDP is reported in both current and real dollars, which is to say that the report also includes a measure of broad-based inflation. You'll find the latest GDP release at http://www. bea.gov/newsreleases/national/gdp/gdpnewsrelease.htm.

Retail Sales: The Census Bureau, which is part of the Department of Commerce, is responsible for reporting on the volume of retail sales. The total is reported, but analysts often subtract auto sales from the total because car sales are very, very volatile. Note that retail sales, by definition, don't include services. Services are included in personal consumption, however, which is reported by the BEA along with personal income. Want to see the retail sales report? Find it at http://www.census. gov/svsd/www/marts_current.html.

International Trade: Exports and imports are broken down by type of good or service in the foreign trade report compiled by Census Bureau. The latest release can be found at http://www. census.gov/foreign-trade/www/press.html.

Productivity: Some things are easy to measure; some things are not. Nonfarm productivity and unit costs (the costs associated with producing a unit of output) fall into the latter category. Nevertheless, the Bureau of Labor Statistics, the same folks who bring you the monthly employment report, make a quarterly stab at it. You'll find the latest release at http://stats.bls.gov/news. release/prod2.toc.htm.

Inflation Measures: No shortage of inflation measures—on the contrary, the difficulty is picking the right one to watch. Inflation at the wholesale level—that is, business to business—is measured by the producer price index, reported monthly by the BLS at http://stats.bls.gov/news.release/ppi.toc.htm. Inflation at the consumer level is reflected by two different measures: the consumer price index, reported by the BLS at http://stats.bls.gov/ news.release/cpi.toc.htm, and the PCE deflator (the price index associated with personal consumption expenditures, which is part of GDP). The CPI is the more commonly used measure. The CPI headlines report the month-to-month percentage change in the index, along with the percentage change in the index excluding food and energy.

10

Who's in Control Here?

A new political movement has been hatched in the past ten years called *antiglobalization*. You've seen antiglobalists on the news, hanging around the headquarters of the International Monetary Fund (IMF) and the World Bank in Washington (which are conveniently located across the street from each other). Or you've seen them on the picket lines at Davos, Switzerland, for the annual meeting of the Global Economic Forum. Or even outside the meetings of APEC, which stands for Asian-Pacific Economic Cooperation.

As their name suggests, these antiglobalists are people who want to stop the forces of globalization, or at the very least, contain them. I'll spare you the economic history lesson, but their movement is very reminiscent of the Luddite movement that began in nineteenth-century England. The Luddites wanted to stop the industrial revolution because it threatened to eliminate jobs in British textile mills. They were right in their forecast of the future: Britain barely has any textile jobs left today, thanks to both the industrial revolution and the availability of cheaper foreign imports. The Luddites were wrong in their proposed solution, however: Britain could no more stop the industrial revolution or international trade than the fictional genie can be put back in the bottle.

Many antiglobalists, as they call themselves, have in fact figured this out. As the author Walter Truett Anderson says, "It
wasn't long after the antiglobalist movement surfaced that its
critics began pointing out that it wasn't exactly un-globalist itself.
A movement that crosses all national boundaries, that relies so
heavily on electronic communications, that so effectively sum-
mons people to come from all over the world to march in the
streets of whatever city might be hosting an economic conference
was clearly a global one, however vigorously its rhetoric might
condemn the evils of globalization."

The movement now calls itself the "true internationalists" or
the "anti-corporate globalization movement" or the "global social
justice movement."

These names are better because they reveal the true motivation of the protest: These protesters are anticapitalist. What
antiglobalists really want is for governments to rein in the political, financial, and economic power of global corporations. Nice
thought, maybe (by which I really mean, no), but it ain't happening. You and I know better: Capitalism produces successful
economies; state-run economies are a mess.

Clearly something's bugging the guys and gals who stand on
the picket line, and I think I know what it is. First off, they don't
like the fact that capitalism produces winners and losers—an issue
we dealt with briefly in chapter 1 of this book and to which we'll
return at the end of this chapter. It's true: Our economy is not
always fair. But you and I know that a capitalist system produces
more equitable results than any other economic system ever created. Either the protestors don't know this fact of life or don't
want to recognize it. Either way, frustration with capitalism's
inadequacies—its failure to redress Third World factories, environmental quality, and child labor—is part of their beef.

Secondly, they don't like change, and they especially don't
like that their lives, the lives of all of us, entail risk. Many

antiglobalists would like to eliminate all risk from life, including bad health, car accidents, or getting jilted by a lover or spouse. But whom are they going to rail against for these things? We all die one way or another; we all experience heartache and pain (sounds like a Country Western ballad, doesn't it?). There's not much they can do to erase physical and emotional risk. But when it comes to economic and financial risk, they see a chance to put their ideas into action. Since government exists as an organ of the people, for the people, government should act to eliminate economic and financial risk, or at least protect people from it.

Therein lies the fundamental difference of opinion. Economists, and by now you, I hope, understand that risk is fundamental to the economy. I'm going to say that again so you'll read it again: Risk is fundamental to the economy. You'll remember from chapter 1 that staring down risk successfully is the way companies make profits. Take away the opportunity to take risks and you take away the profit. Take away profit and you take away the incentive to work hard, to do a good job, and to innovate to make your life better. Indeed, you take away the opportunity to make your life better except by chance.

Countries have tried to eliminate economic and financial risk, and we all know what happens when they go this route. China, North Korea, and Cuba in the second half of the twentieth century are the three glaring examples that we all recognize. Anticapitalist economies either collapse, or, as in the case of Cuba, they're a wreck. Look, many of you are parents like me. We know what it's like to send our kids out into the world each day without a guarantee that they'll come back in one piece. But our anxieties don't—can't—let us stop them from leaving home. We have to learn to manage economic and financial risk appropriately, just as we teach our children to take precautions when they're away from home.

Who's in Control Here?

So are you ready to answer the title question of this chapter? You know the answer, don't you? No one is in charge of the U.S. economy. Nor is anyone in charge of the French, British, Canadian, Mexican, Italian, Spanish, or most other economies. These are economies based on free markets—emphasis on the word *free*.

Is Congress or the White House in control of economic activity in the United States? No. Is the Fed in control of banks? No. Is the SEC in control of financial markets? No. Is the Department of Commerce in control of international trade? No.

At the same time, is GM or Toyota in control of the U.S. or global auto industry? No. Is Citi or Chase or Hong Kong Shanghai Bank (now called HKSB) in control of global banking? No. Is Wal-Mart in control of retailing? Maybe? No! Is AT&T in control of telecommunications, or Dell in control of computer production, or Google in control of the Internet? No, no, and no. No one is in charge.*

Not being in charge is not the same thing as having no influence, however. The White House and Congress and the Fed can and do influence the U.S. economy and the financial markets— just as the decisions made by Wal-Mart, Toyota, Citi, and Google influence the U.S. economy and financial markets. No one denies that these organizations have influence, but they do not dominate their corner of the world (although we've got to give the billionaire from Arkansas extra credit for trying hard).

Saying that no one is in control is not to deny that on occasion the actions of some powerful groups—corporations, unions, or governments—have interfered with the efficient functioning of markets. In this regard, two cases are worth special mention: prices and wages. The federal government, by way of the Federal Reserve, can muscle the nation's inflation rate up or down.

---

* If you're hyperventilating at this point, I think you need to go back and reread chapter 1 on the basics of free markets. They're not as scary as you think.

Unfortunately, as we'll see in just a moment, the Fed hasn't always won the fight against inflation cleanly. The labor market is another place where powerful institutions intervene, with mixed results.

Who's in Control of Inflation?

You know that no one individual or institution is in control of the price of a single good or service, but what about inflation? Inflation comes about from an excess of money in the economy— too much money chasing too few goods. Isn't the Fed, which is responsible for the money supply, in control of inflation? The answer to this question is yes. More so than the president or Congress, Wal-Mart or OPEC, the Fed is in control of inflation— but that answer assumes that you want to upgrade what they do from "influence" to "control."

No consumer likes high prices. Let's take that as a given. We tolerate high prices when the situation is long-standing and we've gotten used to it. After all, in most cases the market has tossed out these prices as being the most fair to both consumers and suppliers. Every once in a while, though, something big comes along to overturn the apple cart.

For a variety of reasons, including the Vietnam War, the creation of OPEC, and President Nixon's distaste for economics (can you believe it?), the United States suffered from rising inflation in the late 1960s and early 1970s.* As a lawyer and politician, Nixon's solution was simple: He decided to set prices the way he ordered troops in Vietnam. (He assumed that prices would respond as well as privates and admirals—ha!) Nixon created the Cost of Living Council to set the prices of all sorts of goods and services—and wages—in the U.S. economy. Marx, I'm sure, chuckled in his grave with delight. Living Russians, I know, had

---

* For more on Nixonian economics, read "Nixon Tries Price Controls," an excerpt from *The Commanding Heights* by Daniel Yergin and Joseph Stanislaw (New York: Simon & Schuster, 1998), pp. 60–64.

a good laugh. Needless to say, it took barely any time at all until the error of Nixon's ways became painfully apparent. The economy plunged to even worse depths as prices and wages deviated further and further from those that free markets would have determined.

Here's the continuation of this story, which has an interesting twist. One of the first major accomplishments (if you want to call it that) of OPEC was to use oil to punish the United States and other Western nations for siding with Israel during the Yom Kippur War, started by Syria and Egypt in 1973. OPEC placed an embargo on oil to Israeli sympathizers, and presto whammo, the oil market fell to pieces in just a few short weeks (the price of oil roughly tripled, from below $15 a barrel to over $40 a barrel). Here in the United States, oil prices were permitted to rise, but not enough to counter the shortage of oil itself. The result was long lines at the gas pumps. Prices were not allocating the scarce supply of oil, long lines were, which is to say that gasoline went to those who could wait.

Allowing the prices of oil and gasoline to rise, and negotiating for more oil, eventually led to more orderly markets: Lines gradually disappeared and fewer people got punched in the face while filling the tank (although, on the downside, fewer recipes were exchanged while women waited for hours on end). Problem was, ordinary people were now paying through the roof for oil and gasoline. That crimped their spending on other items. Fearful of a recession, the Fed, with support from Congress and the White House, began the process of stimulating the economy by adding money to the financial system. They weren't alone. Most of Western Europe and Great Britain followed suit.

Soon enough, most of these economies were staring down the barrel of worse inflation and recession. Unemployment was up, and national income was falling in real, inflation-adjusted terms. What to do?

By that point, the White House had a new occupant: Jimmy Carter. One of then-President Carter's bright ideas was to make the United States a more fuel-efficient place, to reduce our demand for oil and take pressure off oil prices. He encouraged Americans to set our thermostats to 65 degrees Fahrenheit (18°C) in the winter and 78 degrees Fahrenheit (25.5°C) in the summer. He wore sweaters in the White House. He cut the lights on Christmas. But when none of that worked well enough, he appointed a career central banker from New York named Paul Volcker as chairman of the Fed. Chairman Volcker set the forces of free markets loose on the problem: He pushed up short-term interest rates near 20 percent and sharply controlled the amount of money sloshing around in the system.* It worked. Eventually, inflation came down and the recession itself passed. Don't let me mislead you: It took time, lots of it. But the only real solution to the problem was the market-based approach engineered by the gutsy Volcker.

So who's in control of inflation? Not the president, not OPEC, and not Wal-Mart. The person or organization that has the most control over inflation rates in the United States is the Fed because it controls the U.S. money supply. But even the Fed's influence is imprecise—Fed policy has long lags and policymakers have no surefire way to calibrate the Fed's actions. Still, when inflation rears its ugly head in the United States, the solution doesn't lie at 1600 Pennsylvania Avenue or in the Middle East. The Fed must taketh away what the Fed has in all likelihood caused.

Who's in Control of Wages?

Having read this far in the book, your natural instinct is to answer that no one is in control of wages. You've learned well, but in this case, your answer gets a B+, not an A.

---

* The Noble prize–winning economist Milton Friedman must have heartily approved of Volcker's tactics. He once likened an indecisive Fed to a "fool in the shower" fumbling with the hot and cold water taps.

In all likelihood, no one does control your salary, except your employer and you. Your employer hired you at a given wage or salary, and every so often—hopefully often—this figure gets bumped higher. You need not be a passive player in this game, however. You have the option of asking for a raise (ha!) or, better yet, finding a new job—inside the company or at another company—that pays more. And so we return to the laws of supply and demand. You are a supplier of labor, and you can and should earn the going wage. The same principle applies to selling football souvenirs outside Arrowhead Stadium.*

I'm sure this was your answer, perhaps without the reference to the Kansas City Chiefs, which is why you got a B+. Here's why you didn't get an A. More so than other markets, the labor market *is* affected by outside influences. Unions are one example. Union leaders work very hard to ensure that union workers get paid exactly what the market will bear. Sometimes the unions get a bit greedy, though, and push for more. Unions have been known to push a company so far that the company ends up in bankruptcy— I'm thinking the airlines here—which does no one any good. Unions have also been known to trade away job growth as payment for increased job and income security for their current members. Because unions have had a checkered record, and because manufacturing jobs are on the wane, union membership has been steadily declining in the United States over the past twenty to thirty years. Still, any discussion of who controls wages would be incomplete without recognizing the bargaining power of unions.

The government-controlled minimum wage is another outside influence on wages. Did you know that in some Latin American countries, young, inexperienced workers actually pay their

---

* If you try to charge more (for the same quality) as the other hawkers, you'll be forced to change your price when your stuff doesn't sell. Likewise, you'd be stupid to sell your banners and gear for less than the going price.

employer to work? Gee whiz, that sounds like the internships American high school and college kids now scramble for every summer. They're called internships because this moniker allows the employer to skirt minimum wage laws.

Employees don't and can't pay employers to work in the United States, because in this country we have minimum wage laws. There is a certain minimum amount that every worker must earn per hour; and each state gets to decide what that wage will be within their boundaries. At whatever level it's set, the purpose of the minimum wage is to allow workers at the bottom rung of the employment ladder to earn enough to live on. While it doesn't quite accomplish that goal, the minimum wage law does prevent McDonald's from paying its employees $2 an hour, which is not enough for anyone to live on anywhere in the United States.

Recognizing that the minimum wage lifts the wages of some, is it a good or a bad thing? That's up for grabs. Conservative economists have always contended that by setting a wage that's above what employers would pay in the absence of minimum wage laws, the minimum wage prompts employers to cut back on hiring so they can pay the mandated minimum to those they do hire. Theoretically, that rings true. However, recent research doesn't prove that beyond a shadow of a doubt. While most studies do point in this direction, not many muster the reliability that statisticians and economists expect to find. And there is some research to suggest that, at the very least, the minimum wage is neutral with respect to employment. If that's the case, then it's a benefit to the economy, since a steady level of employment, with some people earning more, is an improvement overall.

One thing I can say with a fair degree of certainty. The minimum wage is not disappearing. Governments will continue to exert some influence on wages for the foreseeable future, especially for those at the low end of the pay scale.

Capitalism's Failures

I've spent the last few pages describing ways in which well-intentioned government officials have responded to problems and at times made things worse, not better. (It's not at all clear whether unions and the government-imposed minimum wage fit that description.) A good dose of free market thinking may have avoided those pitfalls, but we all make mistakes. The bigger the job, the bigger the mistakes, I've always found.

The big problems with the global economy are not limited to people's mistakes, however. Capitalism is not perfect either, especially in the way it has been adopted in Western countries. Our economic history is littered with numerous examples of how capitalism has failed us.* Poverty, illiteracy, patchy medical care, job discrimination, pollution, poisonous foods and additives imported from abroad, the meltdown of the subprime mortgage market. . . . These hot issues of the day have as their root cause, at least in part, a failure of free market capitalism.

One of the big problems with the economy is that not everyone has the same information. Those with more or better information end up taking advantage of those who are less well informed. The mortgage broker who convinces a new homebuyer to take on a risky mortgage surely knows better. He holds back on crucial information that would allow the homeowner to make a better decision. His silence may not be illegal, and one can argue that the homeowner should have informed himself before signing, but come on. . . . It's immoral and destructive, if not actually illegal. Likewise, the brokerage house executive who puts together a bond issue for a client knows better than anyone else how that bond will perform in different market environments. Does she

---

* Be mindful of the way I've stated this: Capitalism has not failed as a whole, but it has failed us—consumers, businesses, savers, and investors—on numerous occasions and in numerous ways.

pass this information on to the salespeople whose job it is to sell the bonds to the public? No.

Bribery is another pitfall. Capitalism is a sort of "do-whatever-it-takes" system. And big money motivates people to do all sorts of illegal and immoral things. Of course, bribery of government officials and corporate executives is illegal. It's considered a white-collar crime. But less drastic forms of bribery are commonplace. Indeed, we have a special name for them: *incentives*. Good and bad incentives are ubiquitous in our society. Parents use incentives in a good way when they offer a weekly allowance to their kids for help in clearing the dinner table. Car companies use incentives to clear the lots of last year's models—no one complains. Employers use incentives well when they offer a trip to the annual sales conference in the Caribbean to sales associates who meet their sales quotas—or when they offer early buyout packages to employees near retirement age.

When incentives are hidden, however, they can be particularly nefarious.* Extra commissions given to brokers who sell unattractive securities that no professional will buy are a good example of a nasty hidden incentive. The investor has no clue that the broker has a special incentive for selling that particular security. As a potential homebuyer, you also don't know if the current homeowners have offered real estate agents a special incentive to sell their house quickly. Smart consumers always look for the hidden motivation behind every transaction, but it's not always visible.

In many ways, virtually every day, capitalist systems create opportunities for people to behave in less than honorable ways. It's an unfortunate fact of life. But let me switch gears and go

---

* Not every hidden incentive is bad. A long wait in the hospital emergency room is meant to deter people from using these services in place of a doctor's office. This is a good thing, but the wait is often mistaken for a shortage of staff.

macro on you for a moment, because capitalism generates big failures, too. Let's talk about poverty.

Greater prosperity—not just here in the United States but around the world, in countries like China and Malaysia, Chile and Costa Rica, Bulgaria and Russia—is allowing more and more people to improve their standards of living to the point where they are no longer poor. And it's not just a numbers game; the percentage of the world's population that is poor is declining as well. But extreme poverty—the poverty that causes over twenty thousand deaths a day for lack of safe water, food, or shelter—is still pervasive in some regions of the world, notably Africa and South America. It's not that the world's rich nations don't have the wealth to eliminate extreme poverty. It's that the capitalist system doesn't give these nations an incentive to do so. Our capitalist system in the United States is not designed to provide incentives for other countries to do anything other than send us goods that are cheaper than those we could make ourselves, or buy goods when our prices are cheaper.

Having gotten this far in the book—this far in what is unabashedly an ode to capitalism—you might think that mainstream economists are satisfied with the good, if not perfect, job that capitalism does. You may think that we pooh-pooh problems like poverty. That's not true. On the contrary, the majority of economists today don't study the stuff of the previous chapters; they work to solve the economic and social problems that governments and market forces have failed to redress.

Jeffrey Sachs is a professor at Columbia University and an expert on global poverty. He's trying to figure out a way for countries to break out of what he calls the "poverty trap," a situation in which the poorest nations "lack the financial means to make the necessary investments in infrastructure, education, health care systems and other vital needs." Sachs is convinced that capitalism has failed these people. He concludes: "Although economic growth has shown a remarkable capacity to lift vast numbers of people out of extreme poverty, progress is neither automatic nor inevitable. Market forces and free trade are not enough."*

Sachs is at the forefront of an effort to get international development agencies, international financial institutions, nongovernmental organizations, and communities throughout the developing world to come together on this issue. He believes that the technological revolution going on in the developed world, and the great wealth it is creating for the innovators, can be harnessed to reduce extreme poverty. His goal, admittedly an aggressive one, is to reduce poverty by 50 percent by 2015. He sees this happening as an add-on to capitalism, not a replacement for it. Some of the suggestions he makes include the use of directed aid, investment incentives, and international funding to address crippling and lethal diseases like smallpox and AIDS.

Of course, poverty is not just in other countries. Here in the United States, the gap between the rich and the poor is widening as well, frighteningly fast at times. The fast pace of globalization and innovation in the fields of information and communication technology has pushed those at the lower end of the income scale further away from the top, to be sure, but the so-called digital divide—between highly skilled, tech-savvy workers and those with limited technological skills—has also hurt those in the middle. Simply put, there aren't enough high-tech workers in the United States, so their wages are rising much faster than average wages. At the same time, globalization has allowed work that requires low-skilled labor to be done outside the United States, where labor costs for unskilled workers are a fraction of what they are here. Bottom line: The income gap between the skilled and

---

* From Sachs's article "Can Extreme Poverty Be Eliminated?" *Scientific American* magazine online, http://www.sciam.com/article.cfm?chanID=sa006&articleID=000E4C4C-F093-1304-ABA283414B7F0000.

unskilled is thus getting bigger. Again, market forces are not enough to reverse this trend in the near term. Thus the solution to this problem also entails a multifaceted approach, including better education for our children (especially in math and science), remedial education and job training for adults, and maybe even a rewrite of the tax code to redistribute wealth. Incentives that work with the market are always the better solution—something like incentives to hire workers who have been unemployed for at least six months.

When incentives fail to solve a problem, however, the American people have shown a willingness to try creative alternatives. Compare the economic situation of the "typical" American family today to what it was fifty years ago. (Yes, I know, the typical American family these days does not always have a mother, father, and two-and-a-half kids all in one place. Humor me.) Today, the woman works outside the home, often in a full-time job. Both adults work longer hours than their parents and grandparents did. Many have chosen to raise fewer kids. And many have tapped the equity in their homes, by refinancing their mortgages, to generate a better monthly cash flow. What are such coping mechanisms if not creative ways to prevent the middle and working classes from slipping further and further away from the top?

Capitalism's other failures require a similar approach: using economic incentives, when possible, and coordinated action, when incentives won't work. The economics of pollution, for instance, is taking fascinating twists and turns. Trying to solve the problem of greenhouse gases using free market principles, economists, traders, and environmentalists have turned to the ingenious notion of carbon credits that allow polluters to buy their way out of the doghouse. Companies and countries that pollute excessively buy the right to do so from countries and companies that pollute little. In so doing, the level of greenhouse gases

is kept under control. Or at least that's how it works in principle.*
The jury's still out on this since the international carbon credits
are a pretty new invention and because, so far, the allowable level
of pollution hasn't left that many companies in the market for
credits. Until the kinks are worked out, the countries that signed
the Kyoto Treaty, and the United States, are hard at work on non-
market alternatives.

Finding the Middle Ground

Capitalism isn't perfect, yet it's clear that it's a darn sight better
bet than any other economic system known to man, woman, or
child. What we have in the United States to address capitalism's
failures are a set of economic rules and regulations, a division of
labor among government bodies, and a delegation of responsibility between federal, state, and local governments that all
together work to plug the gaps that capitalism leaves in its wake.

To try to ensure that everyone in the United States has access
to a good education, the federal Department of Education, along
with each and every state in the country, has numerous safeguards
in place to provide equal access. The rules and regulations, even
the tests many states require for high school graduation, are all
part of the democratic effort to improve our schools and train our
young.

To try to ensure that the food we eat is safe to consume and
that the animals that provided the food were treated humanely,
the FDA has regulations by the truckload. And many states
enhance the federal laws with their own, which is why it seems
like every can or box of food we buy sports a Pennsylvania health
certificate. Even with all this, a capitalist's drive to cut costs may
unknowingly result in our buying cereals made with dangerous

---

* I don't know why, but carbon credits always bring to mind the system in the
Middle Ages where rich landowners hired peasants to perform their military service.

chemicals, our eating unhealthy salads, or our swallowing pills that aren't what they say they are.

To try to ensure that the American people are protected from hidden dangers, the federal government is scurrying as I write this to put in place controls over nonedible imports from China—such as toys—in response to growing evidence that certain Chinese exports contain lead. In their quest to produce goods at the lowest possible cost for the global marketplace, the Chinese have obviously cut corners with quality control. They are now starting to pay the price—toy sales plummeted during the 2007 holiday season, reflecting the fact that most of the toys on U.S. store shelves were made in China. (A friend pointed out that her Hanukkah candles were made in China as well. Can candles contain lead?) Of course, the Chinese manufacturers aren't the only ones at fault, and they're not the only ones paying the price. The importers of those toys are also under pressure—for good reason. They failed to adequately test the safety of the products they imported.

To try to ensure that companies realize that the environment is not an unlimited resource that can be used without cost, the EPA and various state authorities regulate usage and waste. Their job is a difficult one: Some industries use a lot of natural resources or generate a lot of pollution by their very nature. Nuclear power plants and chemical manufacturing plants are good examples. Keeping these industries in business is tricky, especially when competition from abroad—where they may pay less attention to pollution—is nipping at their heels.

To try to ensure that money in the U.S. financial system is handled honestly, fairly, and appropriately, and that credit and investment services are available without discrimination, Congress has passed laws that govern the activities of banks and other financial institutions, like brokerage houses and mutual funds. Some state governments have gone even further, passing laws that affect financial companies doing business in their states. In addition to these laws, the Fed, the SEC, the FDIC, and the U.S. Treasury all have the responsibility to regulate specific aspects of the country's financial affairs. These laws may not succeed in every case—that's inevitable. But the laws and regulations are in place to try to eliminate discriminatory practices, such as redlining (whereby banks refuse to issue mortgages to people in certain neighborhoods because the residents there tend to be people of color). The laws and regulations are there to prevent an investment manager from investing a widow's life savings in very risky securities—and to provide some compensation to the widow when the SOB does just that. The laws are there to make sure that drug money isn't being laundered through U.S. banks so that drugs will be harder to sell here. After 9/11, Americans were outraged that overseas terrorists were using American banks to move cash around to their operatives here in the United States. Naturally, the Fed and the Treasury jumped on the problem.

These are just a few examples of government regulation; the list of regulations that most companies live under is vast, and at times the red tape is overwhelming. I should also say that many regulations eventually run aground either because they don't adapt to the particular industry to which they're being applied or because the incentives are no longer compatible with both the regulated industry and the public at large. Still, almost all the rules result from an honest effort to prevent capitalism from letting something bad happen because it happened once before and the public was outraged that it did. Capitalism does not exist in a vacuum. Here in the United States, at least, it exists in a democracy.

Time to Poke Fun at Corporate America

This chapter started with a rant against the antiglobalists, folks we now know are thinly disguised anticapitalists. To complete the circle, I'm going to end the chapter with a rant against corporate spokespeople. After all, why should the antiglobalists have all the fun?

Do you watch C-SPAN? I don't, although somebody must because the C-SPAN channels take up valuable real estate on my cable box. The reason I don't watch C-SPAN for any length of time is that I find the people they put on to be boring or offensive, or both. Maybe if I watched the whole program, they'd inform or convince me, but, frankly, I've got better things to do.

It seems as if every time I pass by C-SPAN on my way to Britcoms or *M*A*S*H,* I glimpse a hearing that's taking place live in Washington. Inevitably, there's a corporate executive, or an academic who's done "research" for a corporate exec, arguing why the federal government should eliminate or at least relax a certain regulation that's having a negative effect on his business.* And inevitably, the argument ends with the threat that unless this regulation is changed, the *consumer* is going to end up paying higher prices. That's the business equivalent of evoking God and hell in your threats to your mother-in-law.

You can't blame these guys for trying. All they want to do is run their business with less government intervention because the regulation or law in question is either costing them money or it's preventing them from executing a solid business plan. Haven't we all done the same thing at one point with a parent, spouse, or boss? C'mon. Come clean.

What your parent, spouse, or boss no doubt reminded you when you made your plea was that you are part of a family (don't you just love it when bosses talk about the corporate "family"?) and that in this family, decisions are made for the benefit of the group as a whole, not just one member. Therefore, your request to spend the bonus money on a trip to Vegas was nixed by your wife.

---

* No, I haven't resorted to being sexist. It's just that I see mostly white, occasionally African-American, men on this channel. I've been told this occurs because Congress subpoenas CEOs to appear, and these are still mostly men.

Therefore, your request to drive the family car to Florida and back with a few friends over spring break was nixed by your father. Therefore, your request to telecommute from Maui was refused cold.

It's your right, of course, to ask. And it's the right of corporations to approach the government agency restraining their exercise of corporate free will—be that Congress, the Fed, the SEC, or any of the other enforcers who make their home in Washington. It's the government's job to listen and then say no. Politely, of course, since they may want campaign contributions from these very supplicants. But say no, nevertheless.

When antiglobalists rant and rave, they need to be reminded that capitalism basically works. When corporate execs rant and rave, they need to be reminded that democracy basically works. Capitalism provides the highest standard of living. Democracy provides the remedies and safety nets for the times when capitalism isn't enough. Hum the national anthem, will you? Despite all the bitching and moaning we do, the U.S. economy is the best in the world and at no real threat of losing that stature. Why? Because we have figured out how to embed freewheeling capitalism in a strong democracy where property rights are protected and individual freedoms are preserved. That's one mean feat. Thank you. You can stop humming now.

PART II

Explaining the Past, Predicting the Future, and Tackling the Hard Problems

11

The Battle Over Oil

As I stand in the cold wind, pumping gas into my car at the rate of $3 a gallon, it isn't lost on me that something has gone miserably wrong. It doesn't feel natural that gasoline should cost more than milk or beer. At least I could buy a cow or ferment hops—not very attractive options for a city dweller like myself, I'll admit, but options nevertheless. What am I supposed to do when gas becomes prohibitively expensive? Walk the twenty miles (32 km) to work?

This chapter is about how oil took over our lives, and what we can—and can't—do about it. The key players in this drama are the Organization of Petroleum Exporting Countries (OPEC); oil-rich Middle East countries like Saudi Arabia, Iran, Iraq, and Kuwait; "Western" suppliers such as the UK, Alaska, Venezuela, and Russia; global oil companies like Exxon, Mobil, and Aramco; and consumers all over the world. I don't think I'll be ruining the story if I tell you upfront that everyone I've listed is a winner except for one group: consumers.* Feeling outnumbered, outmaneuvered, and outsmarted? Yeah, so am I.

The Birth of OPEC

Compared to the oil that's buried deep below the surface of the earth, OPEC is a fresh new arrival on the scene. Fifty years ago, OPEC was no more than a dream that the oil-producing nations of the Middle

---

* Consumers who don't own stock in the oil companies, that is, are the ones left out in the cold.

East had not yet realized. They dreamed of controlling the oil reserves within their borders cooperatively, so that they could exert control over the supply of oil to the world and, therefore, its price.

Time out! Before moving on, I need to explain how monopolies work. Don't worry; it won't take long.

When we've talked about supply and demand in this book, we have done so in the context of competitive markets where there's always another company, another worker, or another consumer to step in and fulfill the deal at the same terms if one party bails out. In competitive markets, no one company or consumer is able to control both price and quantity. On the contrary, there are so many players on both sides of the market that prices can be taken as a given, give or take a few shekels (cents).

Although relatively rare, there are other circumstances. You probably have the option of buying cable TV service from only one or two providers in your area. If you take the train to work, there's probably only one company that runs the route, although you may have the option of a bus or you could drive or ride a bicycle or walk. If you want electricity delivered to your home, and most of us do, we have no option but to deal with one or two local providers. We informally call such companies monopolies, although some are oligopolies—not a single provider, or monopolist, but a few providers, or oligopolists. Either way, when the number of suppliers of a good or service is limited to such a small number, the suppliers have a noticeable influence over the amount sold and the price.* And, not surprisingly, they set a smaller

---

* Such situations only occur when conditions are ripe for them. For example, when there's a single source of a good, such as Bordeaux wine from France or oil from the Middle East. Many times the issue is not the available supply but the enormous investment it takes to build a new factory or to get the resource to market, such as the enormous cost to build a new power plant or the cost of building the pipeline from interior Alaska to the coast. Monopolies are also helped by demand that is pretty much fixed. We can't do without electricity or gasoline, which is why these industries are monopolistic. We can do without wine from Bordeaux because there are good alternatives from other regions.

output than you'd get in a competitive market, which implies a higher price than you'd get in a competitive market.*

When possible, responsible governments like to rein in monopolies and oligopolies. Still, they tend to get some of the "monopoly profits" they're after: I happen to think that $100 for monthly cable service is a bit high!

When there's no government or international body to rein in the monopolist or oligopolists, there's no restraining force in the marketplace. The result is sky-high prices, thanks to their strict self-imposed controls on output. The only saving grace in a monopoly situation is an alternative to the product, for example, coal-fired power plants instead of oil-powered plants. The oligopoly situation has another out: Sooner or later, one of the parties inevitably gets hungry and tries to grab a larger share of the pie, at which point the whole scheme falls apart. Thus, the only oligopolies that last are ones where there's a strong enforcer to keep everyone in line. Which brings us back to OPEC.

Because of the heavy costs associated with oil exploration, oil is not an industry where just anybody can jump in and play.

OK. Time out's over; back to the story. Before OPEC was formed, there were seven main oil companies that provided most of the oil to the world—the so-called seven sisters. Although small in number, these were Western companies, governed by Western-style boards of directors. Each was angling for a bigger share of the oil market in its quest for profits, and each was more concerned about current-year profits than profits fifteen or twenty-five years down the road. Thus, oil may not have been the most competitive of markets in the days of the seven sisters, but it

---

* Strict control over output, or supply, is the key to a monopoly's success. Those in charge of the monopoly allow only a small amount of the good into the market, and make buyers bid for what's available. Obviously, a buyer has to bid high if he wants to get some.

wasn't dominated by a single group of sellers working in obvious cahoots with one another.*

Ironically, OPEC didn't start in the Middle East at all, but in Venezuela. It was Venezuela that approached the Middle East countries of Iran, Iraq, Saudi Arabia, and Kuwait after World War II to enlist their support for the formation of a nation-based *cartel* to control the revenues from oil and so weaken the seven sisters' alliance.** It took a while, but the five nations met in Baghdad in 1960, and OPEC was officially formed. A little while later, the original five were joined by Qatar, Indonesia, Libya, the United Arab Emirates (UAE), Algeria, and Nigeria.*** Look at a map and tell me which Middle East countries, other than Israel, are missing. The answer is Egypt and Syria. Neither country has major oil reserves.

Since the late 1960s, OPEC's control over the oil market has been a potent weapon for the Arab nations. OPEC made quite a bit of noise after the Six Day War between Israel and her Arab neighbors in 1967, and the syndicate was vocal again after the Yom Kippur War of 1973, when the Arab nations withdrew large amounts of oil from the global oil market to put pressure on nations supporting Israel, namely the United States and countries in Western Europe.

Less than ten years later, Western nations were again forced to pay a high price—quite literally—for their censure of the Iranian Revolution. In November 1979, Iranian students kidnapped and then held fifty-two American hostages for 444 days. A counterpart to the human drama was a sharp rise in the price of crude oil

* In the interests of full disclosure, saying that it was not the most competitive of markets may be an understatement. The industry limited competition in every region to just a small group.
** A *cartel* is an explicit arrangement to restrict output and set prices. It may sound less intimidating, but it's not.
*** Other nations have since joined in, and some, like Ecuador, have joined and left.

to almost $40 a barrel—a level unheard of then and, adjusted for inflation, a record still. It wasn't until the mid-1980s that oil prices fell back to a more normal level (although they spiked again, albeit not so high, with Operation Desert Storm).

The 1970s price hikes wreaked havoc in the West. They also had an effect OPEC wasn't counting on: They caused Western oil companies to open wells in the United States that had been capped when oil prices were lower. And the companies sought out oil in Russia, the North Sea, Alaska, and Mexico to replace oil from the Middle East. Nuclear power was also an option by the 1970s. Obviously, energy from these alternative sources couldn't be brought online immediately, so oil prices didn't get comfortable until the mid-1980s. But, eventually, North Sea, Alaskan, and Russian oil supplies—together with the nuclear power supply pouring out of plants in most of the developed nations—helped to mitigate both the hikes in oil prices and the political influence of OPEC.*

On the demand side, high oil prices actually did have a damp-ening effect on our demand for oil. Oil is not a product that we can stop buying immediately. It takes time for cars and trucks to be made more fuel-efficient; for public transport to be converted to electric power; for extra insulation to be added in the attic and floors; for people to be convinced that 75 degrees Fahrenheit (24°C) is cool in the summer and 65 degrees Fahrenheit (18°C) is warm in the winter. Eventually, however, all these small changes in behavior add up.

---

* Nuclear capacity was 100 gigawatts (GW) in the late 1970s, 300 GW in the late 1980s, and roughly 350 GW in 2005. By the 1980s, falling oil prices and a heavy reg-ulatory burden made nuclear power less viable. The accident at Three Mile Island in Pennsylvania in 1979 and the accident at Chernobyl, Russia, in 1986 also put the brakes on new investment in nuclear power by raising safety concerns. This is why, even with oil prices reaching historic highs nowadays, you don't see many proposals for nuclear energy on the table here in the States, although admittedly a few are creeping onto the drawing boards for Europe.

Skip ahead: Wholesale oil prices were down to around $10 a barrel wholesale by 1999.

From $10 to $100

So what happened to cause oil prices to reverse course with such a vengeance that, as of this writing, oil is trading on the world market for $100 a barrel (or about $3.25 a gallon for regular gasoline at the pump)? In no particular order (because they're all big):

1. Nuclear power plants built during the 1970s and 1980s are now old and many are being shut down. Few new nuclear power plants are under construction globally due to security and safety concerns. The upshot is that nuclear power isn't available to satisfy some of the fast-growing global need for energy.

2. With evidence of global warming impossible to escape, environmental concerns over coal have reached a fever pitch. The effect on the oil market is similar to that of nuclear power: reduced supply of energy amidst growing demand, resulting in higher energy prices globally.

    The one exception to the rule, and admittedly it is a big exception, is China. China is bringing one new coal-fired plant online every week to help satisfy the country's explosive energy needs. Naturally, environmentalists around the globe are horrified. But despite their growing criticism, Chinese officials show no signs of jumping out of the bed they've made for themselves: Chinese officials are obviously willing to accept astronomically high levels of pollution as a necessary cost of economic growth.

3. Oil companies have only limited access to the vast Middle East reserves, so their ability to tap into unused oil fields to stabilize prices is limited.

4. OPEC nations have restricted oil extraction because they want their oil—and oil revenues—to last. Many of these countries would be dirt poor if it weren't for oil. More so than immediate profits, the goal of these nations is to stretch out a steady stream of oil revenues over time to be able to maintain gains in their standards of living.

    Don't read this to mean that oil profits have been widely distributed. . . . Extreme poverty remains widespread in many oil-producing nations in the absence of true democracy. The wealthy families that run the governments and control the oil are getting richer by the day while the poor are growing in number by the day. The growing disparity between the incomes of the rich and poor is a major source of concern. As the poor fall further behind, and their numbers grow, the possibility of political upheaval rises exponentially. In this, the Arab world is no different from other nations around the world.

5. The easily (read: cheaply) extracted oil from the North Sea and Alaska has been tapped. Likewise, oil extraction from the continental United States is low. Our dependence on oil relative to economic output (GDP) is shrinking—that is, we're getting more energy-efficient. In this sense we are less dependent on oil imports than we were twenty years ago. But Western-controlled oil is more difficult and costly to extract now than it was in the 1980s. In this sense we are more dependent on oil imports.

6. New construction of oil refineries has been dauntingly slow globally. Indeed, no refinery has been built from scratch in the United States since the mid-1970s! As a result, the United States is vulnerable to even minor shocks to oil supply or heating oil and gasoline production. We saw this vulnerability up close and personal after Hurricane Katrina temporarily took out Gulf Coast refineries. Prices at the gas pump spiked higher because there was no slack in the system.

7. The global economy has been on a tear, with many nations like China growing by more than 10 percent a year. Global demand for oil, in other words, has gone through the roof. (I lied: This is a bigger factor than all the rest.)

Sounds like a train wreck waiting to happen, doesn't it? Yup.

Now What?

I deliberately laid out the factors affecting oil prices in the early 2000s one by one so we could look back at the list and see what might change. Let's do that now. A cool, stiff drink is in order, don't you agree? (Make that root beer for anyone under age.)

I don't see any of the contributing factors I listed above changing anytime in the near future. But I like to be optimistic, so let me suggest a few things that might save our butts.

First, the world economy is getting much better about using energy. World GDP is one-third less reliant on oil than it was at its peak in 1973.* If we can get China, in particular, to become more efficient in its energy use, global demand may soften in the near future even without a pullback in economic growth. I see you shaking your head. Just remember that China is flagrantly inefficient in its energy use; just a small change in such a vast country could mean a lot.

Second, also working in our favor is our increasing consumption of services. Services now account for roughly 65 percent of world GDP. Services generally use less energy than manufacturing (haircuts don't get trucked across the country), so this trend is energy-friendly.

Third, OPEC may come to realize that sky-high oil prices will only accelerate the switch to other forms of energy and energy

---

* Alan Greenspan, *The Age of Turbulence: Adventures in a New World* (New York: The Penguin Press, 2007), p. 447.

conservation overall. (The higher the price, the more incentive we have to buy sweaters and hybrids.) Sure, OPEC *wants* to keep prices high, but they *have* to keep prices low enough that we don't go out and invent ways around oil that would be devastating to their economies, their nations, and their power.

Fourth, demographics and technology are working in our favor. Population is growing the fastest in the developing world, and the developing world has lagged in its adoption of modern energy technology. So if countries in the developing world can upgrade their facilities and methods to state-of-the-art technology, their demand can be less wasteful, that is, their future economic output will be more energy-efficient.[*]

Fifth, we may win the Iraq war and see a friendly government take shape there that's more generous with Iraqi supplies. Hey, I warned you I was being optimistic.

I hate to say it, and I hate even more to put it down in writing, but our best shot at a reduction in oil prices in the near future is a recession—preferably a global recession. That sort of puts the whole issue in context, though, doesn't it? Are we willing to put up with slower income growth, higher unemployment, and reduced wealth to pay less for heating oil, gasoline, natural gas, and electricity? I don't think so, at least not at the current price of oil.

Just as well, then, that we get used to near-record high oil prices. You see, today's prices aren't the work of an oligopoly suddenly constricting supply, as it was in 1973, or a crisis in Iran, as it was in the early 1980s. Today's price is the result of growing, and sometimes wasteful, global demand colliding with intransient, but long-standing, supply restraints. What makes today's $3.25 a gallon of gas, $100 a barrel of oil, so unbearable, in other words, is that it's probably here to stay. Unless it goes up, of course.

---

[*] See Greenspan, cited above, p. 459.

12

Over, Under, and Through: The Economics of Immigration

Talk about a hot potato! Immigration reform is always being tossed around Congress, state legislatures, and city councils but little, if any, reform is enacted. The issue splits the nation, splits Congress, splits political parties, and even splits families, which is a big reason why, despite all the talking—oh, let's be honest, arguing—nothing gets done and nothing changes.

Business people are generally in favor of open borders. Companies want an ample, preferably overflowing, supply of labor at a reasonable cost at their doorsteps. In the Republican Party, the business contingent has to fight for more "liberal" immigration policies against a conservative front that believes it is staunchly defending the jobs and lifestyles of native-born Americans. Immigration reform enjoys more widespread support among Democrats. Still, the immigrants who vote Democratic (the majority of them) don't necessarily see eye to eye on immigration issues with the union members who represent a powerful voting block within the Democratic Party.

Another reason why legislation to reform our nation's immigration policies has a hard time getting off the Hill is that, from an economic standpoint, it's not at all clear what the economic cost is of the status quo. The best economics studies indicate only the barest impact of illegal immigration on wages and national income. The biggest dollar cost, in other words, might be the hours our elected officials have racked up debating the issue without anything to show for it.

As far as I can tell, our national discussion about immigration revolves around four main concerns:

- Illegal immigrants take jobs from Americans.
- Illegal immigrants put a strain on social services.
- Illegal immigrants endanger homeland security.
- Illegal immigrants change the character of the nation.

I am in no position to assess the impact on homeland security of unauthorized individuals crossing the border, although I feel compelled to remind readers that no terrorist suspect to date has used the U.S.-Mexican border to enter the country, which is where the vast majority of illegal immigrants come in. Likewise, I am neither able nor willing to address the social, psychological, or political ramifications of immigration. My expertise is economics and if it's all right with you, I'll stick to what I know. That leaves us with the task of assessing the economics of illegal immigration from the standpoint of jobs and government services.

Here to Work

In an economist's dream world, immigrants would be lined up at our door, ready to serve the U.S. economy. If we needed workers to harvest grapes, they'd be there. If we needed computer programmers for a particular application, they'd be there. If we needed immigrants to build a concrete southern border barrier, they'd be there. And when these tasks were over, they'd be gone. So how far off is reality from this scenario?

If we're talking legal immigrants, people who apply for a visa and a worker's permit in advance of their entry, then the answer is that immigration trends are far from the economic ideal. Some legal immigrants are highly educated individuals who are drawn to the United States for the high quality of jobs here. Once in the system, they are productive and successful. But these people are in the minority because our immigration policies are not designed for them. By design, the majority of legal immigrants come to the United States to join family members who have already settled here. Serving an economic need is a small part of the decision to immigrate—not that they don't find work once they're here.

Perhaps counterintuitively, *illegal* immigrants are more responsive to the nation's economic needs—they are the ones who come to the United States primarily to work. Studies show that the number of illegal immigrants entering the United States increases when the U.S. economy is doing well. Conversely, during U.S. recessions, illegal immigration falls off. The ups and downs of illegal immigration confirm that illegal immigrants are here to work. Illegal immigrants are also more mobile than legal immigrants once they're here. Since reuniting with family is not the reason they've come, they are more willing to move to where the jobs are.

At this point it's worth recognizing that illegal immigrants fall into two camps, one much larger than the other. A relatively small number of highly educated individuals from places like India and Asia come to the United States for high-tech jobs, even if they've been denied a green card. However, the bulk of people entering the United States illegally cross the Mexican border, and they don't have either the education or the skills that would land them high-paying jobs.

Why do unskilled workers jump our southern border? The answer is that on this side of the border there are better-paying jobs. Opportunities for unskilled, uneducated Mexicans are limited back home, and competition for the existing jobs is fierce. In Mexico, the school dropout rate is an alarming 35 percent, and

roughly 25 percent of the country is not fully employed.*
Unskilled workers in Mexico definitely have a hard time of it.

But here in the United States, unskilled illegal immigrants find
a niche. They take low-end jobs that Americans don't want, such
as child care, housekeeping, farm work, landscaping, dry
cleaning, and the like. These jobs at the low end of the totem pole
are ripe for the picking because the United States now graduates
93 percent of young adults from high school and 28 percent from
college. Look at it this way: Between 1960 and 2000, the percentage of working-age, native-born Americans without a high
school degree fell from 50 percent to 12 percent.** Low-skilled jobs
in this country haven't disappeared; on the contrary, there are many
more of these positions available thanks to the economy's growth.
What has disappeared are native-born Americans to fill these jobs.
America's young adults today aim higher, as they should.

Whereas illegal immigrants account for 5 percent of the U.S.
labor force, they represent 10 percent of the low-skilled labor force
nationally. In states abutting the U.S.-Mexican border, such as
California, Texas, Arizona, and New Mexico, illegal immigrants
comprise an even larger share of the workforce. Heading farther
from the border, the influence of illegal immigration is less pronounced, but it doesn't vanish entirely. Remember, illegal immigrants come to the United States for the jobs, and they are mobile.
Cities and towns in states as far away from the Mexican border as
Maine and Illinois consider themselves just as much at the forefront of the immigration debate as El Paso and San Diego.

The Impact on Wages

The illegal immigrants who work in jobs requiring neither skill
nor education accept wages that are at the rock bottom of the pay

---

* Source: UNICEF.
** Gordon H. Hanson, "The Economic Logic of Illegal Immigration," *Council on
Foreign Relations* (April 2007).

scale. In 2000, the average wages of male Mexican immigrants—legal and illegal—were 41 percent lower than the average wages for males in the United States; for female Mexicans, the average was 33 percent less.*

Knowing this, and knowing that the business community is in favor of letting immigrants in to work, labor economists have sought to measure the impact of immigration on the U.S. standard of living. Their results may surprise you—they certainly surprised me. The Kennedy School's George Borjas is perhaps the best-known guru on the subject of immigration economics. Borjas, a Cuban-born immigrant himself, argues strenuously that immigration leads to fewer opportunities, and lower wages, for native workers. But, he admits that, statistically, the effect is minimal. In one research study, he finds that the impact of illegal immigration on overall wages is very small—a 3 percent decline in average wages nationally over the twenty years from 1980 to 2000. In another study with Harvard colleague Larry Katz, he finds that immigration has led to a 5 percent drop in the wages of high school dropouts in the United States, but the impact on the wages of high school graduates is considerably less pronounced, and the impact on the wages of workers with higher degrees is actually positive.**

Another immigration expert, David Card, disagrees with Borjas's conclusion that illegal immigration reduces opportunities and wages for native-born Americans. The University of California economics professor makes a logical point, namely, that illegal immigrants end up creating just as many jobs as they take. After all, illegal immigrants eat at restaurants, rent apartments, drive

---

* See Hanson, cited previously.
** George J. Borjas, *Heaven's Door: Imigration Policy and the American Economy* (Princeton, N.J.: Princeton University Press, 1999). The one caveat I'd mention is that with immigration picking up rapidly toward the end of the twenty-year period, and running high now, such estimates may be on the low side for the current environment.

cars, and have babies here in the United States. Not surprisingly, though, Card doesn't take issue with Borjas's results. The net result is that illegal immigrants have a negligible impact on our overall average income.*

Borjas, Card, and other labor economists here and abroad have looked to other countries and other times to further their knowledge about the effects of massive immigration on the receiving country's standard of living. Over and over again, the data in these studies support the conclusion that only the lowest stratum of native-born workers is affected adversely by a flood of immigrants, and even then, the impact is small and temporary. The studies also confirm that native-born workers who have higher levels of education or skills than immigrants actually experience a net gain in their standard of living during periods of heavy immigration.

What we know, then, about immigration's effect on per capita national income is that a small, positive benefit from having legal immigrants working in high-end jobs (because their numbers are small) is offset by a very small negative impact from having illegal immigrants working in low-paying jobs (despite the large number of them).

Stolen Jobs?

I know what you're thinking: Even though the aggregate impact is nil, isn't it still true that illegal immigrants take jobs away from Americans? Let me address this question again head-on. The answer is no. Illegal immigrants are taking jobs that Americans won't do for the wages companies are willing to pay, which isn't always the minimum wage, by the way. One of the things I found most surprising when I researched this topic was that illegal immi-

---

* It is true that many illegal immigrants send a portion of their earnings to family back home, thus they spend a smaller portion of their income in this country in comparison to native-born workers. Still, they do have to survive here in the United States, and this requires outlays.

grants are often working jobs for \$10–\$12 an hour. This is far above the minimum wage in every state, but still employers have no choice but to fill the vacant positions with illegal immigrants.

I know that some of you are chomping at the bit, waiting to see if I raise the issue that's lurking just below the surface: Why not pay a higher wage for unskilled work? Then native-born Americans would take these jobs and we'd enjoy a higher standing of living. Obviously.

Well, let me tell you, it ain't so obvious. Nor is that bit about a higher standard of living correct. Here's why. If companies have to pay more to fill unskilled jobs, they'll first try to eliminate the jobs—for example, by laying artificial turf instead of grass; by dismantling the cafeteria; by asking everyone to do their own photocopying. The result will be a rise in the unemployment rate, which is not at all good for our standard of living. Alternatively, companies will try to pass on the higher cost of labor to the consumer in the form of higher prices.

Business understands that immigrant labor keeps prices low, and so do most American consumers. I believe that Americans don't want to pay more for things produced or prepared by illegal immigrants—food, child care, photocopying, laundry, house-cleaning, gardening, roofing, painting, car washes, parking, and the like.

Besides, this notion that we have the power to set wages and prices indiscriminately, at levels we deem socially appropriate, is dead wrong. If the last twenty years of globalization have taught us anything, it is that our wages must be in line with those of the global labor market, and the prices of our goods and services must be in line with those of the global marketplace. We know what happens when American producers have higher costs that they try to pass on—we lose business to overseas competitors. And we know what happens when Americans get paid more for the same work—we lose jobs overseas. Long gone is our ability to set wages domestically, irrespective of wages for similar work outside the United States. Even for services that we can't import, wages are forced into line because unskilled workers can change industries at will.

The bottom line is this: Illegal immigrants are not taking jobs from Americans; they're mostly doing jobs we don't want. Moreover, the impact they are having on the U.S. national income is negligible. Efforts to raise the wages paid to domestic unskilled laborers, in order to reduce our dependence on illegal immigrants, would surely backfire. In the meantime, we enjoy the benefit of immigrant labor in the form of lower prices for the goods and services they produce.

That said, it is important for the health of the U.S. economy to ensure a level playing field. One of the frequently heard complaints against the illegal immigrants who gain some footing in the economy is that they continue to work outside the system, whereas American employers and employees must play by the rules. For example, a locally owned electrical contractor will pay taxes for social security and unemployment compensation on behalf of his workers, not to mention health insurance premiums and other benefits to remain competitive in the local labor market. Licensed electricians also must adhere to local regulations designed to safeguard the public. By contrast, illegal immigrants don't pay employee benefits, nor do they pay into the unemployment or social security pools. They don't incur the costs of certification, either. As a result, illegal immigrants can, and commonly do, undercut the prices charged by licensed electricians. Clearly that's not fair; clearly it's not right. Fixing it, however, is a bear. After all, illegal immigrants are in this country illegally; by definition, they're not playing by the rules.

There's another side to this issue that gets people equally riled up. By allowing immigrants to remain in this country illegally, are we essentially creating a caste of second-class citizens? Are illegal immigrants the modern equivalent of the slaves brought over from

Africa in the eighteenth and nineteenth centuries? To some degree the answer to these questions has to be yes. Illegal immigrants are not full-fledged members of society; clearly they do not have the same rights and privileges as legal immigrants and citizens—they are not eligible for social security, Medicare, or Medicaid, and state-run unemployment compensation programs are outside their reach. But, and it's a big *but,* illegal immigrants crossed the border of their own volition. That makes a difference.

The issue I'm doing an admittedly bad job of skirting around is whether illegal immigrants should be granted legal status in the United States; whether they should be accepted into American society in the same way they've been accepted into the American labor force; whether we should expect from them the same things we expect from legal citizens. Well, I know this is going to sound like a copout, but this is the point at which I bow out. As an economist, I can say that it is government's role to ensure that everyone plays by the same rules, to ensure that illegal influence, bribery, racism, and even the threat of violence are not part of business decision-making in this country. As an economist, I can say that unfair trade and hiring practices lead to distortions in the economy, which, in turn, lead to inefficiencies and lost growth. But that's where economics ends. I warned you at the outset that I'd be leaving some things on the table.

Sharing Social Services

Not all illegal immigrants operate under the radar. Some pay taxes to federal, state, and city governments. Most also pay real estate taxes indirectly in their rent check every month. Nevertheless, no one really disagrees with the contention that illegal immigrants get more out of the system than they pay in. Illegal immigrants drive on roads, benefit from police and fire protection, and get their garbage picked up along with everyone else's. Moreover, the Supreme Court has ruled that illegal immigrants are entitled to emergency medical services and their children are entitled to public education. It's also federal law that the children of illegal immigrants be eligible for social safety net programs designed to help children, such as the school lunch and Women, Infants and Children (WIC) programs.

Illegal immigrants create what economists call a *fiscal burden* and it is real, if incredibly difficult to measure. We can make a few observations, though. First, the net loss to the federal government is minor, if it's a loss at all. The federal government receives the lion's share of the taxes paid by illegal immigrants, as it does from all of us, but it provides few of the services they use. Illegal immigrants aren't covered by unemployment insurance; they're not part of the social security system (most don't have social security numbers), and they don't receive Medicare or Medicaid (although their children may qualify for Medicaid). State and local governments shoulder the burden of providing the services that immigrants rely on while in the United States. Inevitably, then, native-born Americans are paying higher state and local taxes than they would if illegal immigration were stopped. The disparity in the fiscal burden between the federal government, on the one hand, and state and local governments, on the other, is the main reason that state and city governments have been quicker to pass and enforce immigration reform than Washington.

But don't leave with the impression that the fiscal burden is huge. Even organizations that would like to see illegal immigration curtailed admit that the figures involved are minuscule in comparison to the nation's annual income (the GDP). Admittedly, though, that may not be the right benchmark since the number of illegal immigrants is largest in just a few states. Perhaps in Minnesota and Mississippi taxpayers wouldn't see much benefit from a reduction in illegal immigration, but I have to believe that the extra cost of social services for the illegal immigrant populations in Arizona and Texas is high and that voters would probably feel a nice chunk of extra change in their wallets if the pace of illegal immigration slowed.

Successful Reform

Although Congress is currently stalled on immigration reform, the United States has passed laws in the past to control the flow of immigrants. Most of the policies enforced today are a result of the Immigration Reform and Control Act (IRCA) of 1986 and Supreme Court rulings since then.

IRCA did something that many business leaders and politicians would like to see reversed: It put the burden on businesses to check the legal immigration status of their workforce. Companies anxious to see their work get done are the wrong players to be enforcing the rules. They are also not trained to spot forgeries of green cards and social security cards, which are what illegal immigrants use to skirt the rules. The system that's been put in place is inefficient and ineffective. That said, however, the business community is strongly in favor of letting low-skilled workers through the door.

Perhaps the near-term solution is to do a better job of defining the portal. To this end, the Bush administration is overseeing the construction of a wall along the U.S.-Mexico border to gain better control of the flow across the border. It's certainly not a cheap proposal—it's going to cost over $1 billion. Yet it's part of a $13 billion request the president has made to beef up security along our borders. Yes, $1 billion—and certainly $13 billion—seems like a lot of money to spend in the absence of evidence that illegal immigration has a negative effect on the economy. But then maybe economics never was the real concern.

13

"Made in China"

Made in China. Those three words rarely meet with approval on American soil. For American workers, that phrase signifies manufacturing jobs permanently lost overseas. For American consumers, it means shoddy and potentially dangerous, albeit cheap, merchandise. For American businesses, it threatens cut-rate and cutthroat competition. For U.S. trade representatives, it's the source of our bulging trade deficit. For currency traders, it's part of the reason for the dollar's precipitous fall. For economists, it's a reminder that the United States has experienced only a fraction of the rapid growth that the world economy has generated these past six or seven years. For environmentalists, well, it's the work of the devil incarnate.

China has become the lightning rod for all that is wrong with the U.S. economy. The continued decline in manufacturing output and employment. Sluggish employment growth. And then there's rising inflation, the record-high trade deficit, the falling dollar, and, perhaps most significantly, the decline of the middle class.

Wait just a minute! Isn't the United States experiencing economic growth? Aren't more people working today than at any time in the nation's history? Aren't inflation and interest rates pretty darn low? All these things are true, but everything I wrote in the last paragraph is true as well. If you take a close look, there is no contradiction. The economy and employment are both growing, but neither as fast as in Asia nor as fast as our economy can or should. Employment growth in the United States, by any measure, has been a disappointment.* Inflation has picked up, although it's still far from being a threat to stability. The dollar's fall, on the other hand, is truly remarkable—remarkable in the sense a radiologist uses the word when he sees something awful on an X-ray. As for the decline in the middle class . . . you don't seriously want to contest that, do you?

Let's compromise. Thankfully the U.S. economy is not in crisis due to trade with China (the subprime mortgage mess is another story). Not a serious short-term crisis, in any case. But I think we all agree that there are long-term trade trends that are worrisome. The reason for this chapter is that in the minds of many Americans, rightly or wrongly, China's contribution to our economic problems is large and growing.

Yao Ming Big

I like to start with the numbers so that we're all on the same page—and so that we have our facts straight. Not a lot of numbers, mind you. Fortunately, or perhaps unfortunately, it doesn't take many to describe our fear factor. The issues we're dealing with here are not subtle.

How Big? You know that China is big. That's incorrect: China is not big. China is *massive*. The population of China is 1,321,852,000. I had to stop and think myself when reading this number. It's one billion, three hundred and twenty-one million, eight hundred and fifty-two thousand. Well over 1 billion people. The United States has 301,140,000 people. The comparison is thus easy: Both countries have roughly three hundred million residents; China just has a billion people on top of that.

---

* Go back to chapter 9, "Multiply by a Gazillion," to refresh your memory about the tricks that are played with employment numbers and other economic indicators.

Here comes the rub (the first of many, actually). All those Chinese are squeezed into a country that's geographically about the same size as the United States. China measures 9,596,960 square kilometers, which is only a smidgeon smaller than the continental United States, which measures 9,826,630 square kilometers. Calculating the number of persons per square kilometer is a bit difficult because of all the digits. If I did it correctly, China has 138 people per km². Oh, spacious skies . . . the United States has 31!

Is it possible for Chinese agriculture to be four times as productive as ours in the United States? Not even with the benefit of the most up-to-date machinery, which Chinese farmers don't have. No, China needs to have a much larger agricultural sector than the United States—and it does. Almost one out of every two workers (45 percent to be exact) in China is a farmer.

Let's divide the population in half, then, to get a better measure of the human resources China can devote to the nonfarm economy. That's roughly 661 million—still double the population of the United States—not living on farms. These stats also foretell one of my favorite facts about China: China has forty-nine cities with a population exceeding 1 million—and I bet you can't name more than three or four of them. The United States has nine.

How Desperate? With over 450 million people living in cities, China has its work cut out for it to keep these people profitably employed. Under strict communism, from 1949 to 1982, China did a pretty bad job of it. Many people were underemployed, if not actually unemployed (the state did not allow unemployment as a matter of policy). The majority of city dwellers were, like their rural counterparts who worked on collective farms, shockingly poor. A severe drought in 1978, which made it that much more difficult for China to feed its masses, brought the nation to the tipping point.

Starting in the late 1970s, therefore, the Communist Party in China began to relax some of the strict guidelines under which the economy had been forced to operate. (It was that or deal with civil rebellion. Remember, by the late 1970s, the information age was upon us. China could no longer keep the evidence of a better world from its people.) Farms were decollectivized and, for the first time, farmers were allowed to keep some of their harvest for personal consumption or sale. The results of this action were so incredibly good that, having learned its lesson, China gradually opened the rest of the economy to capitalism.

Still, China today is a very poor country. Its output totals $10.17 trillion, which puts it right behind the United States and ahead of the country that used to hold the number two position, Japan. The Chinese figure translates to just about $7,700 per person per year, however, which ranks eighty-sixth in the world, right ahead of Algeria.

There's one more set of statistics that's awfully telling: the incomes of the top 10 percent and the bottom 10 percent of the country. In China today, the top 10 percent of the nation—that is, the 10 percent with the biggest paychecks—accounts for 33 percent of national income. The bottom 10 percent gets just 1.8 percent. That is an incredibly uneven distribution of income that is, in almost all cases, a strong destabilizing force in society. No wonder, then, that China has had to retain some of the less palatable elements of communism to keep the country under control.

How So? As poor as China is today, it is much better off than it was in 1980 when income per person ranked 130th in the world. How has it managed to partially reverse in just a few decades the extreme poverty of centuries and modernize what was a backward country? You will not be surprised by the answer: China began experimenting with capitalism. Of course, China doesn't call it capitalism. The official term is *socialism with Chinese characteristics*. But if it looks like a duck, walks like a duck, and quacks like a duck. . . . You get my point.

To be sure, the capitalism we see today in China is not the same unbridled drive for profits that exists in the United States or even Western Europe. China still puts together ten-year plans, ratified by the National People's Congress, that guide the economy going forward. The key difference is that today Chinese officials guide—and often react—rather than dictate. Fewer businesses are state-owned and those that are enjoy more autonomy. Employment is no longer guaranteed. Prices are somewhat flexible. And, most important of all, the Chinese are able to trade with the rest of the world. Put all this together with an improved banking system and a new stock market, and you've got China's recipe for success.

How Fast? I promised you just a few numbers and I don't want to renege on that promise. But there's one more statistical comparison I feel compelled to make, one more point I need to bring out. The Chinese economy is moving forward at lightning speed. Here in the United States, we're happy when the economy, after inflation, grows by 3–4 percent. China's growth rate has recently settled back down (I kid you not) to 10 percent. Let me tell you, when an economy grows by 10 percent a year—and China's growth was even stronger than that earlier in the decade—it will rise in the standings in no time. Maybe China is in eighty-sixth place now. Want to venture a guess where it'll be in 2010? 2020?

A-Rod Strong

You remember my bellyaching in an earlier chapter about Alex Rodriguez's mega-million ten-year contract with the Yankees? Well, in the 2007 season, A-Rod proved he was worth every penny. He ended the year with a .314 batting average—and that after batting .235 in May and .206 in July. A-Rod's bat was a key reason the Yankees came back after the All-Star break to win fifty-one of their remaining seventy-six games (67 percent) and secure a place in the American League playoffs. As much as I hate to admit it as a Red Sox fan, Steinbrenner's deal for A-Rod makes Red Sox general manager Theo Epstein look like a chump for spending $52 million to sign Daisuke Matsuzaka for six years, after spending $51 million just for the right to negotiate with him. (I know; it was Matsuzaka's first season in the United States. I'm willing to give him time, but at $100+ million, we fans have a right to expect him to make the adjustment faster than he has.)

What does A-Rod have to do with China? Only that in the global marketplace, China is becoming just as strong as A-Rod's bat. In 2003, China surpassed Mexico to win the "Most Imports to the United States" title. The very next year, China edged ahead of the UK and Germany to become the fourth-largest market for U.S. exports. Trade with China is strong, coming and going.

Anyone who thinks that China's exports are cheap toys and clothing had better jump into the twenty-first century. The biggest volume of Chinese exports to the United States now comprises office machinery, data processing and telecom equipment, toys, and, believe it or not, furniture—not all of it the kind of stuff that we usually associate with cheap-labor China. Apparel is also up there, admittedly, but the cheap, cheap stuff like paper products are way down on the list. Another interesting development is that the same types of goods show up on both the import and export ledgers: electrical machinery, office machines, and plastics. Clearly, trade with China has come a long way from what it was in the 1960s and 1970s (more about this in the final section of the chapter).

Bill Belichick Smart

China hasn't gotten everything right since the late 1970s—as we'll see in a moment—but I want to emphasize the one thing on the list of what it did right that has made all the difference in the world. It was the push for exports over domestic consumption in the early days of the changeover. China knew that its population would eventually prove fertile ground for businesses of almost every stripe, from the construction of apartment blocks to fashion to personal technology. China held back on encouraging consumption, however, until it had established itself as a global source for manufacturing and mining output. These exports provided China with the hard dollars (not yuan) that it needed to buy machinery and expertise from abroad. It wasn't until the new millennium, more than twenty years into the process, that China acquired a bulging middle class that's now gobbling up dishwashers and iPhones almost faster than manufacturers can supply them.

The Chinese were also smart when it came to maintaining political stability. With all the economic reforms taking place in China, you'd think that its system of government, with dictatorial power squarely lodged in the Communist Party, would have had to change. But philosophically and practically, Chinese officials have managed to make the Chinese versions of communism and socialism coexist with the free market.* One of their tricks has been to reject the moniker of capitalism, as I said earlier. They maintain that the new economic structure they're adopting is an enhancement of socialism and thus entirely consistent with Marx's writings. But their accomplishment also stems from a willingness to put ideology aside and focus on what works, and a willingness to move forward in steps. It is the latter strategy that frustrates many Americans, for we often expect more (e.g., better environmental habits) from a nation that is succeeding in other areas.

What Exactly Is Our Gripe?

With all this data and history as background, we can now lay out the issues that most concern Americans. The list I've devised has five items: the first three have to do with the gaping trade imbalance

---

* In many cases, the Chinese set up separate geographic zones for their market-based industries, thus reducing the potential for conflict.

with China, the fourth relates to their holdings of U.S. securities, and the fifth reflects our concerns about intellectual property.

1. We Americans don't like it that Chinese companies, rather than American companies, are selling to Americans. It implies that Chinese workers are employed producing the goods instead of Americans. It also means that the banking, trucking, and packaging services that are used, even services on the periphery of the manufacturing process, such as waste removal, custodial services, and HR, are all being provided by Chinese companies.

2. We Americans distrust the strategies Chinese companies may be using to undercut the prices of American goods. China has cheap labor, so any good that demands a lot of labor in the production process is going to be more cheaply made in China than in the United States. Fair enough. But as I said above, a lot of the imports from China these days are not labor-intensive goods but rather goods higher up the food chain, for example, printers and sound equipment. Some business people in the United States suspect that Chinese companies are selling goods in the United States at prices that are below their manufacturing costs, a policy called *dumping*. This is a losing proposition for the exporter at this time, but that's not its purpose. A company that dumps is trying to knock out competitors from the market so that in the future, the business will be all theirs (at which point they'll raise prices). Dumping is illegal, dumping is immoral—and dumping is pervasive in international markets.

3. Dumping isn't the only strategy we're concerned about, however. Chinese manufacturers may also be taking business away from American companies because they've managed to cut their costs. One way to cut costs is to use cheaper inputs—

lead paint, for example, in toys. Another way to cut costs is to cut corners, skimping on parts of the production process, such as quality control and environmental safeguards. No one who's read the newspapers in 2007—or who's smelled the air over Beijing—can deny that some Chinese manufacturers are guilty as charged.

4. The trade deficit has a flip side, that is the large number of dollars that the Chinese are holding. Remember that every transaction has two hands outstretched, the seller's and the buyer's. With a big trade deficit, we are usually the buyer of goods and we're handing over dollars to the Chinese. Now we know that they're not turning around and using those dollars to buy American-made products (if they were, there wouldn't be a trade deficit). So they end up holding onto the dollars instead. Of course, they're not holding fistfuls of dollars, but investing the dollars in dollar assets, that is, U.S. Treasury bonds. This raises our biggest fear: What if some day the Chinese decide to dump the U.S. Treasury securities they own? The extra supply of Treasuries on the market would lower their price, which would mean interest rate rise.* It would also weaken the dollar, which would boost prices on everything we buy from abroad. In short, if the Chinese choose to exercise the option, China has the ability to throw the U.S. economy toward recession and inflation simultaneously. Insert the expletive of your choice!

5. Another major problem we have with the Chinese is the safety of our intellectual property. Is China respecting our inventions, our proprietary technology, or our talent? Take a stroll down the street in Shanghai—and nowadays in Los Angeles as

---

* Remember from chapter 3, that the interest rate and price of a bond move in opposite directions.

well—and you'll see vendors hawking cheap, pirated software, CDs, and DVDs all "made in China." This is theft. In the United States, where we have a strong judicial system, thieves who steal intellectual property are prosecuted. China is not subject to U.S. laws; international laws are hard to enforce; and the Chinese legal system is weak. This problem cuts across almost every industry in the United States, from record companies to drug manufacturers to software developers to cleaning products that splash the words NEW AND IMPROVED on their labels.

Right from Wrong

I purposefully laid out the problems Americans have with China over trade in a way that suggests there's not another side to the story. But there is; there always is. My purpose now is to evaluate each of the claims made from an economic perspective, leaving politics and emotions out of it.

First, let's take up the issue of the decline in manufacturing jobs in the United States. Truth be told, the United States has been losing factory jobs for more than fifty years, and politicians, union officials, and workers have been warning of the damage it would cause the economy long before *made in China* became household words.

Recent research by two very well-respected economists, Martin Bailey and Robert Lawrence, for the McKinsey Global Institute, takes a look at the decline in manufacturing jobs since 2000 with an eye toward the trade imbalance.* They conclude that only 11 percent of the jobs lost in manufacturing since 2000 are due to rising imports and falling exports. An even smaller percentage of service-sector job losses can be attributed to trade. In

---

* Martin Neil Bailey and Robert Z. Lawrence, "Don't Blame Trade for U.S. Job Losses," *McKinsey Quarterly* (January 2005).

other words, the trade deficit is not to blame for the latest acceleration in the exodus in manufacturing employment.

What really caused employers to lay off factory workers and be slow to hire when sales increased were three different events/trends: (1) slow growth in consumer spending here in the United States, which has translated into sluggish increases in demand for manufactured goods; (2) rapid growth in worker productivity (probably due to technology) that has allowed employers to get more from each worker; and (3) a strengthening of the dollar (until 2007), which had made it harder for foreigners to afford American output.

The real solutions to the problem, Bailey and Lawrence conclude, are to stimulate U.S. consumer demand and do whatever's possible to reduce interest rates (i.e., rein in government spending so the U.S. Treasury doesn't have to borrow as much). The wrong solutions are to pass laws that will prevent China from exporting to the United States, or to punish financially or emotionally those Americans who buy foreign-made goods.

Fact is, we Americans are better off for being able to buy some Chinese goods more cheaply than their American competition (goods without lead paint, of course!). Wal-Mart advertises that it saves the average family who shops in its stores $2,500 a year! How do you think it does that? By searching out the cheapest goods to bring to the U.S. market. By definition, most of these goods will be made in low-cost labor spots like China. In fact, Wal-Mart is the single largest U.S. importer of Chinese consumer goods, larger even than Germany or Russia.

Our consumption of Chinese-made products may be just the tip of the iceberg, though. As communist societies like China's embrace capitalism, they encourage (sometimes by force) rural laborers' migration into the cities. There they supply manufacturers with cheap labor to produce goods for the global markets. As we know, this phenomenon depresses wages globally for unskilled labor, and it also depresses the prices of goods all over the global markets. The migration of these workers is thus responsible in large part for the broad-based *disinflation* (declining rates of inflation) that we enjoyed in the 1990s and still, to some extent, benefit from today.

When disinflation is taken to its extreme and prices actually fall—a condition known as *deflation*—bad things happen in the economy.* Disinflation itself, however, has some real benefits, namely declining inflation and declining interest rates. Americans are better off living in a world without high or variable inflation. And Americans are better off living in a world of lower interest rates. Anyone who refinanced her mortgage in the past two decades has the Chinese partly to thank for the lower rate and the extra cash in her pocket. Similarly, anyone who's bought a car with 0.9 percent financing, or 1.9 percent or 2.9 percent, has the Chinese to thank, in part, for making that car more affordable. What I'm trying to say is that Americans benefit more than you might think from the low prices China has helped to establish globally.

To be sure, no wants to see an American worker lose his job. But let's understand that buying cheaper Chinese-made telephones and coats were not the real reason he did. If we didn't buy these goods from China, we'd turn to the output of a different country with low-cost labor, maybe Vietnam, Eastern Europe, or the Middle East. Given that the problem is that our labor costs are higher than those of the developing nations, the problem isn't easily fixed by ostracizing Chinese goods. There's an almost unlimited supply of alternatives to China out there. Face it: Americans don't have a future producing goods or services that require unskilled labor.

---

* Deflation feeds upon itself, creating a downward spiral in economic activity. Everyone puts off purchasing all but the most essential items, figuring that goods and services will be cheaper in the future. The more this occurs, the faster prices fall and the more purchases are put off.

One more consideration: China is growing so fast, and turning into such a major purchaser in the global marketplace, that the days of our running a trade deficit with China may be numbered on their own. China is already the third-largest trader in the world, and the United States has many goods the Chinese will want as their economy matures, such as Jeeps, advanced medical care, and airplanes.

Moving on, let's stop for a moment and think about all those dollars in the hands of the Chinese. Not knowing how old you are, or how much you read the paper, I'm going to assume this issue about foreigners holding dollars is all new to you. Let me tell you, it ain't new. Back in the 1970s, when we lined up in our cars for hours on end to buy a single tankful of gas, our concern was the dollars held by OPEC nations. We had a huge trade deficit with OPEC, just as we have now with China. OPEC ended up owning lots of U.S. Treasury securities, just as China does now. The same pattern repeated itself with Japan in the 1980s and early 1990s, before the Japanese economy came apart at the seams. Japanese investors held massive amounts of U.S. Treasury securities when we ran an outrageously large trade deficit with Japan. And we were worried then, too, about what would happen if the Japanese sold their holdings.

At some point in the 1980s, OPEC nations sold some of their bonds. Did anyone notice? Only the traders on Wall Street. At some point in the 1990s, the Japanese sold some of their bonds. Did anyone notice? Only the traders on Wall Street. In fact, interest rates have been tracking down since the 1980s.

What's wrong with the assumption that China's going to dump our bonds in a blaze of glory is that it's not in the best interest of China to sell their holdings in one fell swoop. Given the size of China's holdings—they hold the largest share, having eclipsed the Japanese over the last decade—any sale would have to occur over time. Thus, if China wants to sell some U.S.

Treasuries, perhaps to hold more euro-denominated notes, it is in their best interests to sell quietly and slowly so as not to lower the price of the remaining bonds in their portfolio—just as OPEC and Japan did.

But don't rush to the conclusion that China's selling its U.S. dollar holdings is right around the corner. Political risk, which is credit risk at the national level, is at its lowest in the United States and higher virtually everywhere else in the world. That's not going to change any time soon—indeed I'm inclined to say it won't happen in your lifetime. The Chinese may reduce their U.S. holdings, but it's highly unlikely that they'd liquidate their entire portfolio.

That neither OPEC's nor Japan's holdings of U.S. securities impaired U.S. economic growth is another reason to calm down. We often read that China's accumulation of U.S. paper is a dangerous situation for the U.S. economy, but it's not really. Perhaps the people who write these articles forget that the United States runs not only a trade deficit but a federal government deficit as well (meaning that the U.S. government spends more than it takes in). Because of our "twin deficits," the trade deficit may actually be helping Uncle Sam. You see, with foreigners accumulating dollars when they export to the United States, the U.S. Treasury has a natural buyer for its paper (i.e., a natural source of funding for the U.S. government). If the U.S. trade deficit were to shrink, foreigners would have fewer dollars, and there would be fewer overseas buyers for U.S. government bonds. This could mean higher interest rates in the United States to induce Americans to pony up more savings. Since low interest rates have been supporting the economy's expansion, you can imagine the effect of higher interest rates—not good.

Another related concern often raised is the effect on the dollar that foreigners' holdings of U.S. securities, or their sale, might have. Economics teaches that when a nation like the United States has a large trade deficit, its currency should fall so that American citizens find imports more expensive and buy fewer of them while foreigners find U.S. products less expensive and buy more of them. (Read that sentence again if you need to; it does make sense.) Economics teaches, in other words, that the currency itself, if it's free to fluctuate, should take care of the trade deficit (and the problem of foreigners accumulating dollars) without any outside intervention.

This is one of those cases where economic theory, while air- and watertight, nevertheless fails to explain reality. The trade deficit has pretty much been on a steady course higher in the past forty years; meanwhile, the dollar has appreciated and depreciated without so much as a glance at the trade statistics. So you can argue that the trade deficit is going to do harm to the dollar, but I have no reason to believe it will. And you can argue that when foreigners tire of holding dollars they will do harm to the dollar, but again I have no reason to think they will. (I'm afraid the dollar's decline in 2006 and 2007 had more to do with the world's dissatisfaction with Bush's policy in Iraq, and then the debacle in the sub-prime mortgage market and ensuing period of slow growth, than with the trade deficit.)

Although economists are noticeably divided on the issue, many business leaders and politicians in the United States argue that the Chinese should let their currency rise—they say the Chinese are keeping the value of the yuan artificially low, which means foreigners (like the United States) are paying artificially low prices for Chinese goods. Maybe so. Here's a sobering thought, though: Since many of the things we import from China are no longer produced here, a rise in the yuan and a decline in the dollar will make the trade deficit worse because it will simply cause us to pay more for the imports we can't do without, like toys and shoes (we can't substitute American-made goods because we no longer make them). Combine that with the prospect of higher interest rates and the likelihood that a stronger yuan wouldn't make a dent in the U.S. trade deficit anyway (as described above), and you've got some pretty strong reasons to jump down off that high horse.

If some of what we hear about China is poppycock, however, some of it is undoubtedly true. Although we may never be able to prove it, it is likely that Chinese companies have engaged in dumping on occasion and that the Chinese government has restricted the import of certain U.S.-made goods at times. Chinese officials have done so in the interests of accelerating their country's development from backwater economy to first-world powerhouse, which probably justifies a lot of funny stuff in their minds. Surely they are not the first ones to employ such tactics—there is a school of thought in economics that suggests that developing countries follow that course at times—and they are certainly not the last. And as I said earlier, none of us doubts that China has used less-than-desirable means to cut manufacturing costs. Maybe at some point in the future, if the Chinese manage to see through the pollution, they'll see their way clear to realizing that such actions are counterproductive.

As for China's bending the rules—all right, breaking the rules—over intellectual property, again there is no doubt they've done so. The question is how much have their actions hurt the U.S. economy. Many experts believe that China's theft costs us very little. Illegally copied CDs and DVDs are all over Chinese cities, for sure, but with the quality what it often is, it's not likely that these copies represent lost sales yet for U.S. companies in China.

What Now?

So where do all these arguments leave us? Maybe it's time to learn from Hong Kong. After China took control of Hong Kong from the British, virtually all the manufacturing jobs in the country went bye-bye. But today Hong Kong has a gargantuan and fast-growing service sector. Hong Kong shrugged off China and went on with the job of making money, employing their population, and living well. We should do the same, which is why the next chapter of this book is devoted to job migration.

In the meantime, I have to say that, like most economists, I think we'd be better off putting our own house in order than bashing China. Our to-do list is not trivial: Reducing the federal deficit, keeping inflation in check, and providing effective support for workers laid off top my list.

Addendum to Chapter 13: Is China Invincible?

It used to be we thought that Japan was invincible. American companies even sent representatives (and sometimes spies) over there to copy the ways of Japanese business. What a difference a few decades—and Japan's severe recession—make.

China is not invincible, either. Its laundry list of problems includes pollution, manufacturing inefficiency (even among the new private enterprises), a rapidly aging labor force (thanks in part to the country's one-child policy), the growing disparity between the rich and poor (gotta give Mao his due on this one; he kept everyone poor), an immature and ineffectual financial system (which has already left the country with a huge volume of bad loans), a central bank that is hardly independent, widespread corruption, and an authoritarian government that is only gradually allowing for political freedom.

Say what you will about the United States, these are not problems we face. Maybe that's why the U.S. economy has weathered many a storm, indeed many storms we were told our economy couldn't survive.

Addendum 2 to Chapter 13: Straight-Up Economics

Lurking just under the surface in this chapter is some hard-nosed economic theory that most people don't want to hear. If you have the appetite, however, I'm ready to serve it up.

Trade around the world generally fits into one of two patterns. The first pattern is dictated by what economists call *comparative advantage*. Basically, this is the common-sense rule that when two countries trade in two goods, each should focus on the good it can produce more cheaply. It gets a bit more complicated when one of the two trading partners produces both goods more efficiently. In this case, each country should focus on the good that within its own borders has the smaller opportunity cost, that is, the good it can produce more efficiently than the other. This is why the theory is called *comparative advantage*, not *absolute advantage*.

The U.S. economy has expensive but well-educated labor and lots of capital equipment. As a result, we are efficient at producing products that require skill and technologically advanced machinery. One would expect the United States to sell expensive products. By contrast, China has lots of cheap labor and unproductive land (because the Chinese often employ ancient methods of farming). It has much less capital equipment in place than the United States. One would thus expect China to sell to the United States goods that require a lot of human input. Trade between the United States and China prior to the 1980s followed this pattern, and still does so, to some extent.

The second pattern of trade is more frequently seen between developed nations, both with the ability to produce goods efficiently. In this more advanced trade scenario, dubbed *intra-industry* or *intra-sectoral trade,* countries trade with each other because they're after a specific brand name. So the UK imports

Mercedes cars from Germany and Germany imports Rolls Royce cars from the UK.

It's unusual to see a large trade deficit or surplus in a particular industry or sector when there are efficient two-way trade flows taking place. When it does appear, it may suggest that there is some obstacle preventing goods from being sold—an obstacle like an import tax or an export quota. In trade between the United States and China, a large deficit exists in certain industries, such as office equipment, leading some to question whether China has indeed put into place restrictions on imports from the United States. Another sign of unfair practices may be the fact that the United States runs a deficit with China and China alone in some sectors like optical and medical instruments.

14

Where's My Job? Finding Cheaper Labor Overseas

The voice on the other end of the phone has a familiar, if foreign, accent. "Is this Mrs. Kim-el-man?" Each syllable is anatomically correct but barely recognizable. The whole is incomprehensible. Still, I answer, "Yes, this is she." "Mrs. Kim-el-man, I am calling about your overdue bill with American Express . . ." Before I respond, I pause to wonder: Why in hell is a bloke seven thousand miles (11,250 km) away who can't pronounce my name inquiring into the private life of my American Express card?

Why indeed? He's doing so at the request of American Express, headquartered in the World Financial Center in downtown New York. He may be an employee of American Express directly, or an employee of a firm that's contracted with American Express to handle the company's wayward accounts. Either way, my name and account information came by legitimate means to his desk in India.

My frustration in dealing with the foreign call center employee is only partly explained by his mangling my name and my embarrassment over having not paid my bill. Sometimes it's due to my not getting any resolution to the problem because we're not speaking the same English language. I have not-so-fond memories of trying to get help with a notebook computer and printer to no avail.* Sometimes it's due to the caller's ignorance of what's important to me. Nobody in Boston should be called when the Red Sox are playing the Yankees. However, I suspect I'm most upset by these calls because I know that the job used to be handled by an American. I'm an economist; I know better. And still I feel this way.

Outsourcing versus Offshoring

Let me lay out the concerns that Americans have over outsourcing and then look at those concerns from an economic standpoint. I can't emphasize enough the last four words of the last sentence. Outsourcing wouldn't be controversial if it didn't spark anger, fear, and other raw emotions that I don't even want to think about, much less write about. I can't, and won't, address the emotional side of the issue. I leave that for you and your yoga instructor to work out.

Before the globalization of business put American executives on overseas flights to India and Brazil, these guys and gals were crisscrossing the United States to accomplish much the same goal: finding someone else to do some of their work. Outsourcing is not new, in other words, nor is it, by definition, global. When I was younger, my dad would walk me through the garment district in New York (I think we were looking for corned beef on rye), and I'd see racks and racks of clothes being led from one building to another. The designer had farmed out production to a different firm, and that firm was delivering the finished goods back to the designer's showroom/warehouse. Originally both firms were in the same city. Then they were in the same country (design still in New York but production often in the South). Then production moved overseas to China, the Philippines, Eastern Europe, wherever.

If companies have been outsourcing forever, it is also true that the tasks being outsourced have changed. Production was out-

---

* My solution, by the way, was to keep calling at weird times until by chance my call was passed on to an American or Canadian center. Thought I'd pass the tip along.

sourced first because labor was so much cheaper in other parts of the country or the world. Way back in the '50s and '60s, it was common to pick up toys made in Japan or shoes made in Italy. Then the craze for "competencies" arose, and companies sought to outsource functions that weren't among their "core competencies." This meant that accounting companies, for instance, would bring Marriott in to run the cafeteria and Xerox in to maintain the copiers. Such practices became widespread, and few people argued against them—they made too much common sense.

Having found ample cost savings from outsourcing food, copier, landscaping, janitorial, and a host of other low-level service functions, business threw the net wider in the 1990s and turned over IT operations, accounting, human resources, computer programming, engineering, legal, and customer service. At first, businesses chose companies across town or at the other end of the state to do the work since the tasks often involved data of a sensitive and proprietary nature. That decision helped to keep the riots under control. But as globalization has opened up new opportunities to save money on labor costs, more and more companies have farmed out even highly proprietary work, such as research and development, to overseas vendors. Focusing on the company's core competencies has never been as profitable—or as controversial!

Although theoretically it can be done, as a matter of practice it is nearly impossible to disentangle the practice of outsourcing— obtaining goods or services from an outside source—from the practice of offshoring—shifting work overseas. It's true; these days the two practices often go hand in hand. This need not be the case, however, and indeed many protestors call for firms to offshore but not outsource, that is, take a portion of their business overseas to lower costs but keep it just as much a part of the company as if it were located in Kalamazoo. The hope is that this setup will give American companies greater control over the security of their work and a greater ability to manage the overseas workforce.

Also, this way the profits from the overseas location will come back to the shareholders of the American company. Actually, most big American banks are set up this way. Banks have "branches" all over the world that are, in point of fact, overseas companies. But they are overseas companies owned by their American parent: They're usually headed by an American, they are capitalized by the American parent, they use the same account and trading software as the American parent, and they answer, ultimately, to a boss in New York, Chicago, or San Francisco. Now if only companies could figure out a way to offshore without actually hiring anyone overseas. . . .

Jobs Are Only Part of It

Hands down, the jobs lost overseas are the biggest concern that Americans raise over the practice of outsourcing/offshoring.* We all know, or should know, that American companies don't have any ulterior motive for relocating some of their work overseas; they simply want to save money on labor costs. A recent study confirmed the obvious: 90 percent of all outsourcing decisions are based on a strict cost comparison.**

It's one thing when the work being outsourced is low-end manufacturing—jobs that Americans don't really want. It's something else again when the work being outsourced is what middle-class Americans produce. Well, maybe it's one and the same for the companies; for them, one job is pretty much like another (except for the CEO, of course). For workers, the two circumstances are as different as night and day.

For unskilled labor, the cost differential is huge between American and foreign workers. So it makes good economic sense

---

* If the problem sounds familiar, that's because it is: We've been down this road before in the chapters on China and immigration.
** Linda Cohen of Gartner, Inc., a consulting company, as reported in *Business Week* (December 11, 2006).

for American firms to outsource work to foreign companies that can tap into cheap labor supplies. In such cases, quality is pretty much a moot point. Unskilled labor rarely generates quality differentials that are noticeable; such labor is, after all, unskilled. Why outsource and not just offshore the work? Good question. Simply because most of the time American companies don't have the requisite local knowledge, language skills, connections, and legal status to own and competently run an overseas operation that relies heavily on unskilled labor.

Outsourcing labor-intensive work isn't bad for the American consumer, either. Obviously the practice benefits the receiving country—they see job growth—but it also benefits the American consumer by reducing the costs associated with the products and services Americans buy. Lower costs are passed on, at least in part, to American consumers in the form of lower prices. Lower costs are also passed onto American shareholders as higher profits and dividends. One way or another, Americans benefit.

Outsourcing labor-intensive work also fits with the makeup of the U.S. workforce. Thanks to a decent educational system, we have relatively few unskilled laborers who are willing to work for low, low wages. That's why companies sought out overseas workers in the first place. That's also one of the reasons why illegal immigrants continue to pour over, under, and through America's borders.

If the U.S. workforce is short of unskilled, low-cost labor, it is chock full of skilled middle-class workers. And there's the rub: These people want to be in high demand so they can earn more and more over time. They don't want to see foreign workers competing for jobs *they want themselves*. That's why, when IT operations, research and development, and engineering jobs are shipped overseas, there is the sense that the very fabric of the American way of life is being torn apart.

The End Around

Before tackling the running back, let's see if we can't take out the blocker. As I explained earlier, American companies have been outsourcing work to other American companies for decades. They've done so to improve costs but also to get a better handle on their workflow—to concentrate on what it is they're all about. When outsourcing of this nature takes place, the folks who lose their jobs are put out by the decision, naturally, but few others in the company or community are. Why? Well, one reason may be that the employees may be offered other jobs within the company. That's not atypical. Another reason is that the company taking over the work may offer to keep the employees in the same jobs (they'll work for a different company, in other words, but do the same job). When the jobs move from one company to another, it feels like a zero-sum game. That is, everyone stays employed.

This doesn't mean that jobs are not sometimes lost. The company taking over the task may have better, more efficient ways to get the job done, which is why its offer was attractive in the first place. Consider the fictional footwear company We Feet. We Feet has no expertise in accounting or taxes; in fact, the software used by its ten-person accounting staff is ancient. The local accounting firm, Risks Taken (also fictional), has state-of-the-art accounting and tax software that actually lets a single entry-level accountant run the accounts for companies like We Feet. It's a no-brainer. We Feet outsources its accounting and tax departments to Risks Taken, in the process of which nine We Feet employees lose their jobs. As you can see from this example, outsourcing is not always a zero-sum game. And even if no one is laid off, outsourcing may hurt the workers if the new jobs pay less. Accountants at We Feet probably got paid more than the accountant at Risks Taken, considering that the latter's principal job is data entry.

Domestic outsourcing is not without risk, in other words, for both workers and the communities in which they live. Most of the time it works out pretty well for all sides; sometimes it doesn't. Despite the occasional job losses, you don't hear as much grumbling about outsourcing as you used to. Is it possible that Americans have come to realize that in a free, open economy, the creation and destruction of jobs is organic?* Outsourcing is just another reason for higher job turnover in this country, and probably not the biggest of all.

Outsourcing Overseas

Maybe Americans are getting accustomed to outsourcing as part of their embrace of all things organic. After all, we now buy boatloads of soy milk and miles of organic beef jerky every year. Maybe, but I think the real reason why the critics have been quiet is that they've decided they have bigger fish to fry: globalization. It seems the only time now that people get up in arms over a decision to outsource is when the work will be done overseas. Outsourcing isn't the enemy any more, or not directly; it's globalization.

If the battle cry of 2007–2008 is that good, well-paid American jobs are being exported to developing nations thanks to globalization, then the protesters have actually got it right. If you look out at the outsourcing/offshoring that companies are doing today, three jobs top the list: data entry, computer programming, and software engineering. Are there plenty of Americans qualified to do this work? Yes. Do these people have fewer jobs open to them because some of the work has shifted overseas? Yes. Are the wages of Americans being negatively affected by outsourcing? Yes. So then how do we economists explain the practice?

Well, it's actually not that difficult. Despite there being ample supplies of workers back home, the work can still be done at a fraction of the cost—sometimes a small fraction—by overseas

---

* It probably helps, too, that outsourcing is growing less quickly in the mid-2000s than it did at the turn of the millennium.

workers. Is there a well-spoken American high school grad or part-time college student who could call me up about my delinquent American Express bill? Of course there is. Problem is, she'll still be getting paid much, much more than the fellow in Bangalore. Indeed, the amount I owe American Express could well be more than his annual salary—no, I'm not that rich; he's that poor!

Is it possible that eventually wages and the standard of living in Bangalore will rise enough to make the United States competitive again?* Right. Want to guess the population of India? It's 1,129,866,154. Hey, at least it's smaller than China! Don't get your hopes up. A lot of outsourcing is moving away from India these days—to China. In fact, the so-called BRICS countries are getting a lot of new business. (*BRICS* stands for Brazil, Russia, India, China, and South Africa.) Not to mention all those ex-Soviet satellites, Vietnam, Argentina. . . .

As if money weren't motivation enough (and it usually is), there's another big reason why fairly technical jobs are being moved overseas. Time. Many business executives in the United States report that thanks to seamless 24/7 global communications, crunch times can be better managed by having multiple offices up and running in each of the major time zones.

Time and money. When the two factors dovetail, as they do here, they're well nigh impossible to stop. Thus, the solution, such as it is, is for American workers and institutions to learn to adjust to the realities of a global workforce.

Globalization: An Unstoppable Force

Here's a trick for you: If you ever have the chance to meet an economist, ask him how he feels about economic analysis being done on contract by economists in India. The outsourcing of economic

---

* In point of fact, wages for high-tech workers are rising over 10 percent a year in Bangalore. But that's just one city.

work is being done routinely by the news services, so it's nothing outrageous. In his answer I think you'll find an economist at odds with himself. As an economist, he'll applaud it; as an economist, he'll decry it.

You know why he'll applaud it: creative destruction and all that; the importance of the profit motive for the efficient functioning of an open economy; the inevitability of globalization. . . . And you know why he'll decry it: They're not as competent as American economists; high-paid jobs (his or his colleague's) have been lost to a foreign nation that imports little from the United States; and the most frequently heard complaint of all: How's a fifty-ish professional economist (or accountant or doctor—plug in the professional of your choice) supposed to find work in a new field?

Your economist friend has raised all the big issues, hasn't he? Leaving quality aside for the moment, because that is of mutual concern, the economist's woes aren't any different from those of the manufacturing worker who lamented the passing (i.e., death) of the U.S. steel industry in the 1950s, the milkman who lost his job with the proliferation of cars in the 1960s, or the computer programmer who lost his job to an Indian or Chinese national in 1998. It's not fun; it's not pretty; but it's inevitable. The modernization of the workforce, the globalization of the workforce, and labor market specialization as an integral part of both, simply can't be stopped.

"Mrs. Kim-el-man? Are You There, Mrs. Kim-el-man?"

I started this discussion lamenting the quality of the call-center services that American Express outsourced overseas. Judging from late-night talk shows and stand-up comics, I'm not alone in my dissatisfaction. But it's wise to remember that American consumers are not without clout. When Dell heard from customers that its support services were not making the grade, the head office listened. When Dell was impacted by lost sales, the executives took action. Today Dell has many support service centers back in the United States.*

Quality concerns may be my issue, but companies have issues with outsourcing as well. Firms have to overcome sometimes enormous anxiety over intellectual property in order to outsource overseas. Developing nations generally don't have the legal safeguards to ensure that property ownership will be respected. Some don't even have a stable government in power. It takes a big leap of faith to outsource research and development, high-end computer code, and customer data to these countries. And then there are language considerations. Outside India, where English is widely spoken, language differences create a big barrier.

Companies can also get themselves into trouble chasing lower costs. Last year Bangalore, this year Bucharest, next year Ho Chi Minh City? All these changes come with start-up costs, but if labor-cost savings are the object, a business's hands may be tied. Globalization is taking root across greater portions of the globe and at a faster clip than at any time in our past. Not so fast that American workers are becoming as cheap as their foreign counterparts—at least I hope not. But fast enough to make today's bargain spot lose its cost advantage faster than you can say, "writeoff."

So maybe companies did get ahead of themselves by outsourcing too much overseas too quickly, before foreigners' language or work habits were up to the job. Are we seriously going to say that companies don't make mistakes? I'm not. But I do have faith, complete faith, that capitalist companies will eventually get it mostly right.

---

* Interestingly, some high-tech companies have concluded that American call centers aren't necessarily of higher quality. When the quality of the technical information provided is more important to the caller than the representative's English accent, the overseas center may be better. U.S. companies have a hard time getting trained and educated workers to staff the phones.

In the meantime, it's our job to make sure that the economists who lose their jobs—and everyone else who does, too—are treated with respect and helped to adjust in meaningful ways. And to ensure that the U.S. economy grows as quickly as is safe. In the final analysis, outsourcing won't be an issue when more good, high-paying jobs are created here than shipped abroad.*

---

* This is exactly what has happened since 2004, although few experts believe it will remain the case. The debate over outsourcing is on hold at this point, not over.

15

All Aboard: Resolving Our Health Care Troubles

As I've argued many times in this book, capitalism is hands-down the most efficient and sustainable economic system in the history of humankind. Yet despite capitalism's recent successes, which include the breakdown of communism, the growing prosperity of China and Asia, and the global trend toward low inflation, some economic problems are no better, possibly even worse, than they were fifty years ago.

Free markets have led to incredible gains here in the United States as well. Yet we know that some of our big problems have been left by the wayside. I've waited until (almost) the end of the book to discuss the biggest of these problems: the U.S. health care system. Was I saving the best for the last? Maybe. You just tell me how to apply the adjective *best* to the mess we've gotten ourselves into.

Right about now is when most experts (I'm not one) and politicians (I'm not one of those, either) start in with the statistics. I could throw enough numbers your way to literally send you into a coma, but I'm not going to do so because I know that one in six of you don't have health insurance, and therefore probably wouldn't be able to afford treatment. Seriously, I have the numbers right here next to me as I write. But I'll let you in on a secret.

Health care is really about life, death, and the quality of one's life. Statistics don't hurt; people do.

The Train Leaves the Station on Time

Medical treatment has advanced by leaps and bounds in the past forty to fifty years. Think about it. More and more AIDS and cancer patients die of other causes. The medications we take for everything from a headache to ADD to arthritis have improved dramatically. Surgery is less invasive and far less debilitating. Prostheses (replacement parts) are a zillion times better. Genetic research is in the process of turning upside-down the entire way doctors think and work. No argument: The tech revolution has left its mark on medicine in bold type.

By rights, we should be living far healthier lives. Some of us are. Outside the developed world, the key to a longer, healthier life is often the availability of clean water, safe and nutritious foods, and the absence of violence. We take these things for granted here in the United States. Here, the key is having access to health care. You can't benefit from what you don't have.

So let's go back to that list of medical advances. What does it mean, in terms of the big picture? First off, it means we have higher expectations than previous generations. We expect to live longer and better. We expect a quick and accurate diagnosis of our problems. When we're ill, we expect to have less pain and to recuperate faster. Wrapped up in these expectations is the belief that advances in medical care are public, not private, property. They should be circulated widely, and as quickly as possible.

These developments also mean that health care has gotten more expensive. Advances in medicine don't fall from the sky. Living and breathing people have to work day after day, year after year, to create new tests, new drugs, new machines, new stuff. All that takes money. The spectacular advances in medical care over the past few decades have cost a spectacular amount of money.

Who supplies the cold, hard cash to fund such research and development work? Well, in a capitalist system like ours, the companies that hope to benefit from the new developments do. Hold on for a second: This part of the equation works. Drug companies like Aventis, Merck, and Pfizer supply the labs and pay the salaries of researchers to develop new drugs for the world's worst illnesses. Companies like HP and Johnson & Johnson are dedicating millions of dollars each year to develop better diagnostic tools. Small startups, backing the idea of a single orthopedist, are creating new prosthetic joints. Others are making synthetic veins and organs. This is not to deny the very real contributions made by the National Institutes of Health (NIH). The NIH, which calls itself the "Nation's Medical Research Agency," is a U.S. government-funded organization that finances over $28 billion in medical research each year. But it does so largely in conjunction with private organizations. According to the organization's Web site, "More than 80 percent of the NIH's funding is awarded through almost 50,000 competitive grants to more than 325,000 researchers at over 3,000 universities, medical schools, and other research institutions in every state and around the world."* That's research the American way.

Having some profit-minded companies involved in the work guarantees that research dollars will be dedicated to the biggest problems in health care. The possibility of finding a cure for cancer keeps the PhDs in the lab, challenging them intellectually and giving them a chance to make a contribution to the world (a Nobel prize would be nice, too). What keeps the companies in the game is the profit motive. The bigger the problem, the more people it affects and the bigger the potential profit. Medical com-

---

* From the NIH Web site: http://www.nih.gov/about/budget.htm.

panies routinely reassess their priorities to make sure they're fighting the right wars. As Martha says, that's a good thing.*

Train Wreck

Yet the first (of many) problem(s) with the U.S. health care system arises right here: Our expectations for better health care collide with the industry's need to recoup the costs of research and development. We expect to have access to the latest in medical care; the industry wants to know how we expect to pay for it.

That's a damn good question: How *do* we pay for it? Well, some of us don't pay for it. So we don't get it.** The rest of us pay for health care in three ways: by qualifying for Medicare or Medicaid, by paying for private health insurance, or by paying by check, credit card, or money order (in other words, paying out of our own pockets, which gets the fancy name "fee for service").

It's an old adage that you can't take money to your grave. For many Americans, that's a moot point. The current health care system will guarantee that we have no money by the time the grim reaper shows up at our door. The blunt fact is that many, many people in the United States—about 50 million, or one in six—don't have health insurance so they must pay for medical care on their own. With the price of medical care today, that puts them in an awfully difficult spot.

---

* Having profit-minded companies determine medical research priorities means that researchers focus on numbers. Unfortunately, this doesn't help people with rare diseases. The question, then, is how to fund research for so-called orphan drugs (those needed by only a small number of patients). Similar to other nations, here in the United States, government and charitable funding is the alternative we've chosen. One can argue that this arrangement should be looked at closely, as part of our revamp of the health care system.

** More precisely, most of us who can't pay for health care don't get it. However, some of us do. Hospital emergency rooms provide very expensive and often high-tech services to those who can't pay. This is part of the problem, of course. And people do get care if they're signed up for a research study or qualify for a government-run medical plan.

Unfortunately, many young and middle-aged Americans are finding themselves in exactly this position. Often they once had insurance, but no longer qualify for it because their medical history includes a condition that might be costly to treat. Many people are in this position because they work for a small company that doesn't offer health insurance because the premiums are prohibitively high. Small companies are the lifeblood of the economy, as long as you don't *need* blood. Some people simply can't afford health insurance; it's not cheap, you know. A bare-bones policy for a family of four could easily run well into the thousands—a month!

You read every day in the papers or see on the news stories of people who've got thousands of dollars worth of debt that they accumulated trying to pay for their own medical care. In fact, one half of all bankruptcies in this country in 2001 were caused by overwhelming medical bills, according to a study by researchers at Harvard University. And more than three-quarters of the people who found themselves in bankruptcy court for this reason had health insurance at the start of the illness that caused their financial decline!

Given the hell that those without insurance go through, those of us with insurance should, and usually do, feel blessed. Blessed, but still very, very nervous. Here's why.

The Station's on Fire

We're nervous about health insurance, first off, because we know it's a tenuous thing. Suppose we lose our job—poof! It's gone just like that. Oh, sure, COBRA (the Consolidated Omnibus Budget Reconciliation Act) will allow you to buy the insurance for a time after you've been laid off. But the cost goes up just at a time when your income has gone down. And COBRA's only good for so many months. If your unemployment lasts too long, you're on your own.

You don't have to lose a job to lose insurance, however. You may have worked for forty years for the same company and been retired with a pension for years—only to wake up one morning and find that the pension's medical coverage has just disappeared. Is it moral? Hell no! Is it legal? Hell yes! Or maybe you work for a small company that decides it can no longer afford health insurance for employees if it wants to stay in business. It's a lousy choice—jobs or health insurance—yet companies are forced to make it every day.

Or maybe you lost your job, lost your insurance, but being the stand-up and loyal employee that you are, you got a new job within days of being laid off. Problem solved, right? Not if there's anything in your medical history that requires continuing treatment. You see, your new insurance coverage probably comes with a restriction on "preexisting conditions," which means the new company won't start to pay for medical expenses for your ongoing illnesses or conditions until a certain time has elapsed (time, in this instance, is usually measured in years). Nice, huh? So if you're a diabetic, don't lose your job.*

Oh, and by the way, this business about preexisting conditions isn't just applicable to low-level employees who lost their previous jobs. It's applicable to all new employees, even the highly paid, highly sought-after VP the company just hired. Hope her kids don't get any sports injuries that require physical therapy.

Now, lest you be inclined to say to the people who've lost their insurance, "Buck up. You can buy insurance," I refer you to the previous section. It's expensive! How many people do you know who can afford to pay out an extra few grand each month? Even if your answer is a lot, that's not the correct answer for the vast majority of Americans.

---

* Some states disallow restrictions on preexisting conditions.

Unfortunately, it's not just the loss of insurance that makes us nervous. For many Americans, the bigger fear is that the insurance company won't cover the medicines and treatments needed to make us well. Or we worry that if they do cover our needs initially, then the insurance company will subsequently find an excuse to dump us as clients as soon as technically possible. Every day, every insurance company in the United States denies claims or drops paying customers—probably hundreds, if not thousands of times—to better control costs.

As for medical breakthroughs, ha! New tests? New medicines? New protocols? If they're new, they're expensive—we've established that, right? And if they're expensive, the insurance companies don't want to pay for them. So where does that leave us? Just fine if we get sick with an age-old problem that has an over-the-counter cure. For anything else, we risk extinction. (I exaggerate, of course, to make a point. Insurance comes through for millions of people each day, and the vast majority do not lose their insurance when they get sick. But all of us know people who have floundered; and as I said earlier, for this reason all of us with insurance are nervous.)

Don't Blame the Insurance Companies

By this time you've got the arrows out, pointed straight at the nation's health insurers. Please, put those arrows away. It's not their fault. Yes, I do believe that: It's not their fault. And don't turn and aim those arrows at the drug companies—it's not their fault, either.

Have you ever read your automobile or homeowner's insurance policy? Probably not. It's the size of a small book and, instinctively, you know what's inside: pages and pages of exceptions—circumstances and conditions under which the insurance company will not cover your claim. One of my favorite ads of recent years shows a guy on the phone with his insurance company. Outside a massive tree has just fallen on his parked car. The insurance agent on the phone is telling the guy he's covered only if his car has been damaged by a ficus tree.* The guy has no clue what a ficus tree looks like, but readily agrees that the tree that fell on his car must be a ficus tree. His wife breaks the bad news to him.

Your health insurance policy is just as long, if not longer than, the policy on your car. Actually, you may not even get a full copy of it. It's online and, if you get your insurance from work, probably on file in the HR department office (assuming your HR department is in-house). Reading it won't necessarily help you, however. Health insurance companies give themselves a wide berth when it comes to applying the rules.

Why, then, do I say it's not "their fault" when they refuse someone treatment? The answer is simple: They are private companies whose purpose is to earn profits for their shareholders. Given the speed and diversity of new medical advances, insurance companies couldn't—even if they wanted to—nail down exactly what they will and won't cover in their policies. But in any case they wouldn't want to, because the cutting edge is where their risks lie. New treatments, tests, and procedures make life unpredictable for insurance companies—and unpredictability is any insurance company's nemesis.

A similar sort of business model applies to the drug companies: They, too, are private companies whose purpose is to earn profits for their shareholders. Selling drugs below cost—or even selling drugs at a constant price globally—is inconsistent with the business model of drug companies.

Our outrage at insurance and drug companies is misplaced. We are angry with profit-motivated companies because they refuse to act in ways that would reduce their profits, something

---

* A ficus tree is maybe five feet (1.5 m) tall and lives happily potted inside the house.

that is clearly not in the best interests of their shareholders. We should direct our outrage at ourselves—we're the ones who are dense.

How Do Hospitals Fit into the Picture?

Just as the American people are caught up in the struggle for affordable health care, so are hospitals—only from the other side of the operating table. Many hospitals in the United States are private, profit-oriented companies. It's no surprise then that their behavior is similar to that of drug companies and insurance companies. When you see pictures on TV of indigent, sick people being pushed out of taxis onto the pavement, the culprit is invariably a for-profit hospital. Caring for people who can't pay for medical services is not profit-friendly.

The majority of hospitals in the United States are nonprofit or community-run organizations, however, and making profits is not their first concern. Administrators of most public hospitals would say they have a moral and legal responsibility to care for the sick of their community, and they do the best job they can of rationing their resources to accomplish that goal. Nevertheless, they have to keep their doors open, which means they can't give out care without regard to their operating budget. To be sure, nonprofit and community hospitals do a better job of caring for the uninsured, thanks in large part to limited government financial aid, but they're far from perfect.

Delving into the Business of Making and Selling Drugs

As I've just described them, the outward manifestations of our sickly health care system truly are frightening. I'm not convinced that the fear of dealing with the system doesn't cause illness in and of itself—sort of like your blood pressure rising as soon as the doctor or nurse straps the cuff onto your arm.

Queasiness may be part of the reason why few want to dig deeper to analyze the health care system. Or maybe it's just easier for people to decry the profit motive than fix the underlying problems. Well, you know me—I'm not going to buy that line of reasoning. What I *am* going to do is offer up a more in-depth economic analysis of both the drug and health insurance industries. (If it helps, picture a spiral staircase. We're going to cover much the same ground, but at a higher level.)

Warning: Not reading this rest of this chapter may be hazardous to your health.*

I'm going to start with the drug industry—it's tackling the more difficult bit first. We've touched on the drug industry briefly above, but there's a whole lot more that once understood, provides a better understanding of why drug companies act the way they do.

Viewed from thirty thousand feet, drug companies have two halves to them: research and development, which concocts new drugs, tests them, and gets approval for their sale; and production and sales, which produces and distributes the drugs to consumers, hospitals, and clinics. Now I won't say that production, sales, and distribution costs are miniscule, because they are not. But compared to the costs of discovering and testing new drugs, production and marketing outlays are small.

An economist might look at a drug company's costs as such: The cost of producing pills two through ten million is a fraction of the cost of producing the very first pill for human consumption. That's because all the work that went into discovering and testing the new drug had to be completed before the first pill went on sale. Research and development are "fixed" costs, meaning these costs don't change whether one pill or one hundred million

---

* In other words, don't skip this just because it gets into more economics than you think you can stomach. You've made it this far, after all. You can handle a wee bit more.

pills are subsequently made. If you assign the fixed costs to the first unit produced, then—to take a hypothetical example—the first pill sold of a cholesterol-lowering drug might have cost the drug company $10 million to produce. By contrast, the second through millionth pill might cost the company $2 a pop to produce.*

Now put yourself in the shoes of the drug company. How do you establish a retail price for your product? Do you charge consumers what it costs to produce the pills in their container, $2 per pill? Of course not, because that wouldn't touch the enormous amount of money you spent discovering the drug and getting it ready for market. No, you're going to establish a price that lies somewhere between $2.00 and $10 million. Gee, that was helpful.

Let's see if we can get closer to an answer. The U.S. patent office will issue a patent for new drugs that lasts in practice about ten to fifteen years.** To make my life simple, let's say the company's patent for our hypothetical drug will last ten years. And let's say the company expects to sell 500,000 pills per year. OK, then, its production costs will be $1 million a year (500,000 pills at $2 each). And let's add in one-tenth of the research and development costs incurred in developing the drug, another $1 million.*** So, in any of the first ten years it will cost the company in total $2 million to produce 500,000 pills—or $4 a pill. Problem solved, right? The company should charge $4 a pill.

Did you really think it would be this easy?

First off, recognize that the company's overall research costs far exceeded the $10 million it spent on this particular drug. Research in the drug industry is, well, research. And by defini-

---

* Please recognize that all the numbers in these examples are fictional; I made them up.
** The patent actually lasts longer; however, the clock starts ticking on the date the company first applies, and in reality, it takes drug companies years to get a drug past all the hurdles, such as FDA approval, that are required to bring it to market.
*** Since the patent lasts ten years, I assigned one-tenth of the firm's research and development costs to each year.

tion, research doesn't always pan out. (Remember all those experiments in high school chemistry lab?) For every $10 million that the company spent developing this specific product, it spent oodles more researching drugs that never made the final cut. How does a drug company get paid for research that doesn't end up changing someone's life? Good question. The answer is that it covers these research costs by lifting the prices of the drugs it does sell. And so that $4 for our cholesterol-lowering drug is a pipe dream.

As I said earlier, the drug companies need to be able to recoup the research costs on drugs that don't make it; otherwise, they're going to pull back on their research efforts. That's not something we want to happen. But we also don't want companies to fleece the people who need their drugs. There's part of the rub.

Let me go back a few paragraphs to that patent I spoke of. Without a patent, any old chemical company could steal another's formula (without spending a dime on research) and produce the pill. That would accomplish a quick end to research and development. No, the nation needs to offer the drug companies protection; we need to let the drug company be the *only* seller of a particular drug for a specific period of time. But hold on a minute: only a single seller in the market? That's not free markets! That's a monopoly!

Bingo.

A vital part of the drug industry model, aided and abetted by well-intentioned public policies, is monopoly control over non-generic drug prices. If you remember back to our discussion of monopolies in the oil chapter, you'll remember that in monopoly situations prices are higher than they are in free markets. One other fact about monopolies didn't come up in the oil chapter because it wasn't relevant there, but it is here: Monopolies set different prices in different markets to take advantage of differences in the buyers' economic circumstances. If the market will bear $10 a pill in Saudi Arabia and only $2.25 in Chad, then the monopolist will set two different prices. Market segmentation, as this is called, can't exist in the oil market because oil is easily shipped across borders. But medicine doesn't flow across borders with ease, so market segmentation is feasible.

In fact, market segmentation doesn't even need borders. The U.S. Veterans Administration negotiates a price with drug companies independently. The price at which medicine is sold to the VA probably isn't the same as that negotiated by your health insurance company, and it's certainly not the same price you'd pay without insurance. Now you've gotten the full body rubdown!

Here, then, is a fuller description of the drug industry today:

- New drugs come to market with huge baggage: the cost of their research and testing. The drug companies have to be able to recover these funds.

- Drug companies also spend a lot of money on research and development for drugs that fail. If drug companies are to continue researching new treatments, it is imperative that they be able to recoup these expenditures one way or another.

- Drug companies are protected by patents; the patents allow the companies to own the rights to a new medication and thus avoid competition. But patents create monopolies, and monopoly suppliers charge monopoly prices (i.e., high prices) and they segment markets to eke out every last dollar from consumers.

And so the challenge is how to restructure the drug industry so that shareholder interests are maintained and companies are encouraged to undertake research, while at the same time making drugs more affordable for the people who need them. (Hint: Something's gotta give.)

Off Our Backs and Into Our Corner

Switching over to the insurance industry requires a change in mindset: the issues are of an entirely different nature, although equally as critical. With drug companies, the issue is how to cover the costs of their research so they'll stay in the game and generate a steady flow of new drugs for an ever-widening array of diseases. With insurance companies, the challenge is how to keep them profitable and sustainable in a period of rapid medical advances—or, to use the vernacular, how to get them off our backs and into our corner.

For reasons I won't go into in the text (but are briefly summarized in the footnote below), the U.S. chose some fifty years ago to deliver health care insurance through employers.* Until insurance premiums began to go through the roof in the 1980s, the system worked for the majority of Americans. Now it barely works for half—as of this writing, the number of individuals covered by their employer's health insurance plan was 59 percent and falling fast.**

I don't expect you to feel sorry for private-sector insurers, many of whom make good money, but it would be helpful to see things from their perspective for a moment. Their business faces the following challenges:

- The companies insure new employees (sooner or later) without the right of refusal. If the employer that has purchased an insurer's policy wants a particular individual hired, then it doesn't matter that her husband is fighting a rare form of

---

* During World War II, Washington didn't want companies bidding up the price of labor. Instead of higher wages, companies offered health care insurance.

** The difference between the 59 percent who are covered by an employer-sponsored plan and the one in six, or 17 percent, who have no insurance is 24 percent. These 24 percent of Americans are covered by health insurance they pay for themselves or by Medicare, Medicaid, or some other publicly-funded plan.

cancer or is eventually going to need a kidney transplant. Now, the insurance companies have often instituted a waiting period for care for pre-existing conditions to alleviate financial risk, and you and I are free to find that morally reprehensible, or not. But the fact is that health insurance companies insure people they don't choose to insure. That's risk.

• Insurance companies try very hard to predict what good health care will cost in the future for different sicknesses. They incorporate their estimate of future costs into their financial plans, and set insurance premiums so they'll be able to cover costs. Problem is, insurance companies can't predict the future of health care. Think about it: the antibiotic-resistant infection known as MRSA, obesity surgery, 9/11-related health problems, the bird flu. . . . The chance for their companies' cost estimates to be wide off the mark is huge. But that's nothing compared to the steady stream of new drugs, new diagnostic tools, and new treatments that are being made available. It's wonderful that we live in a time of such rapid medical advances. Just understand that from the perspective of the insurance company, that's risk, too.*

A common metaphor makes sense here. The insurance companies are the keepers of the gate—they determine when the gates will open and how many people will pass through. It seems to us consumers that they're opening the gates less, partly because they're closing the gates earlier and partly because they aren't opening the gates as widely as they had. The gatekeepers argue that they have no control over who enters (healthy or sick) and

---

* Raising the insurance premiums charged so that the insurer can afford more expensive treatments isn't an option. Healthy people would defect to a cheaper plan, leaving the health insurance company with only those who require more expensive care. The cost of insurance in this case would be astronomical since everyone in the insurance pool would have astronomical expenses.

that the gates are being pushed open wider (thanks to medical advances). One thing we agree on: No one is happy with the status quo.

How Do We Get Ourselves Out of This Mess?

I offer no prescription (pun intended) for the health care system. That's not my job, thankfully. But as an objective outsider and economist, it seems to me that we have two ways to solve this problem, and we should work on both of them simultaneously.

First, we need to address the root causes, as described above. Our nation is firmly committed to free markets, which is to say that we have a system in which individuals are used to doing what's best for themselves and their families, and businesses are used to doing what's best for their bottom line. We know that free markets have not solved, but have probably contributed to, the health care mess. Yet asking American families and companies to accept a health care system that limits choice is not going to go over well. We're skeptical of socialized medicine, to be sure, but if you remember we didn't even take kindly to health maintenance organizations (HMOs) ordering us about. I believe our solution has to entail the least number of deviations from the capitalist mold (not to mention the status quo).

Many Americans favor tax incentives to expand private insurance and restrain medical costs through market forces. If these strategies would work, they'd be the most consistent with the American economic model. The problem is, I don't see how they really would work since companies and consumers have different goals. Tax incentives alone are not enough to align the interests of private insurance companies with those of health care consumers. Their drive for profits collides with our need for care.

Look at the problem this way: I think we all agree that the national goal that has emerged over the past few years is to improve health care access for all Americans. And we know that individual freedom—a patient's right to choose—is integral to our satisfaction with the system. Let's figure it out, then. There are basically four types of private "institutions" involved in health care: doctors, hospitals, drug companies, and insurance companies. How could they change to meet that goal?

Is taking the profit motive away from doctors going to solve our problems? No, it's clear that we want doctors to earn a nice living because we want our medical practitioners to be smart, and smart people have well-paid alternatives on Wall Street or in Silicon Valley. If we were to artificially restrict physician salaries, we'd push more doctors out of medicine, which is just the opposite of what we want. Besides, while the great majority of physicians do well, they aren't earning obscene amounts of money. According to the U.S. Department of Labor, the average salary in the United States for a general practitioner is about $170,000. No, I don't think a restriction on doctor's earnings is the solution—the costs outweigh the benefits.

Is taking the profit motive away from hospitals going to solve our problems? It may help, but with so many American hospitals already operating for the community, the impact will be modest unless other more substantive changes are enacted at the same time.

How about the drug industry? Is taking the profit motive away from the drug companies going to solve our problems? We all know that one of the big reasons why health care costs have gotten so out of hand is the high price of new medicines—both in hospitals and out. Yes, but again the issue is how to "cap" drug prices while at the same time encouraging drug companies to engage in research. Drug companies have to get their research dollars from somewhere, and I'd argue that padding the prices of successful drugs is a better alternative than getting a grant from the government—I'd rather see the profit motive determine research priorities than the government*. Doing away with, or shortening, patents for new drugs isn't going to help, either. The companies need space and time to recoup the high fixed costs of bringing a new drug to market.

If there's room for change, I think it has to concern the issue of monopoly pricing. Elsewhere in the economy where competition is limited (e.g., telephone or electric service), government regulation prevents private companies in those industries from charging monopoly prices. Such firms can earn profits, to be sure, just not monopoly profits. It's something to consider doing with drug companies.

And so, saving the best for last: Is taking the profit motive out of the insurance industry a solution to our problems? I think so. To explain why, I need to tackle the insurance "solution" in two parts. First, I believe that any real cure for the problem requires universal health care coverage. Everybody having access to health care, and paying into the insurance system to the extent to which they are able, reduces health care costs by reducing expensive treatment and by broadening the insurance pool. We expect that costly emergency room visits would drop off if everyone had insurance because people would be more likely to receive preventative care and see their doctors for less severe illnesses. And insurance companies would have a larger number of payers, and more dollars, to help cover outlays.

There are plenty of ways to go about this. We can have a two-site system: Get your insurance through your employer or from state-sanctioned providers (which may be regulated private companies or a Medicare-style state plan). We can institute national health insurance for anyone not covered by an employer plan. We can scrap private insurance altogether and institute a unified

---

* The NIH is already involved, in any case, in funding some drug research.

insurance plan, like Medicare, for all Americans. These are three ideas; there are plenty of variations to choose from.

However, universal health insurance isn't enough. If the changes stop there, then the problem won't be solved because the insurers, be they private or public, will still want to contain costs while the consumers will still want access to medical care almost regardless of cost. The battle will continue.

Let's take a breath before continuing. What I'm describing here is no different from the garden center that sold me roses way back in chapter 1. The owners of the nursery wanted to sell me roses at as high a price as they could, and I wanted to buy my roses as cheaply as possible. It's the nature of supply and demand that the two sides to the transaction had different objectives. Well, the same is true for health insurance: Insurers and consumers don't have the same objectives. But here's the key point: Health care is increasingly being seen as a fundamental right of every American. We can let buyers and sellers duke it out over roses, but not over something that's considered fundamental for life.

So, second: I also believe that a successful solution to our health care problems must include changing the *modus operandi* of the insurance industry (for those of you not hooked on mysteries, *modus operandi* is Latin for "mode of operation"). The profit motive is, to my economist's mind, inconsistent with the task of satisfying Americans' fundamental right to good health care.

If the profit motive isn't going to guide decision-making in health care, who or what is? Truth is, medical care has to be rationed at times, and if price/profit isn't going to do it, something or somebody else has to play the villain. In all likelihood, doctors will end up making such decisions. Doctors are a much better choice than bureaucrats, I think, but they won't please everyone and therefore will come under a lot of flak (we can only hope the flak isn't so bad that they quit their profession).

It's time to wrap up this section. But before I do, we have one more bit of work to accomplish. I said at the outset of this discussion on health care solutions that there are two paths to investigate simultaneously. The second is this: We need to see how other developed nations like ours, with populations and expectations and economic systems similar to ours, have solved the problem. Because they have. We're the last ones onboard.

France, Germany, Canada, and the UK are all good models to review because they're all capitalist countries with citizens who expect state-of-the-art health care. My guess is that we'll reject the UK model out of hand; the UK model is the closest to socialized medicine. The whole kit and caboodle is government-run, from doctors to hospitals to insurance. From a patient's perspective, the French system, which earns a top rating from the World Health Organization, looks a lot like our Medicare system. Only the French government owns many hospitals and dictates doctors' salaries. Not a great fit. The Canadian and German systems are better role models. Germany's even figured out a way to keep private insurance companies in the picture.

Foreign nations offer some important lessons about cost as well as structure. At last estimate (2004), the United States spent $6,096 on health care for every person in the country. Are you ready? That's about twice as much as other countries with universal health care, including Canada at $3,173 (with their Tim Hortons), France at $3,040 (with their fancy pastries), and Germany at $3,171 (with their knockwurst and beer).* Hey, change may not be so painful after all.

---

* Source: World Health Organization. Our plans will inevitably cost more than theirs because we don't spend as much as they do on preventative care. Being proactive against disease, and treating illnesses in their early stages, goes a long way toward keeping medical costs down. Another reason our care is bound to cost more is that we take worse care of ourselves (how many times did you eat at McDonald's or Burger King in the last week?).

16

The More Things Change, the More Things Change

Economics isn't known for bringing families together. But by now you realize that this is no ordinary economics book. So here's what I want you to do. Call the oldest relative you have or, even better, sit down with her. I'm talking about someone in her nineties; late eighties will do. If there's no one in your family that old, borrow someone from a neighbor or friend. If worse comes to worst, swing by a retirement home and chat up one of the old folks sitting on the porch. The only requirements are that your person still has her memory and can speak without an interpreter.

I have a few questions for you to ask to get the conversation going.

- Do you remember your family's first car? What were the first few days like when your father and mother brought it home? How did you get around before the car?

- When did you get your first washing machine? Dryer? Dishwasher? Did these appliances change your parents' lives—or yours?

- When did you take your first airplane flight? Do you remember the first-ever jet flight by American Airlines in 1959?

- Can you use a computer? Do you surf the Internet? Has the computer changed your life more or less than previous inventions?

This exercise is motivated by my own curiosity as to what life must have been like for my own mother. She was born in New York City in 1910 and lived for eighty-nine years. The subway had opened in New York just six years before her birth, so I presume that she and my grandparents got around the city via subway or taxi. Yes, real cabs. In 1900, a New York City cab company imported six hundred green-and-white gas-powered cars from France to compete with the city's horse-drawn carriages. By the time my mother was a toddler, there were half a dozen large taxi fleets and thousands of independent owner/drivers. My mother told me that my grandfather was one of the first in the city to buy his own car, although he worked just blocks from his apartment. (A show-off, he liked riding in cars.)

Over the years, my mother would witness a complete change in methods of transportation, including airplane and jet service. But that's not all. She also got to use the very first washing machines and dishwashers, mixers, and blenders. My father got to use the first power tools and garage door openers. He rode an electric elevator at work. It's funny: We always think of the older generations as being resistant to change, but think of all the changes that passed before their eyes and into their hands.

And that was before the computer. How can someone who saw the first jet plane cope with an MRI machine or 24/7 seamless global communications? One century, two revolutions.

Economic Revolutions

If you listen to the commercials for Chevrolet, they'll tell you that the new lineup of Chevy cars and trucks constitute an "American Revolution." Oil of Olay promises a revolutionary change in skin care. Come to think of it, every skin-care company offers that. The word *revolution* is so commonly thrown about that it's almost lost its meaning. To me, a revolution implies a radical and pervasive change in the world; revolutions change the course of history. Sorry, Chevrolet and Oil of Olay—yours don't make the cut.

The industrial revolution of the late 1800s and early 1900s was a real revolution. Farming, manufacturing, and transportation were radically changed by the advent of gas-, water-, steam-, and electrical-powered machinery. Economies were redrawn, societies reorganized, family life recast. Indeed, virtually no aspect of life in the developed nations was unaffected. I hope you gathered as much from your conversation with your old relative or friend. Although the technological advances we see today are often mind-boggling, I think the changes that were the result of the industrial revolution were in many ways more significant for Uncle Eugene or Aunt Erma.

That said, there's no doubt that the revolution in information technology that started in earnest thirty years ago is also the real McCoy. What aspect of life hasn't been affected by advances in information technology? Grocery shopping? Nope. Car buying? Nope. Car production? Nope. Dating? Nope. Everything and every activity you can possibly imagine has been changed one way or another by new technology (yes, even bathrooms).

But if life in general seems much the same, although improved, by the advances of the past thirty years or so, we're told that the changes coming down the pike will make our world virtually unrecognizable. A recent report by the Rand Corporation (a private think tank that does work for big companies and Uncle Sam) says that going forward the effects may include significant improvements in:

- human quality of life and life span

- high rates of industrial turnover

- lifetime worker training

- continued globalization

- reshuffling of wealth

- cultural amalgamation or invasion with potential for increased tension and conflict

- shifts in power from nation-states to nongovernmental organizations and individuals

- mixed environmental effects

- improvements in quality of life with accompanying prosperity and reduced tension

- the possibility of human eugenics and cloning.*

If I get this right, I or one of my clones may live forever in a constantly changing world in which I will fluctuate between rich and poor; be governed by a revolving door of legitimate and illegitimate, benevolent and malevolent creatures; and breath air and drink water that may or may not be genetically engineered. Okey dokey.

Technology and Productivity

Before we take off for the wild blue yonder, let's step back to earth, shall we? Let's look at three areas where, to date, the economy has been—or should be—measurably affected by recent technological advances: productivity; the anatomy of the labor market (where the jobs are); and organizational structure (how organizations themselves have changed). When I've done that, my day job, I'll be happy to don my spacesuit and meet you in the capsule.

---

* http://www.rand.org/pubs/monograph_reports/MR1307/MR1307.sum.html.

You'll remember, I hope, that productivity is the amount of work produced by an individual over a given period of time. If Mark makes ten bows an hour and Julie makes five, Mark is twice as productive as Julie. Simple. Most of the time, though, we don't compare the productivity of two people but rather the productivity of the entire national workforce, or a particular company's workforce, over time.* For example, over the twelve months ended June 2007, productivity in the nonfarm sector of the U.S. economy grew by 2.7 percent, which is to say that U.S. workers became 2.7 percent more productive over this time.

What causes a worker to become more productive? Think of yourself. Is it a new computer or a better-working cell phone? Depending on your job, these may very well improve your productivity. If you work as a waiter or waitress, having one of those computers to send customer orders to the kitchen would be a big boon, saving you steps and saving your back. If you work in a factory, upgrading to state-of-the-art machinery would be a great help. If you work as a broker on Wall Street, having faster communications between the front and back offices would make you more productive. What all these examples have in common is that productivity increases when there's more or better equipment provided. This is exactly my point. There are other ways to improve worker productivity—like on-the-job training or graduate courses, a more efficient organization, or a more effective boss—but productivity gains come first from improved capital equipment and better technology.

In light of the tech revolution, productivity must have advanced rapidly these past twenty years, right? Well, actually, no. And herein lies one of the problems that concerns economists

---

* Companies with multiple locations will often compare the productivity of different factories or offices. Problem is, the comparisons are not valid if the two shops have different machinery, different organizational structures, different bosses. . . .

most: Why, with all that's changed to make people so much more productive, have the data failed to register an improvement in the nation's productivity growth rate? Or is it possible that productivity growth really hasn't improved?

I am going to dismiss the latter question out of hand. We know people have become much more productive: We do more, read more, talk more, write more, produce more each and every working hour of the day—or at least we have the ability to do so (maybe some people finish their work by 11 a.m. and take the rest of the day off, but I wouldn't know about that). We also know that companies are continuing to invest in new technologies. They wouldn't do so for fun or to keep up with the Joneses; they're doing so because they reap higher profits from the investment. Economists also look at falling prices for high-tech equipment. Prices wouldn't be falling unless labor costs per unit produced were declining, and unit labor costs wouldn't be declining in the United States unless workers were more productive (their wages aren't declining, in other words). So there's plenty of tangential evidence that productivity growth must be on the rise, even if the official stats don't capture it.

To explain why the official stats don't reflect what we know to be reality, economists have come up with several possible hypotheses. Now before I lay out a few of them, let me say that none of them is going to sound particularly good. That's because logic doesn't enter into it, really. Logically, the data should show what it's supposed to show and that's the end of it.

One reason why the data doesn't comply, we think, is that we're doing an increasingly bad job of measuring output. That's not as crazy as it seems. It's one thing to measure output when the output is bows made, tiles laid, or dogs spayed, but it's much harder to measure output when the individual is debugging computer code, providing customer assistance, or running a security check. The number of lines of code debugged, the number of calls taken, or the number of contacts investigated is a poor measure of the job getting done. Service output is a bear to measure, and so is service-sector productivity. Unfortunately, the global economy is becoming increasingly service-oriented.

Another reason why the data doesn't comply is that it probably takes time for new equipment and technology to yield the expected benefits. When Excel first hit computers, the only change was that numbers were entered into a computerized spreadsheet rather than on a tablet of paper. Managers pored over printouts instead of typed columns of numbers. Big deal. It wasn't until spreadsheets allowed for new analyses to be performed quickly and accurately that productivity started to improve. Likewise, big improvements came when the financial gurus were able to discern trends that had been too hard to see before. Or another example: At first, grocery stores put in electronic cash registers that printed out the tally for each customer. The old cash register did the same thing, only without as much information about which good cost $4.97. It wasn't until the data in the cash register was tied to the store's inventories and subsequently the grocer's orders to wholesalers that the store managers became more productive.

A third reason why the data doesn't comply may be that the government statisticians aren't going about it in the right way. Lorin Hitt, a professor at the Wharton School of Business, and a colleague from MIT, Erik Brynjolfsson, defined a smaller, more manageable test case. They "examined data from 599 firms across a broad spectrum of industries, calculating productivity levels and growth from 1987 to 1994. [They then] estimated the relationship between changes in productivity and changes in computerization at these firms. [They] concluded that companies that invested heavily in computers were in fact more productive than their industry competitors. Further, these returns were two to five times greater over a seven year, versus one year, period."[*] Their work suggests that, given the nature of the technology involved, maybe economists and statisticians should head back to the drawing board to devise better tests of productivity growth.

Another conclusion found in Hitt and Brynjolfsson's work is that the companies in their study that simply replaced one piece of machinery with a newer, better piece of machinery didn't get much out of it. However, the companies that used the introduction of high-tech equipment to revamp the organization (that is, move away from a traditional hierarchical structure reminiscent of the industrial age) reaped great rewards in terms of productivity. This is a variation on my second point: Improvements take time. The faster companies usher in a "new world" way of doing business, the better their operations will function. Take that to your boss!

Where the Jobs Are

We're almost at the end of the book now, so I feel entirely justified in breaking my promise that there would be no tables or charts in this book. So here's just one. It shows the composition of the workforce—people employed—in 1960 and May 2006.[**]

Whoa! Look at all those people now employed in what the U.S. Department of Labor calls *Professional and Business Services*, which is where IT jobs are listed. (Obviously, there's been explosive growth in health care as well.) While more people still work in health care, education, and trade and transport, today computer-related careers are commonplace. That wasn't the case in 1960.

Why am I pointing out the obvious? In the early days of the high-tech revolution, America's big fear was that workers would lose their jobs to computers. It was an updated version of the complaint industrialists heard in the early 1900s, that workers would

---

[*] http://www.wharton.upenn.edu/alum_mag/issues/winter2000/feature_3.html.
[**] Data source for chart: U.S. Department of Labor, Bureau of Labor Statistics.

Composition of Workforce	1960	2006
Nondurable Manufacturing	12%	4%
Durable Manufacturing	16%	7%
Construction	5%	6%
Education & Health	6%	13%
Government	16%	16%
Trade & Transport	21%	19%
Financial Services	5%	6%
Information	3%	2%
Professional & Bus Services	7%	13%
Other	10%	14%
Total	100%	100%

be replaced by machines. In both cases, workers' fears were justified; job losses did occur. To be perfectly upfront about it, people are still losing their jobs to high-tech innovations. Take the proliferation in the last few years of E-Z Pass, Fast Lane, Smart Tag, I-Pass, or whatever your state calls its toll collection technology. If you count the number of toll collectors out there, it's declining thanks to the introduction of these transponder-based systems. (I'm not even sure what a transponder is, although I know where it goes on the windshield.)

However, worrying about the jobs lost to innovation ignores the reality of change. Yes, some jobs will be eliminated, but others will be created. It's what economists call *creative destruction,* which defines the ups and downs of a dynamic capitalist economy to a tee.* Things are in flux. Some companies are succeeding and others are failing. Some workers are rising through the ranks, others are staying put, still others are being laid off. The share

---

* The term was popularized by the most famous economic historian of all time, Joseph Schumpeter.

prices of some companies are rising, the prices of others are falling. It's entrepreneurial, it's profit-motivated, it's terrifying and exhilarating all at the same time.

The high-tech revolution has had a dramatic effect on the labor market. And to the extent that technology has enabled globalization, the impact is greater still. It's likely that the changes we've seen to date are just the tip of the iceberg.

The New Economy

The term *New Economy* took off in the 1990s. It was used to signify the new world economic order: rapidly changing technology, 24/7 global communications, a single global marketplace, a single global workforce, a single global financial system, less value placed on physical property, more value placed on intellectual property. One of the New Economy's most ardent supporters, California Rep. David Dreier, defines the New Economy this way: "Yesterday's industrial order is giving way to a more complex, dynamic and dispersed economy shaped by information technologies, global markets and new communications networks like the Internet. From the way we educate our children and organize our workplaces to how we improve our health, defend our international interest, and clean up the environment, these forces are transforming our society."*

Not surprisingly, the New Economy of the 1990s was epitomized by the dot-coms. These newbies grabbed employees and investment capital almost faster than they could be used. Their potential was deemed limitless. The changes they were expected to bring about unimaginable. Naturally, their stocks could only go up, since the New Economy also predicted an end to the business cycle.

---

* http://dreier.house.gov/cdd_tech.htm

We all know that the dot-com boom of the mid-1990s eventually gave way to the dot-com bust. Turns out, neither companies nor people could rewrite the laws of gravity—or of financial prudence. The notion that the markets and the economy would no longer cycle up and down was ultimately put to rest in 2001.

And yet there is something to be said for the New Economy. Not all its attributes were false. New York Times columnist Thomas Friedman continues to insist that the world is flat, by which he means that the playing fields in the developed and developing worlds have evened out. He's right, of course. Among the flattening agents he lists are concepts that are by now familiar: the Internet, googling (that is, using search engines), outsourcing, offshoring, and open sourcing (allowing others access to one's programming source code, thus allowing and abetting collaboration). Globalization, per se, isn't on his list, but it's not very far below the surface.

Researchers like Hitt and Brynjolfsson and management consultants like Peter Drucker also believe that there's something to the notion that today's businesses should be structured differently from their industrial-era predecessors. The rationale is a simple one: With information easy to find and usually free to access, anyone in the organization can contribute creatively to the bottom line. Thus, eliminate the infrastructure—the job titles, the closed meetings and closed doors, the tiers of management—and let good ideas surface organically.

One of the oddities of the 1990s boom is that the office dynamics of the day have lived on. Picnic tables are still outside many factories, Ping-Pong tables take up space in what were once conference rooms, and office cubicles are giving way to open floors. As for middle managers, well, they're mostly gone. Perhaps more to the point, the CEO reads his own e-mails.

I say that if an economy that's driven by entrepreneurial skill, technical ingenuity, and a willingness to take risks is a New Economy, then let's have it. I don't really care what it's called.

The Future

Before I write another word, I insist that you recognize the lunacy, if not utter stupidity, of my trying to say something intelligent about the future of the high-tech revolution. If scientists can't predict which inventions and innovations are going to become the next big thing, what chance do I have?

Yet before I let you go, I wanted to give you an idea of the breadth of scientific research that's under way that will change life for us all before you know it. So this is what I did: I spent an afternoon at the library leafing through a bunch of business, scientific, and popular magazines. It didn't take long for my mouth to drop open (and people to stare). I read about energy from ocean waves; cars near mass production—affordable cars, in other words—that will ride on roads or rivers; planes that double as ships; blinking taillights to communicate between drivers, light bulbs that never burn out . . . the list went on and on.

I, for one, am ready to buy the car that runs in water—have you ever witnessed Boston traffic? And just think: LA may be forced to push water through its concrete rivers to ease congestion on the freeways. Ten years from now, commuting may not look anything like it does today. (I just hope the carmakers can keep these vehicles out of Venice.)

We all know that there are literally thousands of ideas like these being worked on in factories and garages, in medical labs and hospital rooms, on CAD-enabled computers, and Nintendo Game Boys. Although categorization is out, many of these innovations stem from a few discoveries: genetic engineering, nanotechnology, fiber optics, molecular manufacturing, and molecular electronics. (This list carries a pharmacy-style warning: *Not* *intended to be exhaustive.*) Unfortunately, most of us, dare I say all but a few of us, have no clue what many of these terms mean (except for nanotechnology—I know that means very, very, very, very . . . very small particles).*

Which raises a really good question: Who is going to work with these products when they finally come to market? Ah, now we're back to economics.

Now you see firsthand why economists are so worried about the quality of education in America.

Now you understand economists' deep concerns over a growing income gap between highly skilled and unskilled workers.

Now you realize why economists insist that the U.S. economy evolve in ways that best fit our natural, capital, and human resources, because globalization means the competent will be rewarded instantly and the unqualified punished just as fast.

Now you can truly appreciate why capitalism is taking over the world, because it's the only economic system that can keep up with the speed of change.

Aren't you glad you finally know how capitalism works?

---

* This fact has not gone unnoticed by economists. They've coined the term *technical superiority* to describe the fact that the pace of invention at this point is being slowed by the limits of the human mind to adapt to it.

Suggested Reading

The World Is Flat: A Brief History of the Twenty-first Century, by Thomas Friedman. One of the best journalists of our times, Friedman reports back from the front lines of business and commerce to explain the effects of globalization. Filled with personal anecdotes and amusing stories, this book is a wonderful description of the far-reaching impact of new technology. (Picador Press, 3rd ed., 2007)

The Future of Success: Working and Living in the New Economy, by Robert Reich. You wouldn't expect a lawyer who writes economics to produce an easy read, but Reich is unique. His career has taken him to and from academia and government service; along the way he's learned a lot about how regular people live life in the 21st century. This is a must read for anyone who works. (A previous book on the subject, *The Work of Nations*, is also superb even though it was written in 1992.) (Vintage Press, 2002)

Freakonomics: A Rogue Economist Explores the Hidden Side of Everything, by Steven D. Levitt and Stephen J. Dubner. Levitt's an economist, Dubner's a journalist, and together they've created a book that explains for the average Joe and Jane why some things are the way they are. From violent crime to birth trends, the authors uncover the economic incentives that often lurk below the surface. It's an amusing, informative read, and in truth, there's nothing freaky about it at all. (William Morrow, revised and expanded edition, 2006)

The Economics of Life: From Baseball to Affirmative Action to Immigration, How Real-World Issues Affect Our Everyday Life, by Gary Becker and Guity Nashat-Becker. The premise is much the same as the later *Freakonomics*, but Gary Becker won the Nobel Prize for Economics in 1992 and this book, which he authors with his wife, tackles more important issues like trade, social security, and education reform. The book is a compilation of columns originally written for *Business Week* magazine. (McGraw–Hill, 1998)

The Wall Street Journal Complete Personal Finance Guidebook, by Jeff D. Opdyke. This book is informative and offers sound advice. It is part of a series of Guidebooks put out by the most respected business journal in the world. Other titles cover real estate investing, money and investing, and—a sign of the times—identity theft. (Three Rivers Press, 2006)

Online Resources

For economic and business news:
www.wsj.com   The granddaddy (and arguably the best) of economics and business news providers. *The Wall Street Journal* also produces two regional versions, one for Asia and another for Europe. Unfortunately, it all comes at a cost (and a fairly high one at that).

www.nytimes/pages/business/index.html   The home page of the *New York Times* business section offers up-to-the-minute reports on economic and business news. And registration is free. That said, most days it offers less analysis of economic and financial news than the *Wall Street Journal*.

http://www.ft.com/home/us This is the United States home page for the London-based *Financial Times*. The *FT's* main advantage is that its journalists look at the United States from a longer distance. I find this gives their work a fresh perspective on things. I also appreciate that the majority of the website is free.

For economic analysis:

www.economist.com This is the website of *The Economist*, a London-based weekly magazine with offices globally. The site is updated real-time with thoughtful reports on economics, business, and finance. Content is tiered, that is to say, some stories are free, and others require a subscription.

www.businessweek.com *Business Week* claims that it provides business news and stock market and financial advice, but it also does a good job of covering the important economics news stories. Archived articles are free; if you want to read current stories, a subscription is required. (Anyone who reads articles of interest each week from either *The Economist* or *Business Week* can consider herself well informed.)

www.briefing.com This site has different levels, but the basic level is accessible without a fee, providing analysis of economic, market, and company news.

www.economy.com/dismal/ Excellent source of global economic analysis for market professionals and business executives. Fee charged.

And don't forget U.S. government data releases; specific sites for each release are listed at the end of chapter 9.

For personal finance:

www.money.cnn.com/news Here you'll find business and financial news from world news leader CNN. The personal finance section is user-friendly. The site is associated with *Money* magazine, and online access is free.

www.cnbc.com Like CNN Money, CNBC offers online the same captivating stories you see on TV (without the repetition). The site also offers excellent resources for investors. Registration is free.

www.moneycentral.msn.com An offshoot of Microsoft's MSN website, moneycentral offers very user-friendly tools for managing money. I especially like the fact that they pull in reports from briefing.com and other professional services. Registration is free of charge.

ACKNOWLEDGMENTS

Before I name names, I wish to accept full responsibility for all errors and omissions, intentional or not. The colleagues and friends mentioned below tried their best to prevent my mistakes, but unthinkingly, I did not always understand or listen to their advice. My biggest thanks go to Marty Ringo, economist extraordinaire, for challenging everything I wrote. I also received invaluable assistance from Rusty Rusten, Arthur Daemmrich, and a number of economists at the Energy Information Administration. My editor, Meredith Hale, was a wonderful partner throughout the entire process. Laurel Ornitz, Diana Drew, and Sterling's Michael Cea were also great to work with. Last but hardly least, the friends and family who listened and encouraged: Martha, Susan, Jeff, Cassie, and Jessie (and always by my side, Brewster and Curry).

INDEX

Retail sales, 135–136, 149
Revolution
    economic, 248–250
    industrial, 249
    information technology, 249
Risk. *See also* business risk
    economy and, 153
    management, 80
    overview, 102–103
    political, 208
    premium, 38
    volatility of, 101
Rodriguez, Alex, 199–200
Rollover, 125
Roosevelt, Franklin D., 66
Russia, unemployment rate, 131

S
S&L crisis, 63
Sachs, Jeffrey, 162
Sales
    final, 148
    Internet, 135–136
    real, 142
    retail, 135–136, 149
Savings, 136–137
Savings and loan association (S&L), 63–64
Schumpeter, Joseph, 256
Scientific American (magazine), 163
Securities firms, types of, 85
Securities, mutual funds versus, 111–112
Security, 38
Sheehy, Gail, 98
Shell, 18–19
Six Day War, 176
Small business owner, perspective on
    demand, 9–11
Smith, Adam, 15, 17
Social Security Administration spending,
    122
Social security system, inflation and, 66
Social Security Trust Fund, 122
Social services, sharing, 191–193
Spending
    government, 123, 135, 137, 148
    gratification from, 97–98
    overview, 120–121
    real, 142
Spokespeople, corporate, 167–169
Stanislaw, Joseph, Commanding Heights,
    The, 155
Statistics
    corporate profits, 148
    drug industry, 240–241
    employment reports, 147

GDP, 148
    inflation measures, 149
    international trade, 149
    personal income, 147–148
    productivity, 149
    retail sales, 149
Stock market, 44
Stocks
    bonds versus, 45–47, 110–111
    common, 44
    growth, 112–113
    overview, 43
    preferred, 44
    purchases example, 44–45
    types of, 44
    value, 112–113
Supply, 11–12
Supply and demand, credit style, 26–28
Syndicate, 86

T
Tangible assets, 96
Taxes
    consequences of bonds, 42–43
    government spending and, 121
    health care system incentives, 242
    overview, 102
Technology
    catalyst to financial industry change,
        82–83
    oil prices and, 181
    productivity and, 250–254
    productivity growth and, 139–140
    revolution, 140
Ten-year treasury rate, 30
Term life policy, 78–79
Texaco, 18–19
Thirty-year mortgage rate, 30
Three Mile Island, 177
Tracking, U.S. economy, 129–149
Trade
    deficit, 208–210
    international, 137–138, 149
    intra-industry (intra-sectoral), 212–213
    world patterns, 212
True internationalists, 152

U
Unemployment rate
    defined, 131
    statistics, 147
Unions, 158
Universal life policy, 79
U.S. economy
    control, 154–155